D1566814

COMPANION TO THE QUMRAN SCROLLS

8

Editor
Philip R. Davies

Published under

LIBRARY OF SECOND TEMPLE STUDIES

63

formerly the Journal for the Study of the Pseudepigrapha Supplement Series

Editor
Lester L. Grabbe

Editorial Board
Helen K. Bond, Randall D. Chesnutt, Philip R. Davies,
Steven Mason, James R. Mueller, Loren T. Stuckenbruck,
James C. VanderKam, Jan Willem van Henten

Founding Editor
James H. Charlesworth

THE PARABIBLICAL TEXTS:

STRATEGIES FOR EXTENDING THE SCRIPTURES IN THE DEAD SEA SCROLLS

Daniel K. Falk

t&t clark

BM
487
.F360
2007

Published by T&T Clark International
A Continuum imprint
The Tower Building, 11 York Road, London SE1 7NX
80 Maiden Lane, Suite 704, New York, NY 10038

www.tandtclark.com

First published 2007

All rights reserved. No part of this publication may be reproduced or transmitted in any form or
by any means, electronic or mechanical, including photocopying, recording or any information
storage or retrieval system, without permission in writing from the publishers.

Daniel K. Falk has asserted his right under the Copyright, Designs and Patents Act, 1988, to be
identified as the author of this work.

British Library Cataloguing-in-Publication Data
A catalogue record for this book is available from the British Library

ISBN-10: 1-841-27242-6   (hardback)
ISBN-13: 978-1-841-27242-9   (hardback)

Typeset by ISB Typesetting, Sheffield
Printed on acid-free paper in Great Britain by Biddles Ltd, King's Lynn, Norfolk

JKM Library
1100 East 55th Street
Chicago, IL 60615

CONTENTS

ACKNOWLEDGMENTS

Teaching Bible in a university setting, it often feels as though an inordinate amount of time is spent on what many students may perceive as destructive efforts: trying to convince them that a text that seemed perfectly familiar and meaningful is instead foreign and complicated. In the back of my mind as I have written this book have been numerous questions raised by students along the way as they have wrestled with ever more difficult questions encountered in study of the Bible. At the beginning, the enterprise seems to the typical student fairly straightforward: a journey to understand what the text means. It is usually a long process for them to come to terms with the fact that there is no single path or bridge that can take one there, for in the abstract no single destination exists. Meanings exist only in relation to specific contexts, and there are many of them. Do we seek the meaning of a story as told around a tribal campfire? As incorporated into a pro-monarchic narrative? In the context of a Deuteronomistic History? As part of a post-exilic collection of Jewish sacred writings? As part of Christian salvation history? And so on ad infinitum. The early meaning contexts are theoretical, and the beginning student is often wary. There is, after all, no actual 'book of J' to show students, no J community to query. For these reasons, the types of texts explored in this book have a unique advantage: they open a window onto the final stages of the formation of the Hebrew Bible, and the meanings that certain Jewish communities found in these texts – meanings that are often quite distant from both the contexts in which the stories originated and from the contexts of modern readers. Students are often surprised, for example, to discover the enormous importance in Second Temple Judaism of Enoch – a rather marginal figure in the Hebrew Bible and in much of modern Judaism and Christianity. It is satisfying to see light dawn on the faces of students as they study such writings and grasp, perhaps for the first time, the fundamental multivalency of scriptures and start to think about the communities who through many centuries have variously encountered God in them. To my students I dedicate this book, and especially Ryan Stoner and Chris Halverson who read drafts of it.

I wish to express my gratitude to Professor Philip Davies for the original invitation to write this monograph, to Professor Lester Grabbe for accepting the volume in the series Library of Second Temple Studies, and to the editors and staff at Continuum. Throughout the work I benefited from discussions with other scholars who helped me formulate questions and frequently sent me back to the drawing board: thanks to Professors Moshe Bernstein, George Brooke, James Sanders and James Scott; members of the West Coast Qumran Study Group, especially Professors Rob Kugler and Bill Schniedewind, and Dorothy Peters; members of the Nordic Network in Qumran Studies; and Daniel Machiela. I am grateful to Prof. Michael Stone for allowing me to attend his stimulating seminar on the Book of Noah in fall 2006.

Numerous sources of funding generously supported various parts of this research. A Summer Research Award from the University of Oregon enabled me to study photographs of the *Genesis Apocryphon* at the Ancient Biblical Manuscript Center in Claremont and the West Semitic Research Project. I am grateful to Michael Phelps at the ABMC and Bruce Zuckerman and Marilyn Lundberg at the WSRP for their help and warm hospitality, and special thanks to Bruce for guidance on Photoshop techniques for studying digital photographs of manuscripts. Thanks to a Research Fellowship at the Oregon Humanities Center I enjoyed a term free from the responsibilities of teaching to focus on research and writing in a pleasant setting, with the support and friendly interest of director Steve Shankman and his staff. Travel and research were further supported by a Faculty Fellowship funded by Richard A. Bray, and a Summer Stipend grant by the University of Oregon. A research fellowship at the Albright Institute in Jerusalem funded by the National Endowment of the Humanities in 2005–06 allowed the opportunity to examine the fragments of the *Genesis Apocryphon* and the *Reworked Pentateuch* at the Israel Museum. Thanks to the staff at the Israel Museum and the Shrine of the Book for their expert help.

Most of all, I wish to thank my wife Kimberly for her patience and support, and our sons David and Jonathan for welcome diversions.

ABBREVIATIONS

2 Bar.	*2 (Syriac) Baruch*
3 Bar.	*3 (Greek) Baruch*
1 En.	*1 (Ethiopic) Enoch*
2 En.	*2 (Slavonic) Enoch*
1 Macc.	1 Maccabees
2 Macc.	2 Maccabees
4 Macc.	4 Maccabees
1QapGen	*Genesis Apocryphon* from Qumran Cave 1
1Q19	*Noah*
1Q27	*Mysteries*
1QH^a	*Hodayot^c*
1QIsa^a	*The Great Isaiah Scroll*
1QM	*War Scroll*
1QpHab	*Habakkuk Pesher*
1QS	*Community Rule*
4Q158	*Reworked Pentateuch^a*
4Q174	*Florilegium*
4Q177	*Catena A*
4Q180	*Ages of Creation*
4Q201	*Book of Watchers^a*
4Q202	*Book of Watchers^b*
4Q204	*Book of Watchers^c*
4Q206	*Book of Watchers^e*
4Q244	*Pseudo-Daniel*
4Q252	*Commentary on Genesis A*
4Q253	*Commentary on Genesis B*
4Q254	*Commentary on Genesis C*
4Q254a	*Commentary on Genesis D*
4Q364	*Reworked Pentateuch^b*
4Q365	*Reworked Pentateuch^c*
4Q366	*Reworked Pentateuch^a*
4Q367	*Reworked Pentateuch^a*
4Q534–536	*Birth of Noah^{a-c}*
4Q537	*Testament of Jacob*
4Q538	*Testament of Judah*
4Q539	*Testament of Joseph*
4QCommGen	*Genesis Commentary* from Qumran Cave 4
4QEn Giants^a	*Book of Giants*
4QExod-Lev^f	*Exodus-Leviticus*
4QMMT	*Halakhah*
4QpIsa^c	*Isaiah Pesher^c*
4QRP	*Reworked Pentateuch* from Qumran Cave 4

6Q8	*Book of Giants*
11QT[a]	*Temple Scroll[a]*
AGAJU	Arbeiten zur Geschichte des Antiken Judentums und des Urchristentums
AJBA	*Australian Journal of Biblical Archaeology*
ALD	*Aramaic Levi Document*
ARN	*Avot of Rabbi Nathan*
ATTM I	Klaus Beyer, *Die Aramäischen Texte Vom Toten Meer* (Göttingen: Vandenhoeck & Ruprecht, 1984): 165–86.
ATTM II	Klaus Beyer, *Die Aramäischen Texte Vom Toten Meer* (Ergänzungsband; Göttingen: Vandenhoeck & Ruprecht, 1994): 89–101.
b.	Babylonian Talmud
Bar.	Baruch
BETL	Bibliotheca Ephemeridum Theologicarum Lovaniensium
BJS	Brown Judaic Studies
BZAW	Beihefte zur *Zeitschrift für die alttestamentliche Wissenschaft*
CAL	Comprehensive Aramaic Lexicon, edited by Stephen A. Kaufman, Joseph A. Fitzmyer, and Michael Sokoloff (http://cal1.cn.huc.edu)
CBQMS	Catholic Biblical Quarterly Monograph Series
CD	Cairo Geniza *Damascus Document*
CDSSE	Geza Vermes, *The Complete Dead Sea Scrolls in English* (London: Penguin Books, 1997)
CJA	Christianity and Judaism in Antiquity
CQS	Companion to the Qumran Scrolls
CRINT	Compendia Rerum Iudaicarum ad Novum Testamentum.
DJD	Discoveries in the Judaean Desert
DJD 1	D. Barthélemy and J.T. Milik (eds), *Qumran Cave I* (DJD 1; Oxford: Clarendon Press, 1955)
DJD 10	Elisha Qimron and John Strugnell, *Qumran Cave 4, V. Miqsat Ma'aśe Ha-Torah* (DJD 10; in consulation with Y. Sussmann, with contributions by Y. Sussmann and A. Yardeni; Oxford: Clarendon Press, 1994)
DJD 13	Harold W. Attridge *et al.*, *Qumran Cave 4. VIII. Parabiblical Texts, Part I* (DJD 13; Oxford: Clarendon Press, 1994)
DJD 19	Magen Broshi *et al.*, *Qumran Cave 4. XIV. Parabiblical Texts, Part 2* (DJD 19; Oxford: Clarendon Press, 1995).
DJD 22	George J. Brooke *et al.*, *Qumran Cave 4. XVII. Parabiblical Texts, Part 3* (DJD 22; Oxford: Clarendon Press, 1996)
DJD 30	Devorah Dimant, *Qumran Cave 4. XXI. Parabiblical Texts, Part 4. Pseudo-Prophetic Texts* (DJD 30; partially based on earlier texts by John Strugnell; Oxford: Clarendon Press, 2001)
DJD 39	Emanuel Tov (ed.), *The Texts from the Judaean Desert: Indices and an Introduction to the Discoveries in the Judaean Desert Series* (DJD 39; Oxford: Clarendon Press, 2002)
DJD 5	John M. Allegro, in collaboration with A.A. Anderson, *Qumran Cave 4, I (4Q158–4Q186),* (DJD 5; Oxford: Clarendon Press, 1968)
DJPA	Michael Sokoloff, *A Dictionary of Jewish Palestinian Aramaic of the Byzantine Period* (Ramat-Gan, Bar Ilan University Press; Baltimore and London: Johns Hopkins University Press, 2nd edn, 2002)
DSSC	Martin G. Abegg, Jr., *The Dead Sea Scrolls Concordance* (2 vols; with James E. Bowley and Edward M. Cook, in consultation with Emanuel Tov; Leiden: Brill, 2003)
DSSR	Donald W. Parry and Emanuel Tov (eds), *The Dead Sea Scrolls Reader*

	(Leiden: Brill, 2004–2005)
DSSSE	Florentino García Martínez and Eibert J.C. Tigchelaar, *The Dead Sea Scrolls Study Edition* (2 vols; Leiden: Brill, 1997)
DSST	Florentino García Martínez, *The Dead Sea Scrolls Translated: The Qumran Texts in English* (trans. W.G.E. Watson; Leiden: Brill; Grand Rapids: Eerdmans, 2nd edn, 1996)
EDSS	Lawrence H. Schiffman and James C. VanderKam (eds), *Encyclopedia of the Dead Sea Scrolls* (Oxford/New York: Oxford University Press, 2000)
FGA³	Fitzmyer, Joseph A. *The Genesis Apocryphon of Qumran Cave 1 (1Q20)* (Biblica et Orientalia 18B; 3rd edn; Rome: Pontifical Biblical Institute, 2004)
Gen. R.	*Genesis Rabbah*
GQ	Jonas C. Greenfield and Elisha Qimron, 'The Genesis Apocryphon Col. XII', pages 70–77 in T. Muraoka (ed.), *Studies in Qumran Aramaic* (*Abr-Nahrain* Supp. 3; Louvain: Peeters, 1992)
HJP²	Emil Schürer, *The History of the Jewish People in the Age of Jesus Christ. A New English Edition* (3 vols; rev. and ed. G. Vermes, F. Millar, M. Black and M. Goodman; Edinburgh: T & T Clark, 1973–87)
IEJ	*Israel Exploration Journal*
Jastrow	Marcus Jastrow, *A Dictionary of the Targumim, the Targum Babli and Yerushalmi, and the Midrashic Literature* (2 vols; London, 1886–1903; Repr. 2 vols in 1, Jerusalem: Horeb, n.d.).
Jdt.	Judith
Jos. *Ant.*	Josephus *Antiquities of the Jews*
Jos. *Apion*	Josephus *Against Apion*
Jos. *Life*	Josephus *Life*
Jos. *War*	Josephus *The Jewish War*
JSJ	*Journal for the Study of Judaism*
JSS	*Journal of Semitic Studies*
Jub.	*Jubilees*
LAB	*Ps.-Philo Liber antiquitatum biblicarum*
LAE (Apoc.)	*Life of Adam and Eve = Apocalypse of Moses*
LAE (Vit.)	*Life of Adam and Eve*
LEC	Library of Early Christianity
LSTS	Library of Second Temple Studies
LXX	Septuagint
m.	*Mishnah*
Mak.	*Makkot*
Mek.	*Mekilta*
MQS	Matthew Morgenstern, Elisha Qimron, and D. Sivan, 'The Hitherto Unpublished Columns of the Genesis Apocryphon', with Appendix by G. Bearman and S. Spiro, *Abr-Nahrain* 33 (1995): 30–54
MT	Masoretic Text
MVEOL	Mededelingen en Verhandelingen van het Vooraziatisch-Egyptisch Genootschap ex Oriente Lus
Num. R.	*Numbers Rabbah*
OBO	Orbis biblicus et orientalis
Philo	
Abr.	*De Abrahamo*
Agr.	*De agricultura*
Cher.	*De cherubim*

Conf. Ling.	*De confusione linguarum*
Dec.	*De decalogo*
Deus Imm.	*Quod Deus sit immutabilis*
Ebr.	*De ebrietate*
Flacc	*In Flaccum*
Gig.	*De gigantibus*
Leg. Gai.	*Legatio ad Gaium*
Migr. Abr.	*De migratione Abrahami*
Op. Mund.	*De opificio mundi*
Plant.	*De plantatione*
Praem. Poen.	*De praemiis et poenis*
Quaest. In Gen.	*Quaestiones in Genesin*
Spec. Leg.	*De specialibus legibus*
Vit. Cont.	*De vita contemplativa*
Vit. Mos.	*De vita Moses*
PRE	*Pirqe Rabbi Eliezer*
PR	*Pesiqta Rabbati*
PRK	*Pesiqta of Rab Kahana*
Ps.-Eupolemus	*Pseudo-Eupolemus*
Ps.-Philo	*Pseudo-Philo*
S. Olam.	*Seder Olam Rabbah*
Sanh.	*Sanhedrin*
SBLEJL	Society of Biblical Literature Early Judaism and Its Literature
SBLRBS	Society of Biblical Literature Resources for Biblical Study
SC	Sources chrétiennes
ScrHier	Scripta Hierosolymitana
SDSSRL	Studies in the Dead Sea Scrolls and Related Literature
Sib. Or.	*Sibylline Oracles*
Sir.	*Sirach*
SP	Samaritan Pentateuch
STDJ	Studies on the Texts of the Desert of Judah
Tanh.	*Tanhuma*
Tanh. Yel.	*Tanhuma Yelamdenu*
T. Sim.	*Testament of Simeon*
T. Levi	*Testament of Levi*
T. Naph.	*Testament of Naphthali*
T. Benj.	*Testament of Benjamin*
Tg.	*Targum*
Tg. Neof.	*Targum Neofiti*
Tg. Ps.-J.	*Targum Pseudo-Jonathan*
Tg. Onk.	*Targum Onkelos*
Tob.	Tobit
TSAJ	Texte und Studien zum Antiken Judentum
VBJ	James C. VanderKam, *The Book of Jubilees* (CSCO 511, Scriptores Aethiopici 88; Lovanii: Aedibus E. Peeters, 1989)
VTSup	*Vetus Testamentum* Supplement
Wis.	Wisdom

Chapter 1

INTRODUCTION

The subject of this book is a body of writings among the Dead Sea Scrolls that in various ways extend the Scriptures in terms of content, meaning and/or application. In recent years, a vast range of such writings have been grouped together under the rubric 'parabiblical' texts – after 'biblical' texts, these now constitute by far the largest category of the Dead Sea Scrolls.[1] Studying these writings collectively as representing a broad phenomenon is still relatively new, and efforts to understand the significance of the phenomenon they represent are just beginning.

So far, the major questions asked of these writings have to do with the text of 'the Bible', biblical interpretation, and the history of traditions, and significant contributions have been made. It has become apparent that these writings reflect the variety of biblical textual forms recognized by scholars in the Dead Sea Scrolls.[2] Geza Vermes (1973) has shown that they attest strands of tradition that can be traced through to much later rabbinic writings. James Kugel (1998) and others have demonstrated that they need to be taken seriously as products of thoughtful interpretation of Scripture, and Michael Fishbane (1988) has stressed that this carries on developments attested in 'biblical' texts. But lying between 'biblical' text and commentary as this category does, it greatly complicates the matter of identifying what is a 'biblical' text.

As scholars have come to terms with the textual plurality at Qumran, they have mostly abandoned the pursuit of a pristine text of the Hebrew Bible and – with less unanimity – the privileging of a certain text (especially the Masoretic type).[3] Most pointedly, Eugene Ulrich has argued that the Hebrew Bible in the Second Temple period should be understood to be characterized by pluriformity (see p. 17 below). These recognitions, together with a greater awareness of a broad spectrum of writings that variously retell, rework, and interpret scriptural traditions have made it necessary for scholars to wrestle explicitly with the difficulty of distinguishing 'biblical' texts from other works, especially those often designated 'parabiblical' texts. But it has proven notoriously difficult to describe a neat boundary between the two. When one

---

1. In the six volume *The Dead Sea Scrolls Reader* (*DSSR*), the largest volume is 650 pages devoted to parabiblical texts, roughly 28% of the total pages in the series (2306 pages). This volume includes 44 works in approximately 115 manuscripts, out of approximately 900 manuscripts from Qumran, about 200 of which are 'biblical'. Such estimates can only be very rough, since they depend on subjective judgments in counting and classifying manuscripts. *The Dead Sea Scrolls Reader* (*DSSR* 3.x, n. 3) generally follows but diverges somewhat from the classification by Armin Lange and Mittman-Richert in DJD 39 (2002a: 117–31).

2. For example, VanderKam 2002b; 1978; Tov 1992; 1998a; Brooke 2002d.

3. Ulrich 2003b: 63; Tov also has more recently moved away from focus on MT (see Tov 2002: 246).

acknowledges inner-biblical interpretation (e.g., Deuteronomy versus Exodus) and variant editions of biblical texts with interpretative modifications (e.g., the Samaritan Pentateuch, MT Jeremiah; Tov 2001: 313–50; Ulrich 1999b), with what criteria does one designate other interpretative renderings of scriptural traditions as 'para-' (and hence *not*) biblical? The question is particularly confounding when dealing with works only fragmentarily preserved. Debates in recent literature reflect an increasing frustration with the Procrustean task of trying to fit the texts into current categories and terminology (e.g., biblical, parabiblical, rewritten Bible; e.g., Campbell 2005; Chiesa 1998). Such questions of classification and definition are part of a larger set of questions having to do with what it means to view these writings as a group representing a phenomenon. What was the purpose of such writings? How were they read and used? These questions may also be turned to ask about the social context of the communities represented (e.g., Nickelsburg 2003a; Schuller 2003; Nickelsburg 2003b).

The data calls, however, for consideration of an even more fundamental question: what is Scripture in Second Temple Judaism? By this I mean not just what should be categorized as Scripture, but what is the conception underlying the phenomenon (or better, phenomena) we might call Scripture? This question picks up a line of inquiry urged since the 1970s by Wilfred Cantwell Smith and his students from a history of religions perspective (Smith 1993; Graham 1987; Levering 1989). These complain that the academic study of Scripture has been dominated by Western – and most specifically Protestant Christian – conceptions of what Scripture is, and they seek instead to describe generic understandings of the phenomena of Scripture and to trace developments of the process of scripturalizing. It will be of great value to the present topic to be informed by such a perspective. On the one hand, the data under consideration offers a unique opportunity: with the Dead Sea Scrolls we are privileged to have a spectrum of texts that clearly reflect a 'Scripture consciousness', and to have glimpses of crucial stages in the scripturalizing process. That is, our data is of both diachronic and synchronic importance. On the other hand, I suspect that a more open approach to what is Scripture – without assuming that what Scripture came to be and mean and function as later in Judaism and Christianity was fully operative in the Second Temple period – will ease some of the difficulties in coming to terms with the data.

In this book I offer studies of three representative texts across the diversity of the corpus: an extended examination of the *Genesis Apocryphon*, and shorter surveys of the *Reworked Pentateuch* and *Genesis Commentary*. In each case, I seek to describe the relationships of the work with known versions of scriptural texts and other writings, and methods of extending scriptural traditions. It should be noted that the language of 'extending' Scripture is used here deliberately to remain non-committal with regard to whether these texts were intended as or functioned as supplementary or complementary to Scripture. With regard to these texts we face two initial questions, which are related. The first has to do with categorization. Where does this material fit? In the broadest sense, are they to be regarded as 'biblical' texts or 'extra-biblical' texts? The second question is really a refinement of the first, but addresses the issue of function. What is the purpose or function of this material? Did these texts function as Scripture, or as interpretation of Scripture, or something else? Thus, before examining the texts, we must survey the state of discussions about classification and genre, Scripture and canon, and the extension and interpretation of Scripture. A concluding chapter will seek to synthesize the insights gained with regard to the driving questions:

what is the significance of these methods of extending Scripture for understanding the scripturalizing process and the function of Scripture in the religious communities represented.

1. *Classification and Genre*

Early scholarship on the Dead Sea Scrolls tended to divide the manuscripts among four main categories: Bible, Apocrypha, Pseudepigrapha, and sectarian texts (e.g., Cross 1995: 44–45, Milik 1959: 20–43). That is, the texts were classified according to categories traditional in Protestant Christian scholarship, defined in relation to a canonical Bible. The *Genesis Apocryphon*, among the first texts discovered, was classified as pseudepigraphical and described as 'a sort of apocryphal version of stories from *Genesis*' (Avigad and Yadin 1956: 38). This text was also compared with – and sometimes classified as – targum, midrash, and haggadah, categories drawn from rabbinic literature (see; Fitzmyer 2004: 18–20; cf. Vermes 1986 3.1: 308). In his pioneering study of haggadic traditions in 1961, Vermes recognized a common strategy among a number of writings that he termed 'rewritten Bible' (Vermes 1973: 95). By this he defined a distinctive corpus of texts that included the *Genesis Apocryphon* along with the Palestinian Targum, Josephus's *Jewish Antiquities, Pseudo-Philo, Jubilees,* and the medieval *Sefer ha-Yashar*. Ginsberg also perceived commonality among the *Genesis Apocryphon, Pseudo-Philo* and *Jubilees* and proposed the term 'parabiblical literature' for the literary genre of such works 'which paraphrase and/or supplement the canonical Scriptures' (Ginsberg 1967: 574). Both of these latter categories have come to be adopted quite broadly in scholarship on early Jewish literature, and used in divergent and at times conflicting ways.

We may notice here the movement from the use of existing categories to the creation of new categories. In this way, scholarly classification is not that dissimilar to household organization. As items accumulate, one naturally adds first to current drawers and boxes with similar items. At some point, the old storage system is no longer adequate and one must add new boxes, perhaps subdividing and rearranging. Eventually, however, this makeshift approach may prove unwieldy and the entire organization system need to be rethought from the beginning (cf. the streamlined taxonomy of Carolus Linnaeus). Taking the analogy of organizational boxes, there are three distinct issues relevant to our task. At one level, the task of classification is simply asking in which box an item belongs. A second task is labeling or naming: what are the best labels for the boxes? These are the most immediate tasks, and with regard to our current subject the source of some considerable confusion since scholars use the various labels with rather different meanings and to name different groupings of the texts. This is both a diachronic and synchronic issue, having to do both with changes of terminology and understanding of commonalities among texts, and also different judgments about the nature of the texts and their relationships. For the sake of clarity, I will survey below some of the major scholars and their classifications. There is a third issue, however, that has so far received little explicit consideration, although it is implicit in the increasing complaints of scholars that the categories no longer seem appropriate. This is the matter of conceptualization. In our analogy it is looking at the boxes themselves and asking what it means to have these boxes. Irrespective of labels, peoples at different times and in different cultures would have apportioned the items differently among the boxes. We deal here with the perception of a generic for grouping the particular. How is it that we perceive difference and commonality, and how have these perceptions changed through time and culture? I will return to this issue further below.

It is important to recall that when Vermes introduced the term rewritten Bible, it was not as the title of a distinct literary genre, but as a description of a strategy employed in the genre of midrash (Vermes 1973: 95–96, 124). He recognized this strategy as exemplified in a group of texts that had only recently come to the attention of modern scholars around the middle of the twentieth century – the *Genesis Apocryphon, Pseudo-Philo*, and the Palestinian targums – and proposed that with them one can trace the development of the genre from biblical to rabbinic midrash.

When H. L. Ginsberg introduced the term parabiblical literature in his review of Fitzmyer's edition of the *Genesis Apocryphon*, it was as a title of a distinct literary genre for roughly the same group of texts Vermes described as rewritten Bible (Ginsberg 1967: 574).

> To the question of literary genre, I should like to contribute a proposal for a term to cover works, like GA, Pseudo-Philo, and the Book of Jubilees, which paraphrase and/or supplement the canonical Scriptures: parabiblical literature. The motivation of such literature – like that of midrash – may be more doctrinal, as in the case of the Book of Jubilees, or more artistic, as in at least the preserved parts of GA, but it differs from midrashic literature by not directly quoting and (with more or less arbitrariness) interpreting canonical Scripture.

It should be noted that this definition excludes works with explicit interpretation from the category of parabiblical, and in contrast to Vermes, differentiates the category from midrash.

In recent years, the tendency has been to speak of midrash in the Second Temple period as an interpretative *activity* as distinct from the formal literary *genre* of rabbinic midrash (see Porton 1992; Strack and Stemberger 1996; Brooke 2000c 1: 298). Also we may note a trend to use rewritten Bible as a literary genre and para-biblical literature as a broad category that includes rewritten Bible along with other genres.

The latter trend is represented above all in the series Discoveries in the Judaean Desert, for which Emanuel Tov adopted the designation 'parabiblical texts' for an umbrella category to include 'various compositions which have in common that they are closely related to texts or themes of the Hebrew Bible. Some of these composi-tions present a reworking, rewriting, or paraphrase of biblical books' (DJD 13: ix).[4] Four volumes of the DJD series are entirely devoted to this category – volumes 13, 19, 22, and 30 – but these do not exhaust the grouping, which also includes numerous texts published elsewhere (especially the *Genesis Apocryphon* and some texts in DJD 1, 3, 5, 25, 26, 28, 31, and 36). Compositions included cover a spectrum of relation-ships to biblical books ranging from close correspondence to more remote, and from extensive to works using only a small section or theme from a biblical book as a starting point. At first it was not clear whether Tov intended parabiblical texts as a

---

4.   The introduction of the term 'parabiblical' is sometimes attributed to E. Tov (Lange 2003: 305; García Martínez 2004: 369). This is not entirely correct. To my knowledge, the first to propose its use in relation to the Dead Sea Scrolls was H. Ginsberg, although with a narrower range (Ginsberg 1967: 574). Tov introduced its use for a very broad range of texts.

specific literary genre, as possibly implied in an early comment: 'Beginning with this volume most of the documents from cave 4 will be published according to their literary genre ... parabiblical texts ..., halakhic texts, calendrical texts, poetical and liturgical texts, sectarian-sapiential texts, Aramaic texts' (DJD 13: ix). It was also not clear whether he intended the category to exclude works with explicit interpretation; the *Genesis Commentaries* from cave 4 were included in DJD 22, and in the quote just cited there was no separate category for exegetical texts.

Florentino García Martínez follows Tov's usage of 'parabiblical texts' for his translations of the Dead Sea Scrolls, although he specifically indicates that it is not a genre but embraces numerous genres. It includes

> material differing greatly in literary form and in origin: reports, apocalypses, testaments, etc. Even so, all the compositions from which this material comes could be classed as 'para-biblical literature', literature that begins with the Bible, which retells the biblical text in its own way, intermingling it and expanding it with other, quite different traditions. Every one of these compositions has its starting point in specific texts of the Torah or of the Prophets but, unlike the exegetical literature, rather than interpreting the biblical text, they elaborate on it, augmenting it with other material. (García Martínez 1994: 218, and see x–xii, 218–99)

García Martínez also specifically isolates exegetical literature as a separate category, where he classifies the *Genesis Commentaries*. The basis for the distinction given in this definition, however, is somewhat misleading, by possibly implying that the parabiblical texts are not interpretative. The difficulty in dividing between the two categories is also apparent in that he classifies the targums and *Temple Scroll* as exegetical, but *Reworked Pentateuch* – which has numerous similarities to the *Temple Scroll* including similar interpretative strategies – as parabiblical (see García Martínez 1995: 129).

He does not subdivide parabiblical texts according to genre, but differentiates among the material in terms of 'fidelity to the original biblical text' (García Martínez 1994: 218). His first category comprises texts that more and less closely follow the plot of the biblical text: the *Genesis Apocryphon*, *Jubilees*, and various other 'paraphrases of the Pentateuch' including *Reworked Pentateuch*, *Apocryphon of David*, *Admonition Based on the Flood*, and *Apocryphon of Joseph*, among others (4Q458, 4Q462, 4Q522, 4Q559, 6Q19, 6Q20).[5] This category is roughly equivalent to what others often refer to as rewritten Bible, but García Martínez seems to avoid the term. It is not clear whether this reflects a deliberate hesitation to regard rewritten Bible as a literary genre.[6]

His second category encompasses compositions that start with the biblical text but result in an independent work. This includes works that take as their starting point a biblical episode or motif (the *Books of Enoch* and *Book of Giants*) or focus on biblical characters: Noah (1Q19; 4Q534–36); the Patriarchs (*Apocryphon of Jacob*, *T. Judah*, *T. Joseph*, *T. Naphtali*, *Aramaic Levi*, *T. Qahat*, *Visions of Amram*); Moses (*Words of Moses*, *Liturgy of the Three Tongues of Fire*, *Apocryphon of Moses*, *Pseudo-Moses*);

5. In this and other lists of texts, for better-known works I normally give the standard name as adopted in DJD and represented in *DSSR*. This means on occasion altering the name of a text as used by a particular author. For the Qumran numbers, see either the author cited, the index in DJD 39, or the table of contents of *DSSR*.
6. See also García Martínez 1995: 127–30 and 2004: 369–71.

Joshua (*Psalms of Joshua*); Samuel (*Vision of Samuel, Apocryphon of Samuel-Kings*);
Jeremiah (*Apocryphon of Jeremiah*); Ezekiel (*Pseudo-Ezekiel*); Daniel (*Pseudo-Daniel,
Prayer of Nabonidus, Daniel-Susannah*). A third category includes texts that are paral-
lel to but with no direct connection to the biblical text, such as *Proto-Esther* and Tobit.

The most comprehensive attempt at classifying the Dead Sea Scrolls manuscripts
is that by Armin Lange, incorporated into DJD 39.[7] Lange states that parabiblical is
not a literary genre, but is the designation for a large category of texts that includes
various literary genres.

> On the basis of biblical texts or themes, the authors of parabiblical texts employ exege-
> tical techniques to provide answers to questions of their own time, phrased as answers
> by God through Moses or the prophets. The result of their exegetical effort is commu-
> nicated in the form of a new book. Therefore, parabiblical literature should not be
> understood as a pseudepigraphic phenomenon, i.e., the ascription of a literary work to a
> biblical author, but as a form of scriptural revelation, comparable to the phenomenon of
> literary prophecy. For this purpose, the authors of parabiblical literature used different
> genres: Rewritten Bible, new stories or novellas created on the basis of biblical items or
> topics, different types of apocalypses, and testaments. (Lange 2002a: 117–18)

The texts included in each genre are as follows:

1. Rewritten Bible: the *Genesis Apocryphon, Discourse on the Exodus/Conquest
    Tradition, Jubilees, Pseudo-Jubilees, Apocryphon of Moses, Pentateuch
    Apocryphon, Temple Scroll, Apocryphon of Joshua, Prophecy of Joshua,
    Work with Place Names, Visions of Samuel, Pseudo-Ezekiel, Prayer of Enosh*
2. Stories based on biblical items: *Book of Giants*, the 'Birth of Noah' in the
    Genesis Apocryphon, Birth of Noah, Aramaic Levi Document
3. Apocalypses (sub-divided): *Astronomical Book, Book of Watchers, Book of
    Dreams, Apocryphon of Jeremiah, New Jerusalem, Apocryphon of Daniel,
    Four Kingdoms, Pseudo-Daniel*
4. Testaments: *Testament of Jacob* (?), *Testament of Judah, Testament of Ben-
    jamin, Visions of Amram, Apocryphon of Levi*
5. Texts of mixed genre: *Letter of Enoch, Testament of Naphtali, Testament of
    Joseph, Testament of Qahat, Epistle of Jeremiah*
6. Unclassified: *Paraphrase of Genesis and Exodus, Admonition Based on the
    Flood, Text Mentioning the Flood, Noah, Exposition on the Patriarchs, Text
    Concerning Rachel and Joseph, Apocryphon of Moses* (?), *Paraphrase of
    Exodus, Pentateuch Apocryphon B, Paraphrase of Kings, Apocryphon of
    Samuel–Kings, Text Mentioning Zedekiah*, and several unidentified narrative
    and poetic compositions

Lange expressly uses rewritten Bible as a literary genre, but does not include
Reworked Pentateuch on the argument that it is instead best regarded as a 'biblical'
text (Lange 2002a: 122). He introduces the valuable qualification that parabiblical

---

7. With U. Mittmann-Richert, Lange presents an annotated list of his classification of the Dead
Sea Scrolls in DJD 39 (Lange 2002a); for parabiblical and exegetical texts see 117–18, 122–31. He
will present a more extensive analysis in his forthcoming *Einleitung in die Textfunde vom Toten
Meer*. For a detailed discussion of parabiblical literature more broadly in early Judaism and its
implication for the canonical history of the Hebrew Bible, see Lange 2003.

texts must be related to an existing authoritative text (Lange 2003: 310 Table 2; 320 Table 4). Therefore, in contrast to García Martínez, he does not include *Prayer of Nabonidus*, *Proto-Esther*, or Tobit, classifiying them instead as historical tales (Lange 2002a: 141). He both acknowledges that parabiblical texts are interpretative and clearly distinguishes exegetical texts as a separate group on the basis of implicit versus explicit interpretation. 'In contrast to parabiblical compositions which also employ exegetical techniques, the texts grouped [as exegetical texts] display their exegetical interest even in their respective genres', especially continuous and thematic pesharim (Lange 2002a: 118). The main distinction is that exegetical texts contain features to explicitly mark interpretation. Thus, he classifies the *Genesis Commentaries* as exegetical texts, but in contrast to García Martínez classifies the *Temple Scroll* under parabiblical texts as rewritten Bible. Lange identifies the following genres of exegetical texts:

1. Thematic pesharim: *Midrash on Eschatology*, *Ages of Creation A* and *B*, *Melchizedek*
2. Continuous pesharim: *Pesher Isaiah*, *Pesher Hosea*, *Pesher Micah*, *Pesher Nahum*, *Pesher Habakkuk*, *Pesher Zephaniah*, *Pesher Psalms*
3. Commentaries without pesher formula: *Commentary on Genesis*, *Tanhumim*, *Commentary on Malachi*
4. Halakhic Midrash: *Midrash Sefer Moshe*
5. Other Exegetical Texts: *Testimonia*, *List of False Prophets*, *Biblical Chronology*, and several unclassified texts, including *Pesher on the Apocalypse of Weeks*

Lange's classification is in turn adopted for *The Dead Sea Scrolls Reader* by D. Parry and E. Tov with only a few modifications (*DSSR* 3: see xxiii–xxiv).[8] Most importantly, Parry and Tov include *Reworked Pentateuch* as rewritten Bible. Although they also distinguish exegetical texts from parabiblical texts on the grounds of explicit versus implicit exegesis, they acknowledge a good deal of overlap and note that 'an exact line of distinction cannot be drawn between the two groups of texts' (*DSSR* 2: xxi).

The three examples just cited (Tov, García Martínez, Lange) represent a similar approach to classifying a broad range of compositions that fit between Bible on the one hand and commentary on the other.[9] The boundaries of this in-between category of parabiblical texts are acknowledged as blurry in practice but are distinguished in theory at least.[10]

We may consider together a second diverse group of scholars who, despite considerable differences in details, share in common that they treat rewritten scriptural texts and explicit commentary such as the pesharim more as lying on a continuum of interpretative literature. That is, instead of three categories of Scriptures, parabiblical and

8. They acknowledge that some apocalyptic works can be regarded as parabiblical in agreement with Lange, although they present them together with other apocalyptic works in volume 6 (*DSSR* 3: xxiv) .

9. See also Trebolle Barrera (1998: 184–204, esp. 201), although his use of terminology is inconsistent.

10. On the artificial and overlapping nature of these boundaries, see García Martínez 2004: 370–71; Trebolle Barrera 2000: 100–103. We may also perhaps include here Devorah Dimant who distinguishes between 'expositional' and 'compositional' use of biblical material and states that only the former has as its purpose to interpret the text (Dimant 1988: 382–83, 400). The distinction is similar to Perrot's *texte expliqué* and *texte continué* (Perrot and Bogaert 1976: 24–27).

exegetical texts, they tend to emphasize two categories: Scriptures and a broad category of interpretative literature (sometimes referred to as parabiblical). These place somewhat less stress on the formal distinction between implicit and explicit exegesis, emphasizing that a major purpose of all of these texts is to interpret authoritative Scriptures. An important corollary is that these texts assume an existing body of authoritative Scriptures – although not necessarily a fixed 'canonical Bible' – that they accompany rather than replace.

Vermes is a central example. In his collection of translations, he has two chapters entitled respectively 'Bible interpretation' and 'biblically based apocryphal works', but these do not correspond to the categories of exegetical and parabiblical texts as in the DJD classification. Rather, he regards all of these texts as examples of biblical commentary, which he sub-divides into five types (Vermes 1997: 429–30):[11]

1. 'The first and least developed form of exegesis is contained in the so-called "Reworked Pentateuch" texts, consisting of a quasi-traditional text of the Bible, occasionally rearranged and supplemented' (e.g., *Reworked Pentateuch, Paraphrase of Genesis and Exodus, Temple Scroll*, but also the Aramaic targums and Greek Bible translations)

2. 'The second type ... sets out to render the Bible story more intelligible and attractive by giving it more substance, by reconciling conflicting statements, and by reinterpreting in the light of contemporary standards and beliefs any passages which might seem to give offence' (e.g., the *Genesis Apocryphon, Genesis Commentary*)

3. 'The third type of commentary departs from the biblical text and, relying on one or several passages, creates a new story' (e.g., *Admonition Based on the Flood, Words of Moses, New Jerusalem, Prayer of Nabonidus*)

4. 'The fourth and most characteristic form of exegesis applies prophetic texts to the past, present and future of the sect. Normally the commentator expounds a biblical book verse by verse ... but some works ... follow the traditional Jewish example and assemble passages from different parts of Scripture in order to develop a common theme' (i.e., the continuous pesharim and the thematic pesharim, which include *Florilegium, Testimonia, Ordinances, Melchizedek, Tanhumim, Catanae A* and *B*)

5. His last category is 'a substantial amount of free compositions modelled on the Bible' (e.g., *Jubilees*, books of *Enoch, Book of Giants, Book of Noah, Aramaic Levi Document, Testament of Levi, Testament of Naphtali, Joseph Apocryphon, Testament of Qahat, Testament of Amram, Discourse on the Exodus/Conquest Tradition, Moses Apocryphon, Pseudo-Moses, Pseudo-Daniel*, and *Tobit*)[12]

---

11. In the following list, I modify some of the names to those used in DJD 39, and omit some less well-identified items. For the text numbers, see Vermes 1997: x–xi. Elsewhere, Vermes has used the designation 'biblical midrash' as an umbrella term for such texts (1986).

12. The remaining works presented in his chapter on 'biblically based apocryphal works' would presumably fit into either his third or fifth category: *Prayer of Enosh, Ages of Creation, Words of the Archangel Michael, Joseph Apocryphon, Testament of Qahat, Visions of Amram, Narrative and Poetic Composition, Prophecy of Joshua, Joshua Apocryphon, Visions of Samuel, Elisha Apocryphon, Text Mentioning Zedekiah, Exposition on the Patriarchs, Jeremiah Apocryphon, Pseudo-Ezekiel, Four Kingdoms, Daniel Apocryphon, Proto-Esther*.

Lawrence Schiffman has a very similar classification, dividing a broad category of biblical interpretation into the following genres (1994: 211–41):

1. Translation (including Aramaic targums and Greek translation)
2. Plain sense commentary (e.g., *Genesis Commentary* which involves retelling the Bible, but is distinct from that genre)
3. Retelling the Bible (e.g., the *Genesis Apocryphon*)
4. Harmonizing interpretation (e.g., *Temple Scroll, Rewritten Pentateuch*)
5. Halakhic midrash (e.g., parts of *Damascus Document*)
6. Pesher

Sidnie White Crawford (2000b: 173–74; 2006: 131–32) distinguishes four categories of interpretative literature at Qumran:

1. 'Rewritten Bible', which 'has a close narrative attachment to some book contained in the present Jewish canon of scripture, and some type of reworking, whether through rearrangement, conflation, omission, or supplementation of the present canonical biblical text'
2. '"Parabiblical" texts, which may be tied to some person, event, or pericope in the present canonical text, but do not actually reuse extensively the biblical text'
3. 'Works loosely related to a biblical book, but with no overt tie, such as the *Prayer of Nabonidus* or *Proto-Esther*'
4. 'Commentaries (e.g., pesharim), which make a clear distinction between biblical lemma and interpretation'

In contrast to the classification of Tov and Lange where rewritten Bible is a subcategory of parabiblical, White Crawford views rewritten Bible and parabiblical as sub-categories of the same order on a graded scale from close to more remote from the biblical text.

Considerable attention has been given to attempts to define the category rewritten Bible as a distinct literary genre. The most thorough definition is by Philip Alexander (1988: 116), who describes rewritten Bible texts as 'narratives, which follow a sequential, chronological order. Their framework is an account of events, and so they may be described broadly as histories. They are not theological treatises, though an account of events may incidentally serve theological ends'. On the basis of form, attitude towards the authority of the Bible, use of biblical and non-biblical material, and exegetical methods, he argues that such texts as *Jubilees*, the *Genesis Apocryphon*, *Pseudo-Philo*, and Josephus's *Jewish Antiquities* do represent a definite literary genre, with the following principle characteristics (Alexander 1988: 116–18):

a. They are 'narratives which follow a sequential, chronological order'
b. They are 'free-standing compositions which replicate the form of the biblical books on which they are based'
c. They are 'not intended to replace, or to supersede the Bible'
d. They 'cover a substantial portion of the Bible' and are 'centripetal', reintegrating legends into biblical history
e. They 'follow the Bible serially, in proper order, but they are highly selective in what they represent'
f. 'The intention of the texts is to produce an interpretative reading of Scripture'

g.   'They can impose only a single interpretation on the original'
h.   'The limitations of the narrative form also preclude making clear the exegetical reasoning'
i.   They 'make use of non-biblical tradition and draw on non-biblical sources, whether oral or written'

With regard to the function of these texts, he proposes:

> By fusing this material with the biblical narrative the rewritten Bible texts appear to be aiming at a synthesis of the whole tradition (both biblical and extra-biblical) within a biblical framework: they seek to unify the tradition on a biblical base. Though they accord the Bible priority in the synthesis they have a high regard for non-biblical tradition. As in the case of Jubilees they may even regard it as inspired. So their intention may be seen as both exegetical and eisegetical: they seek to draw out the sense of Scripture and to solve its problems, and at the same time to read non-biblical material into Scripture, thereby validating it and preventing the fragmentation of the tradition. (Alexander 1988: 118)

Moshe Bernstein (2005b) similarly concludes that rewritten Bible is meaningful as a literary genre if it is narrowly defined, but he argues that there is no reason to restrict it to narrative. It should include rewritten legal texts as well, especially the *Temple Scroll*.[13] He too emphasizes the interpretative function of rewritten Bible texts, distinguished from explicit commentary more in terms of diachronic development than function: 'it is possible that "Rewritten Bible" represents the earliest generic attempt to comment on the Bible before the more economical "commentary" form was developed' (Bernstein 2000: 379). Similar to Michael Segal (2000; 2005), Bernstein seeks to define more sharply the border between rewritten Bible as a genre and biblical text.[14] These both distinguish betwen the process of rewriting (or revising) of biblical texts and the genre 'rewritten Bible', which should by definition exclude revised biblical texts (e.g., Deuteronomy, Chronicles, Samaritan Pentateuch) and biblical translations (e.g., targums and the Septuagint). *Reworked Pentateuch* poses a problem as a borderline case: Segal classes it as a revision of a biblical text analogous to the Samaritan Pentateuch – and hence not belonging to the genre rewritten Bible. Bernstein argues that even if it is not clear that one should call it rewritten Bible, it falls on the side of biblical interpretation rather than biblical text, although the authors may have regarded it as Scripture with interpretation in the text.[15] This latter qualification hints at the extreme problems of attempting a Solomonic division here. Like Alexander, Bernstein's definition also differentiates from works more loosely related to the Bible or based on a limited part of a biblical text, for which he accepts the broader term 'parabiblical': rewritten Bible is a 'comprehensive or broad scope rewriting of narrative

---

13. Borgen (1997: 56, 78–79) makes the same point to include Philo's *Exposition on the Laws of Moses* as belonging to a genre of rewritten Bible.

14. Segal (2005) lists the following criteria for rewritten Bible: it must be in the same language as the original (thus, excludes *Genesis Apocryphon*, Josephus's *Jewish Antiquities*, and the targums); it must have a scope relative to the biblical original; a new narrative frame; a different narrative voice; presence of expansion as well as abridgment; tendentious editorial layer; it must contain explicit references to the source composition.

15. To be more precise, it should be noted that both Bernstein and Segal regard 4Q158 to be of a different composition than 4Q364–67. Segal regards 4Q158 to be an example of rewritten Bible, but 4Q364–67 to be biblical manuscripts; Bernstein (2005b: 181–83) regards 4Q364–67 to be possibly rewritten Bible.

and/or legal material with commentary woven into the fabric implicitly, but perhaps *not* merely a biblical text with some superimposed exegesis' (Bernstein 2005b: 195).

Rewritten Bible as a genre of interpretative literature is often viewed from a diachronic perspective in the context of the development of sacred tradition, from late biblical books reinterpreting and rewriting earlier traditions, to rewritten Bible complementary to Scripture, to explicit commentary; that is, as sacred tradition became stabilized, interpretation became increasingly external to the sacred text.[16]

Other scholars do not recognize rewritten Bible as a distinct literary genre, but use the designation rather loosely for a 'literary technique, process or activity' that is expressed in various genres within a broad range of intepretative writings.[17] Thus, Nickelsburg and Harrington use the term to describe a range of texts almost as broad as that for which Tov and Lange use the term 'parabiblical', embracing numerous genres and ranging from texts with large-scale correspondence to a biblical narrative as well as texts that use only a limited story or theme as a jumping point for a new composition.[18] Nickelsburg places this phenomenon of texts closely following biblical works and implicitly commenting on them in a diachronic perspective: it 'may be seen as a reflection of their developing canonical status' (Nickelsburg 1984: 89). Bruce Fisk uses the term to describe a more narrowly circumscribed group of texts – but still too diverse to constitute a literary genre – with the following characteristics:

1. They 'offer a coherent and sustained retelling of sustantial portions of Old Testament narrative, generally in chronological sequence and in accord with the narrative framework of Scripture itself'
2. They integrate extrabiblical traditions into the biblical storyline
3. They contain implicit rather than explicit exegesis, 'by filling gaps, solving problems and explaining connections in the biblical text'
4. They serve as companion to rather than replacement of Scripture (Fisk 2000b: 947–48)

---

16. See Evans (1988: 165), Kugel (1998: 3), Bernstein (2000: 379), and Najman (2000: 212–14; 2003: 7–9 [and nn. 13–14], 16–17 [and n. 33], and 41–50).

17. This summary is from B. Halpern-Amaru (1994: 4, and see 130 nn. 7–8), who differentiates this from use 'for a specific genre of literature'.

18. Nickelsburg describes rewritten Bible as 'literature that is very closely related to the biblical texts, expanding and paraphrasing them and implicitly commenting on them. This tendency to follow the ancient texts more closely may be seen as a reflection of their developing canonical status' (Nickelsburg 1984: 89); and 'a form of biblical exposition that interprets a narrative by retelling it in an elaborated form ... Its purpose is to expound sacred tradition so that it speaks to contemporary times and issues' (Nickelsburg 2001: 29). In a chapter titled 'Bible Rewritten and Expanded', Nickelsburg (1984) includes: *1 Enoch, Book of Giants, Jubilees, Genesis Apocryphon, Biblical Antiquities, Apocalypse of Moses, Life of Adam and Eve, Philo the Epic Poet, Theodotus the Epic Poet, Ezekiel the Tragedian*. Elsewhere (Nickelsburg 2001: 29), he also includes testamentary literature (*Testament of Moses, Testaments of the 12 Patriarchs, Testament of Abraham, Testament of Job*).

Harrington describes as rewritten Bible works that 'take as their literary framework the flow of the biblical text itself and apparently have as their major purpose the clarification and actualization of the biblical story', including such diverse texts as *Jubilees, Assumption/Testament of Moses, Temple Scroll, Genesis Apocryphon*, Pseudo-Philo's *Biblical Antiquities*, and Josephus's *Jewish Antiquities*, and less fully, *Paralipomena of Jeremiah, Life of Adam and Eve/Apocalypse of Moses*, and *Ascension of Isaiah, Enochic* writings, *4 Ezra, 2 Baruch*, and some of Philo's work. 'What holds all of them together is the effort to actualize a religious tradition and make it meaningful within new situations' (Harrington 1986: 239).

Besides the central examples of *Jubilees*, *Pseudo-Philo*, and the *Genesis Apocryphon*, he acknowledges the practice among canonical works such as Deuteronomy and Chronicles (also 1 Esdras), and also includes *Reworked Pentateuch*, *Genesis Commentary*, *Ps-Jubilees* and *Words of Moses* among the Dead Sea Scrolls and *1 Enoch*, *Testament of Moses*, *Ezekiel the Tragedian*, *Demetrius the Chronographer*, Josephus's *Jewish Antiquities*, and Philo's *Life of Moses*. He excludes non-narrative works (e.g., *Temple Scroll*), and interpretative translation and paraphrase such as the Septuagint and the targums (Fisk 2000b: 947; Fisk 2001: 13–14 and n. 3).

George Brooke also uses rewritten Bible more loosely as an activity found in many genres rather than as a literary genre itself,[19] but he introduces the very important clarification that the genre of the new work is related to the genre of the scriptural source. Thus, he identifies the following features:

1. 'The source is thoroughly embedded in its rewrtten form not as explicit citation but as a running text'
2. 'The order of the source is followed extensively'
3. 'The content of the source is followed relatively closely'
4. 'The original genre or genres stays much the same' … 'the source provides the generic model' (Brooke 2002d: 31–33)
5. They 'clearly display an editorial intention that is other than or supplementary to that of the text being altered' (Brooke 2000f: 777–78)

Behind this perspective is that Brooke takes very seriously the textual diversity of Scripture in the Second Temple period and the implications of some 'biblical' writings being the product of rewriting (Brooke 2000f: 778; Brooke 2002d: 31–32). Without prejudicing an anachronistic concept of a canonical Bible, there is no appropriate basis for defining rewritten Bible as distinctly different from 'biblical' writings that are themselves rewritings of earlier works (Brooke 2000f: 778; Brooke 2002d: 35–36). He suggests the term 'rewritten scriptural texts' instead of 'rewritten Bible': 'A rewritten scriptural text is essentially a composition which shows clear dependence on a scriptural text. It must be clearly recognized at the outset that, by virtue of its being dependent on an authoritative scriptural text, a rewritten text is not necessarily thereby non-authoritative, or in anachronistic terms non-canonical' (Brooke 2002d: 31–32). Thus, Brooke upholds the existence of a recognizable body of authoritative Scriptures that are variously appropriated at the same time as downplaying a hard boundary between biblical and rewritten (and parabiblical) texts such as sought by Bernstein, Segal, and White Crawford. In fact, rewritten Bible works 'are a major indicator of the emergence of an authoritative body of Jewish literature after the exile' (Brooke 2002d: 31). They 'generally follow the biblical text closely; the appropriateness of the label depends on discerning that the biblical text acts persistently as the primary control on what is re-presented. Rewritten Bible texts thus reflect a consistent attitude of respect to the authoritative base text. They do not replace the biblical text, but offer alternative or supplementary versions of it' (Brooke 2000f: 780).

---

19. It is 'any representation of an authoritative scriptural text that implicitly incorporates interpretive elements, large or small in the retelling itself'; such retellings 'follow closely their scriptural base text and which clearly display an editorial intention that is other than or supplementary to that of the text being altered' (Brooke 2000f: 777–78).

Common to these diverse scholars is the distinction of an existing biblical text which is interpreted implicitly by creating a new work that is a synthesis of biblical writing and extra-biblical tradition. The problem of delineating the distinction in practice is evident in the work of Bernstein, Segal, and Tov, as well as in White Crawford's reference to 'the present Jewish canon of Scripture' as a standard.[20] There is ultimately no way to distinguish a definitive body of Scriptures for the Second Temple period without the choice being somewhat arbitrary. Although the problem is explicitly acknowledged by most of these scholars, Brooke emphasizes that the boundary between scriptural and rewritten scriptural works (or parascriptural) is so weak as to be virtually meaningless. In this way, Brooke is on the borderline with scholars we may conveniently discuss as a third group.

This third group is represented by scholars who question the very basis for distinguishing between scriptural books and rewritten scriptural works.[21] These emphasize that there is no generic distinction between the rewriting activity in works that came to be included in the Hebrew Bible (especially Deuteronomy, Chronicles, MT Jeremiah, and the base text for the Samaritan Pentateuch) and the rewriting in works that are not part of the succeeding Bible. What especially distinguishes this group from the views discussed in the first two groups is that they tend toward a maximalist position with regard to the body of sacred writings in Second Temple Judaism. Particularly influential here are Ulrich's theories about multiple literary editions and the pluriform nature of Scripture in the Second Temple period; he suggests that *Reworked Pentateuch* may best viewed as a variant 'biblical' edition not fundamentally different from the Samaritan Pentateuch (Ulrich 1998: 88–89; 2000b: 56–57; 2000a: 76).[22]

James VanderKam (2000; 2002a), for example, argues that there was no canon of Scripture in Second Temple Judaism in the sense of an exclusive list of authoritative texts. Furthermore, although there is good evidence that the Torah of Moses was deemed authoritative generally in Judaism of the time, it cannot be assumed that this corresponded to the traditional Pentateuch, especially among the Jews represented at Qumran and among the early Christians. Because of the abundant evidence of textual fluidity among 'biblical' texts, there are no good grounds in terms of form or content to differentiate 'rewritten biblical' works such as the *Reworked Pentateuch*, *Temple Scroll* and *Jubilees* from the 'biblical' texts of Genesis to Deuteronomy. Neither can one reliably distinguish them on the basis of reception: these texts present themselves as divine word and there is no reason to believe they were not received as such. Therefore, he proposes that 'rewritten biblical' texts should not be treated as a separate category from 'biblical' texts, and in fact, that scholars should avoid using the words Bible, biblical and rewritten Bible for the Second Temple period. He suggests instead using the more neutral language of Scriptures and rewritten Scriptures.

---

20. She suggests, 'the criteria for membership in this category include a close attachment, either through narrative or themes, to some book contained in the present Jewish canon of Scripture, and some type of reworking, whether through rearrangement, conflation, or supplementation of the present canonical biblical text' (White Crawford 2000b: 174). She acknowledges that this use of 'Bible' is anachronistic for the time period of these texts, as well as the idea of rewritten, but adopts the categorization as nevertheless useful for modern scholars (176–77; 2006: 132–34).

21. In addition to the scholars discussed below, see Chiesa 1998; Bowley and Reeves 2003; Martone 2004.

22. Also see Ulrich 1999c; 2001; 2002a; 2003a.

Johann Maier also notes that 'Bible' and canon are anachronistic generally for the Second Temple period, and that at Qumran specifically these would be incompatible with their sense of continual revelation (Maier 1996a: 122). Moreover, he argues that it is inappropriate to prejudice biblical *text* as in the use of such terms as paraphrase, re-written Bible, para-biblical, apocrypha, and pseudepigrapha. At this time it was not the textual form itself that was central but the content (Maier 1996b: 12).[23]

Moving away from a privileging of text (i.e., over the tradition itself, including oral) opens up new problems for the category of rewritten Bible – as well as fresh insights. On what basis could one meaningfully exclude retellings of authoritative traditions not later enshrined in the Jewish canon? The problem is relevant, for example, for such works as *Pseudo-Daniel*, *Proto-Esther*, and *Pseudo-Jubilees*.

Jonathan Campbell (2005; see also 2004: 20–30) carries such reasoning perhaps the farthest. Drawing especially on John Barton's argument for an open-ended body of prophetic writings (Barton 1986: 13–95; 1996), Campbell advocates referring simply to 'Scripture' or 'Scriptures' for all literature presented as from ancient Israel (e.g., such works as *Jubilees*, the *Genesis Apocryphon* and *Pseudo-Philo*) on the grounds that they would have been received as prophetic revelation of old. He uses the term para-scriptural for works like Josephus's *Jewish Antiquities* and Ben Sira 44–49 that are fundamentally different since they self-consciously are not presented as ancient reve-lation. Thus, between these two categories he dispenses with rewritten Bible as a cate-gory. What is important about Campbell's definition is that he focuses on the work's reception rather than its composition. This is a useful distinction, but makes problem-atic assumptions about how an audience would have received a composition, and results uncomfortably in calling Scripture numerous works for which there is no evidence that they commanded any acceptance as authoritative while excluding Ben Sira which demonstrably attained a significant degree of authority (see Ulrich 2003a: 19–21). Most problematically, this criterion would seem to be untenable with the two communities from the Second Temple period best represented in textual evidence: the community at Qumran and the early Christians, both of whom accepted contempo-rary revelation (especially in relation to the Teacher of Righteousness and Jesus respectively; see Brooke 2005a: 97–98).

Some of this debate will undoubtedly remain a matter of quibbling over sorting and labeling, and that is not particularly the concern here. I am interested rather in reflecting on the underlying conceptions. In this regard, there are some important threads to pick up from the discussion before we move on.

First, it does seem possible – and necessary – to chart a path between the Scylla of a canon-centred approach and the Charybdis of a pan-Scripture model. Although there do seem to have been varying numbers of authoritative texts among different groups in Second Temple Judaism, including numerous texts not ultimately included in the Jewish canon, it is important to distinguish among levels of authority and to acknowl-edge that authoritative writing – even citation of a text or tradition as authoritative – does not necessarily imply a status we may meaningfully call 'Scripture'. Scripture has

---

23. On this Ulrich (2003b: 59) also makes the point that it is the book not its specific textual form that is 'canonical' at this time. Maier notes that the textual form became important where certain texts were used in debates. For Maier's classification of material closely related to biblical (pesharim, biblical materials, and Torah and rules), and discussion of the relationships, see Maier 1996b: 9–15.

to do not merely with authority but above all with theological status (Alexander 2000: 40–41).[24] There is widely attested in Second Temple Judaism what we might call a Scripture consciousness, and this is above all reflected in appeals to a broadly agreed basis of sacred authority, most especially the Torah of Moses.[25] This does not imply a completely fixed text or closed canon, and it would be a mistake to assume that the Torah of Moses necessarily meant exactly the Pentateuch as known to us, but it is also a mistake to assume that Scripture was merely fluid and amorphous.[26] There is ample attestation – shared widely in Second Temple Judaism – of a special status for Genesis, Exodus, Leviticus, Numbers, and Deuteronomy, treated as a continuous sacred story and in textual form substantially as survives in the major witnesses, in unity with a broader corpus of 'prophetic' writings somewhat less well defined.[27] In any case, however, although our primary evidence is textual, it is important that text and textual form not dominate the focus of our thinking about authoritative sacred traditions. What is authoritative at this time is the sacred tradition more broadly speaking than just specific textual forms (Ulrich 2003b: 59). Thus, the term 'rewritten' is also misleading because it ignores the broader phenomenon of *retelling* sacred tradition.

Philo may illustrate an attitude of utmost reverence for recognizable books of Scripture at the same time as relativizing the written text to the living tradition. On the one hand he shows reverence for five books of Mosaic Torah (Philo *Vit. Mos.* 1.1, 4; 2.292) along with other sacred Scripture in harmony with them.[28] On the other hand, he states that the lives of pious individuals recorded in the most holy scriptures are the 'originals' (ἀρχετύπους) of which laws are the 'copies' (εἰκόνων; Philo, *Abr.* 3).

24. Alexander distinguishes three categories of authoritative text at Qumran: (1) 'divinely inspired, prophetic literature' (Torah, prophets, writings of David), (2) a 'body of tradition which the community believed it had received from antiquity, and to which it accorded great respect, but which it probably did not regard as Scripture in the full sense of the term' (Enochic literature and *Jubilees*) and (3) 'a body of law, regulations, and doctrine which was generated within the community. This is also post-biblical and post-prophetic, since it is commonly presented in the form of commentary on Scripture' (pesharim, probably *Temple Scroll*; *serakhim*). One might disagree with details, but the main assertion that the community would perceive difference is probable.

25. Brooke notes that in MMT (4Q397 14–21 10–11) 'appeal is made to shared authoritative texts *as a whole* to argue the point that the author's community is keeping to the written traditions sufficiently faithfully in order to believe it would be the heir of the blessings promised in those self-same traditions. Thus we understand that the community sees itself as being under the authority of the whole tradition' (Brooke 2000a: 62). On the status and function of Mosaic discourse in Second Temple Judaism, see Najman 2000; 2003.

26. See Alexander (2000: 41; 2002: 65), Brooke (2000a; 2000b; 2005a), Charlesworth (1993).

27. It is not necessary to rehearse the evidence here in detail (see, e.g., Brooke 1997b and p. 19 below). At Qumran, such evidence includes the number and quality of manuscripts, and citation and interpretation, both explicit and implicit. That Genesis–Deuteronomy were viewed as a continuous sacred story is evidenced by manuscripts that cover more than one book (4QGen–Exod[a, l]; 4QExod–Lev[f]; 4QLev–Num[a]), rewritings that harmonize and/or span more than one book (e.g., *Reworked Pentateuch* seems to have covered Genesis through Deuteronomy; *Jubilees* and *Temple Scroll* together treat Genesis through Deuteronomy), and interpretation that displays an intertextual attitude toward these writings. This data is largely consistent with the picture that emerges elsewhere in Judaism (e.g., LXX, Ben Sira, Philo, Josephus, New Testament). The scriptural text assumed in citations, rewritten works and commentaries mostly corresponds to recognizable forms known from the major witnesses, but with freedom; e.g., the pesharim (Brooke 1987); *Jubilees* (VanderKam 1977: 287); *Genesis Apocryphon* (VanderKam 1978); *1 Enoch* (Alexander 2002: 64–65); *Pseudo-Philo* (Jacobson 1996: 1.254–57); Josephus (Feldman 1998a: 23–36); Philo (Borgen 1997: 46–79).

28. See Beckwith 1986: 75–76.

Philo's language here relies on viewing written text as one step removed from living truth, reflecting the type of logic expounded in Plato's *Phaedrus* (274e–276a), where writing is denigrated as external, merely a dead and static reminder, in contrast to the living dynamic discourse of the one who knows, of which the written discourse is only an image (εἴδωλον). Accordingly, when Philo tells the story of Moses (*Vit. Mos.* 1.4; cf. 2.292) he combines what he learned from the sacred books and from the 'elders of the nation', 'for I always interwove what I was told with what I read, and thus believed myself to have a closer knowledge than others of his life's history'. Arguably a similar attitude is reflected at Qumran and in the New Testament (see Brooke 2000a: 61).

Second, rewritten Scripture as a technique is essentially what van Seters (2000) calls 'creative imitation'. He illustrates the technique in Deuteronomy and Chronicles and more broadly with regard to classical texts in the ancient world. It is difficult to argue that there is any generic distinctive to rewritten Scripture as opposed to rewritten Homer. The reference to Bible in 'rewritten Bible' is thus a red herring, and there is not really a meaningful way to speak of rewritten Bible as a literary genre any more than to speak of imitation as a style of painting.[29] Just as 'biblical text' is not a genre, 'rewritten Bible' cannot properly be a genre. It is a strategy of extending scriptural authority by imitation. It is possible to keep the same genre as the scriptural base, or to recast it into a new genre (e.g., contrast *Reworked Pentateuch* with *Jubilees*).[30]

Third, the technique of rewriting or imitation is a strategy for extending or invoking the authority of traditions already accepted as authoritative. As Hindi Najman (2000: 203) notes, since 'authority was inextricably linked to Moses and the ancient tradition of Mosaic Torah … legal or political innovations had to be justified and grounded in terms of this already authoritative tradition of sacred writing'. What constitutes the 'Torah of Moses' cannot be limited simply to a fixed text, but involves this extended dynamic of interpretation, re-application and invocation of authority. 'If we take the term 'Torah of Moses' to designate authoritative sacred writings *and their inherited or innovated authoritative interpretations*, then we can view rewritten Bible as an understandable attempt to authorize certain laws and practices by literally inscribing them back into Mosaic Torah … Just as there was no distinction between citing and interpreting, so too there was no clear distinction between interpreting and interpolating' (Najman 2000: 213–214; emphasis added).[31] As Najman further notes, in the context of authoritative sacred writings but not yet closed canon, the goal of such rewritings may have been 'not to replace, but rather to *accompany* traditions already regarded as authoritative, and thus to provide those traditions with their proper interpretive context' (Najman 2003: 44). We might say that as the moon does not rob from the sun, such texts can extend the authority of Scripture without necessarily aiming to rival or replace it.

29. On imitation, Brooke notes at Qumran there is prominently the 'presentation of new material in a form which looks in most respects like that which is being interpreted. New laws, in themselves matters of legal interpretation, are presented in the form of Torah' (and similarly with narrative and poetry; Brooke 2000a: 69).

30. Variation is available due to different means of imitation. Cf. Aristotle's (*Poetics* 1) distinction of three modes of artistic imitation: the medium (e.g., rhythm, tune, meter); the objects (e.g., people in action, which can be rendered true to life, better than in real life, or worse); and manner (e.g., by narration, assuming a different personality, speaking as one's own person, or presenting all characters as living and moving before the audience).

31. Cf. the example of Philo cited above, p. 15.

In the light of the foregoing, I will attend to features of the phenomena associated with extending Scriptures without attempting to identify the strategies as literary genres. I will use the term 'parascriptural' as an umbrella term for a broad class of texts that in various ways extend the authority of Scripture by imitation and interpretation. Rewritten Bible can be useful as a category (along the lines of Alexander and Bernstein), but it is also misleading in the sense that it is not really a literary genre itself, it implies an anachronistic sense of 'Bible', and 'rewritten' restricts consideration of the larger phenomenon. I will use the term 'rewritten Scripture' occasionally in lieu of a more satisfactory term, but in reference to the activity not a genre.

2. *Scripture and Canon*

A great deal of the growing discomfort with categorizing parascriptural texts, and with labels such as rewritten Bible and parabiblical, has to do with recognition that there is not 'a Bible' properly speaking in the Second Temple period (e.g., Bowley and Reeves 2003: 4, 7, 15–16). Since the discovery of the Dead Sea Scrolls, scholarship on defining Scripture in early Judaism has undergone radical revision in two main areas of research: the development of texts (textual criticism) and the development of a collection of sacred texts (canon). It is necessary here to highlight just a few of the main trends.

With regard to textual criticism the data from the Dead Sea Scrolls have invalidated the pursuit of an *Urtext* for biblical books, at least for any practical purposes.[32] This follows from an acknowledgment of multiple editions of texts synchronically as well as fluid – and possibly non-linear – development of texts diachronically. That is, the transmission and development of the text are inseparable, as the scribe comes into view more actively as interpreter and author (Ulrich 1999a: 11; Brooke 2005b: 31).

As Eugene Ulrich in particular has emphasized, Scripture was characterized by textual pluriformity (Ulrich 1999c; 2001; 2002b; 2003a: 5). This does not seem to be the case just between groups (different groups with their own fixed form) but rather it was probably the case in general. There is no evidence of a sectarian form of scriptural books. Although the Dead Sea Scrolls exhibit many textual variants, not a single one can be described as a sectarian variant (Ulrich 2003b: 64–65), and the situation of textual plurality at Qumran is probably representative of Judaism more broadly. A similar lack of concern for a unified biblical text is found in the New Testament and Josephus (Ulrich 2000a).

Therefore, what are often called rewritten biblical texts may be seen as part of a larger phenomenon of a living tradition that in part became concretized in texts

---

32. Ulrich 1999a: 12–16; Talmon 2000: 149–50. Up until recently, Tov defended the idea of an *Urtext* by sharply distinguishing between literary growth, textual transmission, and later midrashic development (Tov 2001: 171–80), but on this point, his thinking has moved closer to that of Ulrich, at least for practical purposes. Although he still holds theoretically to an *Urtext* on the grounds that development appears to be linear, it is of almost no practical consequence because there are no solid grounds for identifying one particularly stage of development as the target *Urtext*. 'By dissolving the linkage between the assumption of an *Urtext* and the canon of Jewish scripture, we thus assume a sequence of authoritative literary strata of a biblical book. We suggest that we should single out no stage as the presumed *Urtext*. As far as we can ascertain, all these early stages were equally authoritative, probably in different centers and at different times' (Tov 2002: 248).

recognized as 'biblical'. Shemaryahu Talmon (2000: 157), for example, complains that classification of texts as re-told, re-read, re-written, or re-worked:

> reveals that in the background of this attempt to classify the textually widely varying Qumran material 'still lurks the theory of an *Ur-recension* or an *Urtext* from which they presumably derive. In contrast, it is my thesis that the presumably 're-told', 're-read', 're-written', etc. Bible-related works should mostly be viewed as crystallizations of 'living' literary traditions, which parallel presentations of these same traditions in the books of the Hebrew Bible, but do not necessarily spring from them. Rather, the preservation of multiform concretizations of biblical themes again evinces the basic 'biblical ethos' of the pre-divide Covenanters. As already noted, like Israel of the biblical period, so also the Community of the Renewed Covenant tolerated diverse formulations of traditions, stories, themes, etc. which differed to an undefined but evidently permissible degree from their formulations in the handed down corpus of biblical *books*, the culmination of a long process of growth of an earlier diversified biblical *literature* in oral and written transmission [emphasis original].

With regard to canon, scholars now generally accept that the formation of a collection of sacred texts was a long process rather than specifically the product of official decisions.[33] Hand in hand with this is a more functional concept of canonical authority focused on communities for whom the writings serve as normative for religious life (Anderson 1970: 117; Sanders 1992: 847; VanderKam 2000: 3). Thus, one cannot treat canon in a strictly linear fashion or as static since it is dynamically related to specific communities. It is important to distinguish the sense of canon as a body of authoritative tradition from canon as an exclusive and authoritative body of fixed texts.[34] Better yet, for the sake of clarity, is to reserve the term 'canon' for the latter and to simply use the term 'Scripture' for the former (Barton 1986: 55–57; Ulrich 2002a: 29–33).[35] In any case, the *canonical process* overlaps with the development and growth of texts.[36] In discerning a canon in either sense, a key feature is that of intertextuality, the treatment of authoritative traditions as a unity so that they are mutually interpreted (Fishbane 2000: 39; Barton 2000b).

33. For a survey of the most important implications of the Dead Sea Scrolls on the study of canon, see VanderKam 2002a; 2000. Recent scholarship on canon includes Anderson 1970; Leiman 1976; Sanders 1976; 1984: 21–45; 1992; Barr 1983; Barthélemy 1984; 2006; Beckwith 1986; Barton 1986, 1996, 2000a; Ulrich 1992; Carr 1996; Trebolle Barrera 1998; Davies 1998; Evans 2001; Talmon 2002; Lange 2003; Brooke 2005a; Cross 2006; and the various articles in Kaestli and Wermelinger 1984; Kooij and Toorn 1998; McDonald and Sanders 2002; Auwers and de Jonge 2003; Helmer and Landmesser 2004.

34. Sanders (1992: 847) distinguishes between canon as *norma normans* – a 'collection of authoritative books' – and canon as *norma normata* – an 'authoritative collection of books'; he states that 'canon *as function* [the former] antedates canon *as shape* [the latter]' (emphasis original). Cf. VanderKam 2000: 2–3. G. Sheppard (1987: 64) uses the terms 'canon 1' and 'canon 2' for essentially the same distinction; cf. somewhat similarly the 'canon I' and 'canon II' of Folkert 1989: 173.

35. This distinction was proposed by Sundberg 1968: 147–48. Probably the most useful definition of canon is that of Ulrich, who proposes three elements essential to the concept of canon: 'first, the canon involves books, not the textual form of the books; secondly, it requires reflective judgment; and thirdly, it denotes a closed list' (Ulrich 2002a: 31 see also 2006: 97).

36. Ulrich 2006: 96. In this way, Anderson (1970) is able to trace a 'canonical process' beginning in the biblical period: Josiah's reform already treats the Book of the Law as normative, but the Law is still modified and adapted; the preservation and interpretation of the teachings of the prophets by disciples attest their use as normative, but it is at first a living and expanding tradition; and liturgical use of the Psalms is attested in Chronicles. On the process from authoritative writings to canon illustrated by the reworkings of scripture at Qumran, see Brooke 2005a.

A current debate centers on whether to find greater definition and closure to canon earlier (e.g., Beckwith 1986 arguing for an exclusive canon with fixed text under Judas Maccabaeus) or an authoritative body of texts that remained less defined and open later (e.g., Barton 1986, who argues for a defined Pentateuch and a body of prophetic texts that have secondary rank and remain open-ended throughout the Second Temple period). It is inappropriate to seek a singular answer that would apply equally across the board in Second Temple Judaism, but on the whole Barton's theory better suits the relevant data considered here.[37] A few observations seem reasonably secure. (1) There was a core body of texts with supreme authority that could be assumed universally in Second Temple Judaism, specifically the Torah associated with Moses (VanderKam 2002a: 92–93). (2) There were other works of less marked authority that probably varied among communities, and whose authority was apparently seen as related to their perceived harmony with Mosaic Torah.[38] These writings were often regarded as prophetic (especially including Psalms and Daniel),[39] although one should not assume that all groups necessarily would have appealed to or accepted prophetic authority. (3) The larger body of authoritative writings (at least among certain groups) included works that did not become part of the Jewish Bible. It is important to distinguish various levels of authority, but these do not fall neatly between what became the Jewish Bible and other writings. There can be no doubt that some writings not ultimately included in the Jewish Bible functioned with greater authority than some works that were (especially *Jubilees* and *1 Enoch*; see VanderKam 2000: 24–28). (4) There is no evidence at Qumran that the movement set themselves apart by a distinctive collection of Scripture (Lange 2004: 76–77; Ulrich 1999a: 8–9). Indeed, as Brooke notes, the polemical discourse in 4QMMT (4Q397 14–21 10) implies that they submitted to the whole tradition as accepted also by their antagonists (Brooke 2000a: 62). Rather, it was the content of their interpretation that set them apart, not what they regarded as scripture (Brooke 2000b: 119). (5) There is no evidence for an exclusive list of sacred writings (that is, a closed canonical Bible) before the end of the first century CE.[40]

Thus, in Second Temple Judaism there was a recognizable body of authoritative Scripture in considerable continuity with what ultimately became the Jewish Bible, but there was not canon in the sense of 'a list of books that alone were regarded as supremely authoritative, a list from which none could be subtracted and to which none could be added' (VanderKam 2002a: 91).

37. As Davies (1998: 107) notes, though, Barton downplays the evidence that at least in certain contexts another class of writings was distinguished from prophets.

38. Philo, for example, cites from Samuel, Isaiah, Jeremiah, Hosea, Zechariah, Psalms, and Proverbs as inspired works that are part of a unity with Moses (e.g., 'friend' or 'disciple of Moses'): *Deus Imm.* 6; *Quaest. in Gen.* 2.43; *Cher.* 49; *Plant.* 138; *Agr.* 50; *Plant.* 39; *Ebr.* 31; *Conf.* 62 (see Beckwith 1986: 75–76). Cf. the pairing of Moses/Law and the prophets in such texts as Sir. 39.1; 46.1; Sir. Prologue; 1QS 1.1–3; 8:15–16; MMT (4Q397 14–21 10); Josephus *Apion* 1.39–40 and throughout the New Testament (see Barton 1986: 35–55). Also in support of this are intertextual interpretations of Torah and prophets, e.g., in the thematic pesharim (see Dimant 1992: 247–48). See also Najman's excellent discussion of authority grounded in Mosaic discourse (Najman 2003).

39. In addition to the previous note, see Sir 24.33 on wisdom as prophetic.

40. The earliest references to a closed list of scripture are Josephus *Apion* 1.37–40 and *4 Ezra* 14.19–26, 37–48, and even so, the witness of these texts is equivocal (see VanderKam 2000: 8–9, 20–23). But see Cross 2006, who argues for a pharisaic canon established by Hillel in the early 1st cent. CE.

On the basis of such observations about textual development and formation of canon, James Sanders has argued for some years that Scripture is dynamic and can only be defined in relation to specific religious communities, that Scripture as text is secondary to the sacred story, and that adaptability through interpretation is an essential quality of Scripture.[41] In such a context, the place of parascriptural and rewritten scriptural texts is inescapably ambiguous.

Of further insight are studies of Scripture and canon from the perspective of the comparative history of religions. Jonathan Smith argues that there are two complementary features of canon: 'the process of arbitrary limitation and of overcoming limitation through ingenuity'; thus, 'canon cannot exist without a tradition and an interpreter' (Smith 1982: 50). Wilfred Smith and his students emphasize that Scripture is relational, having to do with function and reception in a specific religious community.[42] They also stress that Scripture is inseparable from an interpretative tradition by which it is a living force in the community. Scripture is not only or even primarily a text. Even in religious communities that emphasize textual Scriptures there are important oral and aural aspects.[43] Scripture is functional and dynamic, not statically situated in a text. Smith (1993: ix, 18) states that:

> being scripture is not a quality inherent in a given text, or type of text, so much as an interactive relation between that text and a community of persons ... One might even speak of a widespread tendency to treat texts in a 'scripture-like' way: a human propensity to scripturalize. ... no text is a scripture in itself and as such. People – a given community – make a text into scripture, or keep it scripture: by treating it in a certain way. I suggest: *scripture is a human activity* [emphasis original].

Pointing out that we have developed our concept of Scripture from the Bible, Smith advocates the opposite, that instead we learn our understanding of Bible from the larger concept of Scripture (Smith 1989: 45). Especially useful for the present study are examples of different configurations of Scripture in relation to other traditions. Smith's comparison of two Buddhist movements encourages new reflection on the possible function of parascriptural texts in Second Temple Judaism.[44]

> Theravadins differ from the Mahayana movement in that conceptually they consciously revere a single fixed canon perceived as closed. They attend the local temple or participate in religious festivals and hear the village priest expound a theme normally drawn from that canon but then elaborated from these 'para-scriptural' works or illustrated from these non-canonical but thoroughly familiar and much-loved and richly embellished stories. Just as we noted that Jews have read about the Abraham of the Bible but perceived him as the Abraham of the Talmud, so for Theravada the secondary material has been practically consequential while the primary is theoretically paramount ... The Mahayana, on the other hand ... has developed not only practical involvement with but profound reverence for and conceptual elevation of other – later – writings, not subordinated even theoretically to what went before. (Smith 1993: 152–53)

Smith (1993: 204–205) states that the boundary between what is called Scripture and other writings is far from clear in many contexts. There is a 'fairly widespread pairing

41. See Sanders 1976; 1984; 1991; 1992; 2002.

42. See Smith 1993, Graham 1987, and the articles in Levering 1989. For an application of such views to understanding scripture in the Dead Sea Scrolls, see Kugler 2003. On canon from a cultural perspective, see Davies 1998; 2002.

43. Graham (1987: 156) emphasizes 'the *interpenetration* of the written and spoken word'.

44. On parascriptural texts, see Smith 1993: 152, 204–206.

of materials, with two authoritative bodies of writings of which one is considered loftier in theory, in cosmic status, even while in practice the other may be also decidedly consequential – and at times equally, if not actually more, authoritative'; for example Bible and Talmud, Qur'an and Sunnah (Hadith), *śruti* and *smṛti*.[45] Correspondingly, he notes, there are periodic reformist attempts to eliminate the second and 'go back to' the other (e.g. 'Back to the Vedas' and *sola scriptura*). Sometimes the authority for the secondary work is accounted for in some theory (e.g., oral Torah), but there are also writings that function authoritatively without theoretical backing (e.g., the Book of Common Prayer). With regard to the Hindu Vedas, Graham stresses that it is the oral recitation that is scriptural; the written text is only a copy. Furthermore, whereas the Vedas are most sacred as foundational Scriptures, in popular life other texts play a more prominent role as functional Scriptures (Graham 1987: 71–75).

The scenarios summarized above concerning Theravada and Mahayana Buddhism, and with Hindu Scriptures, caution against assuming that parascriptural writings functioned in a singular way throughout Judaism in the Second Temple period. We must allow that an integral part of the process of story becoming Scripture involves a working of the tradition, and various means of extending the Scriptures are a necessary corollary of the canonical process. Attempts to define neatly the 'relationship' of such writings to 'the Bible' are doomed to frustration because the question is typically framed from a post-canonical perspective and with a limited and anachronistic view of Scripture.[46] For these reasons, I seek to approach these texts as examples of working the tradition and extending Scripture as much as possible without prejudice to whether they are complementary or supplementary, internal or external to scripture.

3. *Extension and Interpretation of Scripture*

In a diachronic perspective, the stage we are considering here represents a mid-point in the process of canonization. Yet even after the establishment of a fixed text of Scripture and an exclusive collection of sacred texts, it would be deficient to think of this as the encapsulation of Scripture. The text and a definitive collection of texts are only the most visible parts of what Scripture is, and to borrow Philo's language, only the εἰκῶν of which the archetype is dynamic function in a living community (see pp. 15–16). That is, Scripture always implies and includes its complex set of interrelationships involving its function, use, and interpretations in a particular community. Ultimately, it is almost meaningless to speak of 'the Bible' or 'Scripture' in the abstract. One can only meaningfully speak of 'the Bible' in relation to particular religious communities that value certain texts in various ways as sacred. To ransack a

---

45. The terms *śruti* and *smṛti* distinguish respectively the most ancient and sacred of the Hindu Vedas as transcendant revelation ('what is heard') from later and less sacred texts of tradition ('what is remembered'). See Graham 1987: 65, 71.

46. In reference to pseudepigraphic literature, A. Reed (2005: 55) comments: 'Taken together, the continued production of "ancient" scriptures and the use of these new/old books by many Jews hints at a more inclusive understanding of scriptural authority than that which would later develop in Judaism and Christianity. It is especially important to remember that the authors (and early readers) of the *Book of Watchers* did not conceive of "the Bible" in the same sense as later Jews and Christians. In the third century BCE, it is likely that the Torah already held a special level of authority amongst almost all Jews, but there was not yet a broader "biblical" canon and the notion of scriptural authority remained fluid'.

different image from the Epistle of James, texts can never be Scripture independent of
their use by an interpreting community any more than one can speak of faith apart from
action (Jas 2.17–26).

   Working the traditions and extending the Scriptures did not start 'after the fact',
that is, after there was a 'Bible'. Rather, it seems that the impetus to clarify, harmonize,
and update is part of the very development of what came to be scripture. Annette Reed
makes this point well with regard to the Enochic literature. Drawing on the work of
Kugel, she notes that:

> The parabiblical literature of Second Temple Judaism did not spring full-formed from
> the imaginations of their authors. The composition of new texts in the names of biblical
> figures seems to have been rooted in a broader matrix of midrashic, aggadic, and
> halakhic traditions, the contours of which were already familiar to their readers/hearers
> … this literature is best seen as the product of a dynamic process that shaped 'biblical'
> texts no less than 'extrabiblical' ones: the interplay between oral interpretative and liter-
> ary traditions, by which older scriptures were continually reinterpreted and new works
> of revealed literature were progressively produced. (Reed 2005: 54–55)

This is effectively a continuation of a process seen already in Deuteronomy's version
of the Sinai laws (Deuteronomy 12–26) compared to that in Exodus (20.22–23.33),
and innumerable other examples documented in Fishbane's extensive study of 'inner-
biblical interpretation' (Fishbane 1985; Najman 2003: 20–40 and n. 39). That is, from
the start, the sacred traditions of Israel were not static text, but dynamic word updated,
clarified, and applied anew in order to be understandable and functional.[47]

   That Scripture should be both intelligible/coherent and relevant/applicable is an
important assumption of the phenomenon we are considering here.[48] To add precision,
Vermes introduced an influential distinction between 'pure exegesis' and 'applied
exegesis' (Vermes 1975a: 63, 80). Pure exegesis seeks to solve difficulties perceived
in the text having to do with unclear language, lack of detail, apparent contradiction,
or because of a possibly unacceptable meaning. This is roughly similar to what is
sometimes called 'simple sense interpretation'. Applied exegesis begins with concerns external to the text itself and seeks to justify them and root them in Scripture.
Most commonly these concerns are ideological, theological, or legal. The distinction
is heuristically useful, but it needs to be noted that the two are not mutually exclusive
and it is doubtful that ancient interpreters would have recognized the distinction
(Bernstein 2000: 378).[49] At the very least, they are frequently in practice not nearly as

---

   47. The original title of Kugel's exploration of interpretative traditions (*The Bible as it Was*)
explicitly reflects his conviction that scripture and interpretation are inseparable, and that a study of
this interpretative activity reveals the nature of Scripture at the time (Kugel 1997: 35–36). He notes
both the phenomenon of interpretation becoming Scripture as well as interpretation becoming effectively canonized by general acceptance (Kugel 1998: 890).
   48. This is not a universal assumption that can be made about Scripture in general. Where the
function of Scripture is more purely ritual or as words of power, it does not necessarily have to be
intelligible in a narrative sense. Perhaps the most obvious example would be the recitation of *mantras*
in the Hindu or Buddhist context (see Smith 1993: 132–33 and 302 nn. 26, 27; Coburn 1989: 119;
Levering 1989: 77–78, 87–88), but one could also think of ritual recitation of Qur'an (Graham 1987:
103–104), and mystical use of Scripture such as the kabbalistic concept of Torah as a series of divine
names (Holdrege 1989: 208–209). See especially Levering's distinction of four modes of reception of
Scripture (Levering 1989: 59–60).
   49. Probably an ancient interpreter would have viewed all of his interpretation as 'pure' – that is,
just making clear what the text 'means' – but as Kugel (1998: 21–22) notes, no interpretation is

easy to differentiate as one might wish. Furthermore, sometimes the two overlap: there really is a simple-sense obscurity in the text, but the interpreter has a vested interest in a particular solution.[50]

For summarizing some of the main strategies of extending scriptures that we will encounter, Bernstein's typology of methods of interpretation is particularly helpful as a basic framework (Bernstein 2000: 380–82).[51] The first method is what Bernstein calls 'thematic association', which includes various techniques of juxtaposition (collating passages with a common theme), harmonization (producing one new narrative or law out of two thematically similar passages), linking (invoking another passage by theme or catchword for analogy, or otherwise evoking some aspect of its signification), and rearrangement (presenting passages in a more orderly sequence or to resolve difficulties). In an example from the *Genesis Apocryphon*, Abram's words to Sarai mentioned in Gen. 20.13 are incorporated into the appropriate place in the narrative of Gen. 12.12–13 (1QapGen 19.20).

Bernstein's second and third methods are 'specification', in which ambiguous terms or references are identified, and 'atomization', in which parts of a passage are assigned meanings as discrete items apart from their literary context. The former is common in the rewritten scriptural texts; for example the *Genesis Apocryphon* identifies the survivor who informs Abram of the capture of Lot as 'one of the herdsmen of the flock which Abram gave to Lot' (1QapGen 22.1–2).

Fourth, Bernstein lists various legal methods, which include reading the text as strictly as possible, expanding the application, and interpreting by analogy to related passages.

The fifth method is the introduction of new material, either interpolated into a passage or added as supplementary to a passage (cf. Fishbane 1985: 423–24). Sometimes the new content has no discernible scriptural basis but comes from haggadic traditions. Other times, the additions are inferred from the scriptural text, and fill perceived gaps or provide antecedents or secondary references anticipated in the text (Bernstein 1996). An example from *Reworked Pentateuch* is the introduction of a song of Miriam modeled on the song of Moses (4Q365 6a ii and c 1–7).

---

simply pure. 'The ancient interpreter *always* had an axe to grind, always had a bit of an ulterior motive: at the very least, this interpreter wished to convince listeners or readers that the text means something other than what it might seem to mean at first glance, that his clever way of explaining things reveals the text's true significance'. Still, he cautions against seeking an ideological motivation everywhere.

50. In such cases, Kugel (1998: 22) notes that often it is difficult to determine whether the author sought out a place to insert a particular view, or whether in seeking to explain the text came up with an interpretation that 'also reflected his own ideology or the issues of his day'.

51. In what follows, I mostly follow Bernstein – including the first two examples cited – with some modifications drawn from summaries of interpretative method by Vermes (1989) and Fishbane (1985: 419–25). The most useful general surveys of forms and methods of interpretation in the Dead Sea Scrolls are those of Vermes (1989), Bernstein (2000), and Brooke (2000a). Studies include Bruce (1959), Betz (1960), Vermes (1973; 1975a; 1976), Gabrion (1979), Horgan (1979: 244–47), Dimant (1984: 503–14; 1988), Brooke (1985; 1997a; 2000e), Kugel (1998: 1–30), Endres (1987: 15–17, 196–225), Fishbane (1988; 1985: esp. 419–31 and summarized in Fisk 2001: 58–68), Brewer (1992: 177–225), Bernstein (1996; 1998), Maier (1996a), Jacobson (1996: 1.224–41), Eshel (1997), Kister (1998), Segal (1998), Mandel (2001), Lim (2002: 24–53), Davies (2003), Campbell (2004: 28–29), and some of the articles in Henze (ed., 2005).

Fishbane (1985: 429–31) identifies three forms that haggadic exegesis takes in the Hebrew Bible that are also found in parascriptural writings and concern us here: lemmatic, embedded, and taxemic. In the *lemmatic* form, the lemma to be interpreted is given followed by its application. This is explicit or overt commentary. It is common in the pesharim but there are also some instances of this in the *Genesis Commentary* along with implicit interpretation.

The second, *embedded* form, is by contrast implicit or covert interpretation.[52] The *traditio* is interwoven into the *traditum*. This is the essence of 'rewritten scriptural' works, and most of the interpretative activity we will be considering is of this form. This can be as subtle as rearranging the text without any addition, producing an edited text that is clearer, more logical or systematic, or otherwise improved upon (Vermes 1989: 185); much of the *Reworked Pentateuch* is of this technique. Additional material in implicit interpretation generally takes the form of substitution: the interpretation is simply substituted for the scriptural text (Kugel 1998: 23–25). As Kugel notes, most of this occurs at the micro-level of individual motifs some of which may be original to the author but more often are probably variously drawn from traditional teaching handed down. The new story serves not so much as a singular interpretation of a scriptural text but as a kind of compendium of independent and sometimes even contradictory interpretative traditions. As an analogy, we might think of the conflated nativity stories that are operative in the mind of many Christians, often to a greater extent than the story told by either Matthew or Luke. Such stories do present somewhat of a singular interpretation, but also by harmonizing the two gospel accounts introduce tensions not present in either gospel on its own (e.g., why they were in Bethlehem), and also serve as carriers for numerous extra-biblical traditions (e.g., three wise men). This compendium feature makes it particularly precarious to seek to discern an ideological aim for a particular work, although sometimes patterns of interpretation reveal an author's special interests, as is clearly evident in *Jubilees* and at least partly in the *Genesis Apocryphon*.

The third form identified by Fishbane, taxemic, involves various types of 'creative combination or recombination of elements from the tradition' (Fishbane 1985: 430). The most important type for our purposes is anthological, in which separate elements of tradition are brought together. This is related to the technique of linking mentioned above which is a favorite technique of ancient Jewish exegesis: interpreting one passage by means of linking with another (Fisk 2000a: 217–21), which reflects an assumption that Scripture is a unity. Parascriptural writings bristle with intricate webs of intertextual allusions. Often such allusions are straightforward and readily recognized by anyone for whom the biblical text is familiar, such as when a significant part of a passage is quoted or paraphrased. But other times, allusions may be more opaque, as when a writer seeks to invoke another passage by a mere word, phrase, or image. Even more problematic is when one suspects that it is the larger context that is being evoked by means of a partial quotation or allusion (see Hays 1989: 18–21, 29–32; Fisk 2001: 68–89, 114–15; Kugler 2001: 88–90). Such cases are often controversial and we will encounter the issue in the debate between Brooke and Bernstein over the *Commentary on Genesis* in Chapter 4. It is important not to underestimate, however,

---

52. This is effectively what Perrot (1976: 24–27) called 'texte continué' in contrast to 'texte expliqué'.

the ability of a native in the immediate cultural context of a living tradition to catch even very subtle evocations and their fine nuances. Perhaps a modern analogy might be the rapid adoption of '9/11' in American discourse as a technical term with an extraordinarily large – and constantly evolving – baggage of meaning. On the surface it is a number that represents a calendar date, but it is used as shorthand for a particular set of events that occurred on 11 September 2001, certain reactions to those events, new attitudes and mindsets consequent on those events and reactions, and so on.[53] Due to the extreme abbreviation, fluidity of usage, and rapid innovation the meanings would be utterly incomprehensible to anyone outside the context where this is a living and developing metaphor, yet no one inside the culture has any difficulty following the diverse and subtle shades of meaning encountered daily in the media.

Fishbane (1985: 425–26) also articulates three strategies of transforming the *traditum* that are applicable in our texts as well: spiritualization of content, nationalization of content, and nomicization and ethicization of content. The most important of these for our purposes is the latter, which Fishbane divides into three subtypes:

1. 'The interpolation into a *traditum* of "Torahistic" values, precepts, or regulations'
2. 'The reinterpretation of a *traditum* in terms of a certain moral standard'
3. 'The concern to repress a violent or aggressive tradition in favour of a more ethical or noble version of it'

All three of these are frequent in the parascriptural works, and particularly in the *Genesis Apocryphon*, which takes pains to demonstrate strict Torah observance and ethical behavior among the patriarchs, such as that Noah observed laws of sacrifice, that he arranged endogamous marriages for his sons, and that Abram acted nobly and generously in relation to Sarai and Lot.

Taking bearings from this walk around part of the larger forest, the rest of this volume will study details of three of the trees: the *Genesis Apocryphon*, *Reworked Pentateuch*, and *Genesis Commentary*.

---

53. Random examples from newspapers include 'before 9/11', 'after 9/11', '9/11 happened', '9/11 relatives', '9/11 trial', 'post-9/11 paranoia', '9/11 recession', '9/11 dust', '9/11 perpetrators', etc.

Chapter 2

THE *GENESIS APOCRYPHON*

1. *Description of the Manuscript*

The manuscript now commonly known as 'a *Genesis Apocryphon*' was one of the first seven scrolls to be discovered in 1947 in Qumran Cave 1. It was also in the worst condition of any of these original scrolls, so brittle that the scroll could not be opened without causing serious damage. In preliminary examination of the scroll, a few loose fragments allowed John Trever to determine that the text was in Aramaic, with Lamech speaking in the first person and referring to his wife Bitenosh. Convinced that the work was the lost apocryphal book of Lamech mentioned in antiquity, Trever named it the *'Ain Feshkha Lamech Scroll* (Trever 1949: 9–10). Not until 1954 when the scroll was purchased by means of undercover negotiations for the State of Israel ($250,000 for this and three other scrolls) was it possible to begin the delicate procedure of unrolling the mysterious scroll, carried out by James Biberkraut.

Portions of 22 columns survived from the middle of the scroll – both the beginning and the end were clearly lost. One side of the scroll had severely deteriorated, probably from contact with the ground, leaving large gaps between pieces of the outer layers, which have also lost lines from the top and/or bottom of columns. Throughout most of the manuscript, the ink had reacted with the leather resulting in illegible black patches, or in many cases had eaten right through the leather (similarly 4QExod-Lev[f] and 4QLev[d]; Tov 1998b: 16). What could be read was often legible only with the use of infra-red photography. Only the last three columns from the innermost layers of the scroll survived in near entirety. So poor was the condition of the scroll that the original editors – Avigad and Yadin – were able to publish only five columns of text: the complete columns 20–22, and the majority of columns 2 and 19, although with many uncertain readings. For the rest of the manuscript, they provided sketchy descriptions of the meager content that could be discerned. Even so, it was readily apparent that the scroll was not a lost book of Lamech but rather a retelling of the stories of several characters in the book of Genesis, and so the editors renamed the work 'A *Genesis Apocryphon*' (Avigad and Yadin 1956: 8).

Some small fragments that had come loose from the outer layers of the scroll were published separately. Milik published eight fragments (1Q20) in 1955 under the title *Apocalypse of Lamech* (Milik 1955: 86–87 and plate XVII). Zuckerman and Wise more recently presented a reconstruction of these fragments together with the so-called 'Trever fragment' (the middle fragment in Trever 1948: 53; Sukenik 1950: plate 4) as belonging to column 1 and the preceding column, now dubbed 'column 0' (Zuckerman and Wise 1991; see Fitzmyer 2004: 115–17, 64–67). A further tiny fragment from the Trever photograph (bottom right) has even more recently been identified among fragments in the Schøyen collection, ms. 1926/2, belonging to columns 0 and 1 or columns 1 and 2 (Lundberg and Zuckerman 1996). Thus, the manuscript as it is now known preserves material from at least 23 columns, but I will continue the convention of referring to that first column as column 0 since the exact position of these fragments is not certain.

In the late 1960s, the scroll suffered further deterioration in the Shrine of the Book museum in Jerusalem (Fitzmyer 2004: 14–15), so that the earliest photographs by John Trever (1948–51, JCT 108–110) and the Shrine of the Book (1954, SHR; for photograph numbers, see Reed 1994: 11–14) are often the only witnesses to some data now lost. On the other hand, the recent application of advanced imaging techniques – image spectrometry and digital enhancement – has produced startling results, revealing a great deal of text previously considered unrecoverable (see Bearman and Spiro 1995; 1999; Zuckerman and Lundberg 2002). New photographs were taken in 1988 by Bruce and Kenneth Zuckerman of the West Semitic Research Project in collaboration with the Princeton Theological Seminary. In further projects sponsored by the Ancient Biblical Manuscript Center, new procedures of narrow-band infrared photography were used to produce in many cases the most useful images yet, both film (by the Zuckermans in 1994) and digital (by Greg Bearman in 1994 and 1997).

Using the new images and original photographs, a team of scholars including E. Qimron in conjunction with others began work towards a critical edition of the scroll (Qimron 1992; 1999). This team produced preliminary publications presenting roughly 50 per cent more of the text than known previously (especially columns 5–6 and 10–17) and corrected many readings (Greenfield and Qimron 1992; Morgenstern, Qimron, and Sivan 1995; subsequently GQ and MQS) which have been incorporated into the third edition of the scroll by J. Fitzmyer (2004; subsequently FGA[3]) and other recent editions (*ATTM* 2.68–70; *DSSSE* 26–49; *DSSR* 2–34). A full *editio princeps* of the scroll is currently being prepared for the DJD series by M. Bernstein and E. Eshel.[1]

All the known fragments of the *Genesis Apocryphon* belong to a single manuscript, a scroll of four sheets of parchment, still sewn together, measuring 31 cm high and with a total length of at least 2.5 m. It is probable that at least column 0 also belonged to the first surviving sheet. It is impossible to determine whether one or more sheets preceded that. M. Morgenstern has argued that the Hebrew letters *pe, sade,* and *qoph* written at the top right of sheets 2, 3, and 4 respectively were intended to number successive sheets 17, 18, 19 (or 16, 17, 18 if *waw* was not counted). He suggests, then, that 14 or 15 sheets have been lost from the beginning of 1QapGen, containing an estimated 70–105 columns (Morgenstern 1996). This would make for an extremely large scroll, originally at least 12–15 m if there were only a single sheet lost from the end (see below). This is considerably longer than the largest intact scrolls attested from Qumran – 1QIsa[a] at 7.34 m; 11QTemple[a] originally at 8.75 m, of which 8.148 m survives (Stegemann 1990: 199) – but it is perhaps not impossible as it has been conjectured that 4QReworked Pentateuch would have been even longer if it covered the content of Genesis–Deuteronomy in a single scroll (Stegemann 1990: 192). The proposal remains highly speculative, however, because this is the only instance of sequential letters found in such a context in the scrolls from Qumran, and numerous

---

1. Dan Machiela is currently writing a doctoral dissertation on the *Genesis Apocryphon* that will include new readings (University of Notre Dame, under the supervision of James VanderKam).

markings appear in the margins whose function remains unclear. Moreover, if the letters were intended to number the sheets, they would not have been for the reader to function as 'page numbers', but would have served in the manufacture of the scroll to indicate the correct sequence for joining inscribed sheets (see Tov 1998b: 13). We could not be certain that the sequence in this scroll began with the letter *aleph* (for number one).

How much may have been lost at the end of the scroll is equally unclear. There was certainly at least one further sheet at the end of the scroll, since column 22 ends in the middle of a sentence, and the seam joining the fourth sheet to the fifth sheet is still intact. If the scroll had been whole when it was rolled in antiquity, there could have been no more than this fifth sheet about the length of sheet 4, that is, about 6 columns (the circumference of the innermost layer is about 5 cm while that of tightly rolled scrolls is as small as 2.5 cm; the difference allows at most about 80 cm [see Stegemann 1990: 196]). But it appears that the end of the scroll was cut off in antiquity – it ends with a straight edge just to the left (3–5 mm) of the seam – and the scroll rolled up without its end, perhaps awaiting repair (Stegemann, cited in Schuller 2003).[2] The theory that the scroll was under repair may also explain the presence of a thin sheet of unidentified white material that covered (and obscured) the lower part of columns 10–15 (Avigad and Yadin 1956: 14).[3] While such mysteries remain, the overall extent and hence character of the scroll are unclear.

It should be noted that K. Beyer regards the fragments of 4Q537, 4Q538, and 4Q539 as belonging to another copy of the *Genesis Apocryphon* from Cave 4 (Beyer 1984: 186–88). These Aramaic fragments include first-person accounts by Jacob of his dream at Bethel, by Benjamin of meeting Joseph in Egypt, and by Joseph of instruction to his sons. There is no compelling evidence to associate these with the *Genesis Apocryphon*, however.

2. *Date and Provenance*

With regard to the date of the sole known manuscript of the *Genesis Apocryphon* (1QapGen), there is remarkable convergence between two different means of dating: the comparative study of the script in which it was written (palaeography), and radiocarbon analysis of the animal skin on which it was written. The writing is careful and in a formal 'Herodian' script, close but not identical to that of 1QM (*War Rule*), and dated to the latter half of the first century BCE or the first half of the first century CE (Avigad 1958: 71–74; Fitzmyer 2004: 25–26). Radiocarbon analysis carried out by the Institut für Mittelenergiephysik in Zurich in 1990 and 1997 points to the same time frame (Doudna 1998: 469). In general, the scribal features of the scroll preparation and writing are common among scrolls found at Qumran, and some of the features are distinctive of the group of scrolls that Tov describes as the 'Qumran scribal school' (Tov 2000): a system of blank spaces divides the text into sense units; letters for deletion are marked with a dot above them; guide dots at the beginning and end of each

---

2. On the basis of my own examination of the scroll at the Shrine of the Book on 10 Jan. 2006, Stegemann's theory that the fifth sheet was intentionally cut off in antiquity is the most probable.

3. The affected columns were cleaned and the white material tested by Michael Magen in Nov. 2003. The bottom half of these columns is now lighter than the top half. I understand that photographs were taken after the cleaning, but I have not seen these.

sheet mark the lines for ruling; the orthography is characteristically 'full', that is, with the use of extra consonants to indicate the pronunciation of vowel sounds (Fitzmyer 2004: 261–71). Thus, the dating, script, and scribal practices all suggest that this scroll was copied at Qumran in the latter first century BCE or early first century CE.

Even though no other copies are known, it is very unlikely either that 1QapGen is the original autograph or that it originated at Qumran. There is wide agreement among scholars that the community at Qumran did not compose new works in Aramaic, although they did copy some. Furthermore, the text shows no clear sectarian language or other distinctive features. Both of these arguments, then, point to an older provenance. The Aramaic language in the scroll – between that of Daniel and that of the official targums (*Onqelos/Jonathan*) – suggests a date in the first century BCE or perhaps the first century CE (Kutscher 1965: 21–22; Fitzmyer 2004: 26, 32, 35–36). This locates the dialect in the context of Middle Aramaic (c. 200 BCE–200 CE), but is of little help in narrowing down an absolute date for the text itself (Cook 1993: 218–19; Wise 1992: 163–67).

There are no reliable historical allusions to help with dating the *Genesis Apocryphon*. The few that have been suggested would point to the early first century BCE (Altheim and Stiehl 1958), for example, proposed allusions to Mithridates VI Eupator, Mithridates II, and Gotarzes I in the account of the war of the Mesopotamian kings (1QapGen 21.23-25), and to the Hasmonaean Hyrcanos II in the named Egyptian noble (1QapGen 20.8). But these are all extremely speculative, and in the end of no real help (Coppens 1959; Fitzmyer 2004: 27–28).

Potentially the most useful means of dating the *Genesis Apocryphon* is its relationship to other literature. It bears a very strong relation to both *Jubilees* and *1 Enoch* – or traditions in common with them – but the matter is very complex and there is little agreement on the conclusions. The strongest arguments seem to favor the view that the *Genesis Apocryphon* draws on both *Jubilees* and parts of *1 Enoch*, incorporating traditions from them and other sources in accordance with the author's particular interests. We must consider this question in detail below as it is one of the major points of interest and controversy. Specific geographic details suggest that the author lived in Palestine (e.g., moving Abram to Mount Hazor for viewing the land, 1QapGen 21.8; Bardtke, cited in Fitzmyer 2004, 220). Thus, perhaps the best estimate of the provenance of the work is that it originated in Palestine, and probably not within the context of the Qumran sect. It should probably be dated in the latter half of the second century BCE to the first half of the first century BCE. Vermes prefers an 'earlier second century date for this work, mainly because of the freshness and simplicity of its haggadah, and because of its freedom from any sectarian bias' (Vermes 1973: 96 n. 2), but these are not strong criteria.

3. *Contents*

The surviving portion of the *Genesis Apocryphon* contains a very lively retelling of the stories of the patriarchs corresponding to Gen. 5.18–15.5, that is, from Enoch to Abram's vision of the stars. A particularly distinctive feature is that the narrative is dominated by first-person speech by the patriarchs Lamech, Methuselah, Enoch, Noah, and Abram. It is reasonable to wonder whether the narrative as a whole was structured around each of the patriarchs in turn telling their own stories, possibly

from Adam through Jacob, or even as far as Moses if its scope was comparable to
Jubilees. This seems unlikely, though, and not only because it would assume an
improbably long scroll. Rather, it is part of the narrative's style to allow characters to
speak in their own words, including: one of the Watchers (col. 0?); Lot (20.22-23);
Melchizedek (22.16-17); Bitenosh (2.9-10, 13-18); Sarai (19.18; 20.10); an Egyptian
official named Hirqanos (20.2-8; 20.24-26); Pharaoh (20.26-28); an angelic messenger
(to Noah 6.15-19; 7.10-?; 14.9–15.20); and God (to Noah 7.1-6; 11.15-12.?; to Abram
21.8-10, 12-14; 22.27-32). This does not differentiate separate stories. Moreover,
only three of the patriarchs take over the *narrative voice*: Lamech, Noah and Abram.

This raises a second possibility, that 1QapGen is structured around three stories: a
story of Lamech, a story of Noah, and a story of Abram. (1) Lamech is the narrator
from 2.1–5.28, telling the story of the Watchers and the birth of Noah (Gen. 5.18–
6.5). He narrates the speeches of Enoch and Methuselah. It is possible that he is also
the narrator of columns 0–1 which seem to report speeches by and/or about the
Watchers. (2) An introduction to a 'book of the words of Noah' marks a transition to
Noah as narrator, whereupon he tells his story from 5.29 to column 17 or 18 (Gen.
5.32–10.32). (3) The transition is lost, but beginning somewhere in column 18 Abram
next narrates his story up to his settlement at Hebron (Gen. 11.26–13.18). However,
at this point (1QapGen 21.23), the narrative abruptly switches to an impersonal
narrative voice until the end of the surviving text (Gen. 14.1–15.4). The reason for
this abrupt shift is uncertain, as is the question of whether the impersonal narration
continued until the end. In any case, the narrative voice does not seem to be an
entirely reliable guide to the intended structure; there is also a lapse to the impersonal
narrator in 5.24-25.

It is preferable to view the *Genesis Apocryphon* – at least as preserved for us – as
structured around two stories: a Noah cycle and an Abram cycle. The Lamech section
is best seen as part of the Noah cycle, and its purpose is to more fully place the story
of Noah in the context of the sons of God myth from Gen. 6.1-5. Lamech's narration
is framed by his anxiety that Noah may be the offspring of one of the Watchers (2.1-
2; 5.26-28). Both the narrations by Lamech and Noah treat the story of the sons of
God from Gen. 6.1-5, and both are further tied together by visions of the sins of the
Watchers (cols. 0–1; 6.11-22) and similar language ('mystery' [1.2; 6.12]; 'messenger' [1.25; 6.13]).

In the following outline, I present the *Genesis Apocryphon* in these two parts: a
Noah cycle (A) and an Abram cycle (B). In each story, I have numbered episodes
sequentially, for the sake of reference (e.g., A14). Where possible and practical, this
division into episodes follows the paragraph division in the manuscript marked by
means of blank spaces. More broadly, what constitutes an 'episode' in this outline
varies considerably and this is for pragmatic reasons: the purpose is to divide the text
up into units of distinctive components *vis-à-vis* the scriptural story to facilitate comparison. Thus, a large unit extraneous to the story in Genesis may be treated as a single
'episode', whereas where the narrative closely follows Genesis, each distinctive com-
ponent may be marked as a separate 'episode'. Hypothesized but uncertain episodes are
set in italics. Correspondences in other texts are generally indicated only where there is
a distinctive element not in Genesis; references in parentheses indicate partial or loose
correspondence, for example a comparable motif; square brackets in the last column
enclose references for which there are no distinctive correspondences discernible that

differ from Genesis, but which are included for the purposes of comparing the order of presentation. Subsequently, I will often refer to passages in the *Genesis Apocryphon* by these episode numbers so that the parallel passages in Genesis and other texts are readily apparent.[4]

Table 1. *Outline of the* Genesis Apocryphon.

Episode	1QapGen	Genesis	Other
A. *Noah Cycle*			
Lamech/Enoch			
1. *Apocalypse of Enoch or Lamech?*	Col. 0–1?	--- (6.1–5)	(*Jub.* 5.1, 6)
Birth of Noah			
2. *Noah's birth*	Col. 1?	5.28–9	(*1 En.* 106.1)
3. *Noah's strange appearance*	Col. 1?	---	*1 En.* 106.2-3
4. Lamech fears Noah is son of angel	2.1-2	--- (6.4)	*1 En.* 106.4-6
5. Lamech confronts Bitenosh	2.3-18	---	(*Jub.* 4.28)
6. Lamech consults Methuselah	2.19-21	---	*1 En.* 106.5-8a
7. Methuselah consults Enoch	2.21–?	---	*1 En.* 106.8b-12
8. Enoch's apocalypse	2.?–5.1	---	*1 En.* 106.13-17, 19; 107.1 (*Jub.* 4.15, 17-19, 21-22)
9. Enoch's answer for Lamech	5.2-23	---	*1 En.* 106.18–107.2 (106.10-12)
10. Methuselah's report to Lamech	5.24-25	---	*1 En.* 107.3
11. Lamech's conclusion	5.26-27	---	
Book of the Words of Noah			
12. Heading	5.29	---	(*Jub.* 10.13; 21.10)
Noah's early life			
13. Noah's growth in truth	5.29–6.5	--- (6.9)	(*Jub.* 10.17; *1 En.* 106.10-12)
14. Noah's marriage	6.6-7	---	*Jub.* 4.33a
15. Noah's children	6.7-8	5.32; 6.10	[*Jub.* 4.33b]
16. Noah arranges marriages for children	6.8-9	---	
Noah's revelation			
17. Noah's vision of the wayward angels	6.9-12	--- (6.1-2)	*1 En.* 60.1 (*Jub.* 5.1)
18. Noah receives angelic messenger	6.13-22	--- (6.3-5)	*1 En.* 60.1-6 (*Jub.* 5.1-18; 7.20-24; 10.3-14; *1 En.* 7; 65.1–68.1)
19. Noah finds favor	6.23	6.8	[*Jub.* 5.5, 19]
20. God's planned destruction	6.24–?	6.6-7, 11-17	*Jub.* 5.2, 20-21
21. God blesses Noah	6.?–7.6	(9.1-2; cf. 6.18-21)	
22. Noah rejoices	7.7–9	---	
23. –*ditto*?	7.10–15	---	
24. –*ditto*?	7.16–?	---	

4.   In the following, I will highlight only readings where I differ from or add to the current editions of the text. See also Bernstein's summary of the Noah narrative (2005)

Episode	1QapGen	Genesis	Other
Noah and the ark			
25. *Noah builds ark?*	7.?–?	(6.22)	[*Jub.* 5.22]
26. Noah enters ark	7.?–8.2	7.6-7, 13-16	*Jub.* 5.23
27. *Noah preaches?*	8.3?–9.1	---	(*Sib. Or.* 1.127-31, 149-57)
28. God grants dominion	9.2–8	---	
29. The flood	9.9–10.1	7.11-12 (7.17–8.3)	[*Jub.* 5.24–27]
30. Noah and family praise God	10.1-10	---	
31. The ark rests on Hurarat	10.11-12	8.4	*Jub.* 5.28
32. Noah offers sacrifices	10.12-13	8.20	*Jub.* 6.1b-2
33. Description of sacrifices	10.13-17	---	*Jub.* 6.2-3
34. God accepts the sacrifice	10.18–?	8.21-22	[*Jub.* 6.4]
35. Noah surveys the land from the ark	11.1–10	---	
Covenant with Noah			
36. Noah exits ark	11.11	8.18	[*Jub.* 6.1a]
37. Noah tours the land	11.11-12	---	
38. Noah blesses God	11.12-14	---	
39. God blesses Noah	11.15–?	9.1-7	*Jub.* 6.5-9 (6.13)
40. Sign of the covenant	11.?–12.6	9.8-17	[*Jub.* 6.15-16]
Noah's grandchildren			
41. Noah descends mountain	12.7-9	(9.18)	
42. Birth of Noah's grandchildren	12.9	10.1 (9.18-19)	
43. Shem's children	12.10-11	10.21-22 11.10-11	*Jub.* 7.18 (cf. *Jub.* 4.33)
44. Ham's children	12.11-12	10.6	[*Jub.* 7.13]
45. Japheth's children	12.12	10.2	[*Jub.* 7.19]
Noah and the vineyard			
46. Noah plants vineyard	12.13	9.20	*Jub.* 7.1
47. Noah observes law of fruit trees	12.13-14	--- Lev. 19.23-25	*Jub.* 7.1–2 (7.34–9)
48. Noah observes feast	12.14-27+	---	*Jub.* 7.3–6
49. Noah has dream visions	12.?–14.?	---	
50. Noah's dreams interpreted	14.?–15.20	---	
51. Noah awakes	15.21–?	(9.24a)	[*Jub.* 7.10]
Division of land			
52. *Noah apportions land* (?)	15.?–?	---	*Jub.* 8.10-11
53. Territory of Japheth	16.?-12	---	*Jub.* 8.25-30
54. Territory of Shem	16.14-25?	---	*Jub.* 8.12-21
55. *Territory of Ham?*	16.26?–17.6	---	*Jub.* 8.22-24
56. Territory of sons of Shem	17.7-15	(10.21–31)	*Jub.* 9.2-6
57. Territory of sons of Japheth	17.16-19	(10.2–5)	*Jub.* 9.7-13
58. *Territory of sons of Ham?*	17.20–?	(10.6–20)	*Jub.* 9.1

B. *Abram Cycle*

Abram in Ur and Haran			
1. *Abram in Ur*	18.?–?	11.27-30	[*Jub.* 11.7–12.14]
2. *Abram's journey to Haran*	18.?–?	11.31-32	[*Jub.* 12.15-21]
3. *Abram's journey to Canaan*	18.?–?	12.1–6	[*Jub.* 12.22-31]

Episode	1QapGen	Genesis	Other
Abram in Canaan			
4. *Abram at Shechem*	18.?–?	12.6	[*Jub.* 13.1-2]
5. *God appears to Abram*	18.?–?	12.7a	[*Jub.* 13.3]
6. *Abram builds altar at Shechem*	18.?–?	12.7b	[*Jub.* 13.4]
7. Abram at Bethel	18.?–19.6	12.8a	[*Jub.* 13.5-7]
8. Abram builds altar at Bethel	19.7	12.8b	[*Jub.* 13.8-9]
9. Abram prays	19.7–8	---	[*Jub.* 13.8b]
10. Abram sets out toward holy mountains	19.8	---	(cf. *Gen. R. 39.15*)
11. Abram travels south	19.8–9	12.9	*Jub.* 13.10
12. Abram dwells 2 years at Hebron	19.9–10	---	*Jub.* 13.10
13. Famine in Canaan	19.10	12.10a	[*Jub.* 13.10]
14. Abram hears of grain in Egypt	19.10	--- (cf. 42.2)	
15. Abram travels to Egypt	19.10-13	12.10b	[*Jub.* 13.11a]
Abram in Egypt			
16. Eve of entering Egypt	19.14	12.11a	
17. Abram has a dream	19.14-17	---	
18. Abram tells Sarai of dream	19.17-19	---	
19. Abram warns of danger	19.19	12.11b-12	
20. Abram instructs Sarai	19.19-21	12.13 (20.13)	
21. Sarai weeps	19.21-23	---	
22. Abram dwells five years in Egypt	19.23	--- (45.6)	*Jub.* 13.11-12
23. Egyptian nobles seek Abram's wisdom	19.24-25	---	(cf. *Jub.* 11.16, 21, 23-24; 12.16-18, 25-27)
24. Abram teaches from book of Enoch	19.25	---	(cf. *Jub.* 21.10)
25. *Banquet?*	19.26–?	---	
26. Nobles praise Sarai's beauty	19.?-20.8	12.15a	
27. Pharaoh takes Sarai	20.8-9	12.15b	[*Jub.* 13.13a]
28. Sarai saves Abram	20.9-10	---	
29. Abram weeps for Sarai	20.10-11	---	
30. Abram prays for Sarai	20.12-16	---	
31. God afflicts Pharaoh	20.16-17	12.17; (20.18)	[*Jub.* 13.13b]
32. Pharaoh unable to approach Sarai	20.17	--- (20.4)	
33. Sarai with Pharaoh two years	20.17–18	--- (cf. 45.6)	(cf. *Jub.* 13.11, 16)
34. Wise men fail to heal Pharaoh	20.18-21	---	
35. Noble seeks Abram's help	20.21-22	---	
36. Pharaoh's dream	20.22	(20.3)	
37. Lot reveals that Sarai is Abram's wife	20.22-23	---	
38. Noble informs Pharaoh	20.24-26	---	
39. Pharaoh rebukes Abram	20.26-28	12.18-19	
40. Pharaoh asks Abram to pray for him	20.28	--- (20.7)	
41. Abram prays for Pharaoh	20.28-29	--- (20.17)	
42. Pharaoh gives gifts to Abram	20.29-30	--- (20.14; cf. 12.16)	[*Jub.* 13.14]
43. Pharaoh's oath [*Sarai untouched*]	20.30	--- (20.16)	
44. Pharaoh returns Sarai	20.30-31	12.19; (20.14)	[*Jub.* 13.15]

Episode	1QapGen	Genesis	Other
45. Pharaoh gives gifts to Sarai	20.31-32	--- (20.16; 16:1)	
46. Abram and Sarai sent away	20.32	12.20	*Jub.* 13.15
Abram in Canaan			
47. Abram departs with riches	20.33-34	13.1-2	[*Jub.* 13.14]
48. Lot acquired riches in Egypt	20.34	(13.5)	[*Jub.* 13.14]
49. Lot got a wife in Egypt	20.34	---	
50. Abram travels to Bethel	20.34-21.1	13.3-4	[*Jub.* 13.15]
51. Abram rebuilds altar	21.1	---	
52. Abram offers sacrifices	21.2	---	*Jub.* 13.16b
53. Abram prays to God	21.2-4	13.4	*Jub.* 13.15-6
Settlement in the Promised Land			
54. Lot parts from Abram	21.5	13.5-10	*Jub.* 13.17
55. Lot settles in Jordan valley	21.5-6	13.11	
56. Abram enriches Lot	21.6	---	
57. Lot moves to Sodom	21.6	13.12	[*Jub.* 13.17]
58. Lot buys house in Sodom	21.6-7	---	*Jub.* 13.17
59. Abram dwells on mountain of Bethel	21.7	---	
60. Abram grieves the departure of Lot	21.7	---	*Jub.* 13.18
61. Abram has a vision	21.8	---	
62. God sends Abram to Ramath-Hazor	21.8	---	
63. God instructs Abram to survey the land	21.9-10	13.14-15	*Jub.* 13.19-20
64. Abram surveys the land	21.10-12	---	
65. God promises land and descendants	21.12-13	13.16 (15.18)	*Jub.* 13.20
66. God instructs Abram to walk the land	21.13-14	13.17	[*Jub.* 13.21]
67. Abram tours the land	21.15-19	---	(cf. *Jub.* 9.2-6)
68. Abram returns to Bethel	21.19	---	
69. Abram settles at Hebron	21.19-20	13.18a	[*Jub.* 13.21]
70. Abram builds altar at Hebron	21.20	13.18b	
71. Abram offers sacrifices	21.20	---	
72. Abram holds feast	21.20-21	---	
73. Abram invites Amorite friends	21.21-22	--- (14.13, 24)	
Abram Defeats Invading Kings			
74. Battle of nine kings	21.23-25	14.1-3	[*Jub.* 13.22]
75. Eastern kings impose tribute	21.25-26	---	(Jos. *Ant.* 1.172)
76. Defeated kings rebel	21.26-27	14.4	
77. Return of eastern kings	21.27-30	14.5-7	[*Jub.* 13.22]
78. Battle of nine kings	21.31-32	14.8-9	
79. Sodom and Gomorrah defeated	21.32-33	14.10	*Jub.*13.22
80. Plunder of Sodom and Gomorrah	21.33-34	14.11	[*Jub.* 13.23a]
81. Capture of Lot	21.34-22.1	14.12	[*Jub.* 13.23b]
82. Abram informed of Lot's capture	22.1-3	14.13-14	[*Jub.* 13.24]
83. Abram informed of kings' movements	22.3-4	---	
84. Abram weeps for Lot	22.5	---	(Jos. *Ant.* 1.176)
85. Abram assembles army	22.5-6	14.14	[*Jub.* 13.25]
86. Amorite allies accompany Abram	22.6-7	(14.13, 24)	
87. Abram defeats eastern kings	22.7--10	14.14-15	
88. Abram rescues captives and plunder	22.10-12	14.16	
89. Abram meets king of Sodom	22.12-14	14.17	
90. Abram meets Melchizedek	22.14-17	14.18-20	[*Jub.* 13.25-27]
91. King of Sodom requests captives	22.18-20	14.21	*Jub.* 13.28
92. Abram swears oath	22.20-24	14.22-24	[*Jub.* 13.29]

Episode	1QapGen	Genesis	Other
93. Abram returns goods and captives	22.24-26	---	
Covenant with Abram			
94. Abram has a vision	22.27	15.1	[*Jub.* 14.1a]
95. God recounts Abram's travels	22.27-29	--- (cf. 16.3; 45.6)	Cf. *Jub.* 13.8, 10-12, 15-16; 14.1
96. Fulfillment of promise of blessing	22.29-30		
97. God promises protection	22.30-32	15.1	[*Jub.* 14.1b]
98. Abram replies	22.32-34	15.2-3	[*Jub.* 14.2]
99. God promises Abram a son	22.34–23.?	15.4-5	[*Jub.* 14.3-4]

Columns 0 and 1 are very fragmentary and it is difficult to determine the content. A few phrases suggest a description of violence and judgment (mostly following the text and translation of Fitzmyer 2004: 64–67): 'you will intensify your anger and will be sustained. But who is there [who can withstand …] the heat of your anger', 'and those who are extinguished and the lowly ones (are) trembling and shuddering … and now, look, we are prisoners', '… in your anger …', 'and now your hand (is) near to strike', 'because of his words the [time] of our imprisonment is coming to an end', '… fire which is seen …', 'and they are being smitten by their brothers …' (column 0); 'and with the women …', 'the mystery of evil', 'medicines, magicians and sooth[sayers …]', 'a strong bond', 'and as a shame for all flesh', 'and by messengers he sent to you', 'to the earth and to descend', 'he did to them and also to all flesh' (column 1).

Given that column 2 begins with Lamech narrating and assuming the story of angels having intercourse with humans (Gen. 6.1-8), it is probable that this material is part of an apocalypse describing the misdeeds of the angels (Gen. 6.2-4) and the resulting wickedness on earth (Gen. 6.5) that occasion God's judgment by flood. The apocalypse may have included the punishment and imprisonment of the wayward angels ('we are prisoners') which was a prominent motif in early Jewish exposition of the 'sons of God' story, and especially in the Enochic traditions that influenced the *Genesis Apocryphon* (Milik 1955: 86; e.g., *1 En.* 10.1-16; 13.1-2; 14.3-5; 18.14-16; 21.1-10; 54.1-6; 56.1-4; 69.28; 88.1; 90.21-24; *Jub.* 5.6; 10.1-14; 4QEn Giants[a] 8 3-15; *T. Levi* 18.12; *2 Bar.* 56.11-16; Jude 6; 1 Pet. 3.19-20; 2 Pet. 2.4; CD 2.18; 1Q27 1 i 5). The recipient of this apocalypse is not clear, but it may be Lamech, who is the narrator immediately following. In support of this, revelations would then be attributed to each focal patriarch in the work: Lamech, Enoch, Noah, and Abram. The reason for attributing an apocalypse to Lamech is apparently creative reflection on Gen. 5.29, finding a reference to divine revelation in the cryptic comment that Lamech named his son Noah for 'this one will bring us comfort from our work and from the toil of our hands because of the ground which the Lord cursed'.

Presumably Noah's birth was narrated toward the bottom of column 1, with a description of unusual phenomena which accompanied his birth such as in *1 En.* 106.1-3. From where we can pick up the narrative in column 2, Lamech tells the story of the birth of his son Noah (1QapGen 1.?–5.27) at great length with material completely extraneous to Genesis. Lamech describes his fear at the strange sight of the infant Noah and confronts his wife Bitenosh with his suspicion that this child has been fathered by an angel. In an emotional exchange, she energetically defends her faithfulness, citing her robust orgasm the last time they had intercourse as evidence that he is indeed the father. Not convinced, Lamech storms off to his father Methuselah and begs him to inquire the truth from Enoch, who lives with the angels. Methuselah and Enoch also speak in the first person, and this gives Enoch the stage to reveal divine mysteries ranging from the source of evil in the world to God's final judgment to consume evil angels and humans alike – and by the way, Lamech is not to worry, he is the legitimate father of Noah. The basic story of this legend appears in a different form in *1 Enoch* 106, and some details such as the name of Lamech's wife are reflected in *Jubilees* (4.28).

In 1QapGen 5.29 Noah takes the stage after the introduction: '[A copy of] the book of the words of Noah' (Steiner 1995). Noah tells of his adherence to truth from his birth, his marriage to Imzera, the birth of three daughters and three sons, and his arrangement of marriage for his sons 'according to the law of the eternal ordinance' (6.1-9). He describes visions and an angelic visitation he received about the corruption of angels and humans, and God's decision to destroy the world and to spare his family (6.23–7.6). Notably, part of God's address to Noah is reconstructed by Fitzmyer (2004: 78–79, 150), '[*you shall rule*] over them, the earth and all that is upon it, in the seas and on the mountains …' (7.1). This is perhaps an allusion to the blessing to Noah in Gen. 9.1-2.

Noah rejoices at the angel's message (1QapGen 7.7-9). It is impossible to determine the content of the next section (7.10-15), but following this there seems to be a speech by Noah (7.16-23+) which mentions 'the beautiful heavens' (7.18-19) and his deliverance from the flood ('to remove me and to build …', 7.19). Together with the preceding section, this may be the content of his rejoicing at the angelic message.

Following this may have been a mention of the construction of the ark, but in any case column 8 seems to begin in the midst of a description of the embarking: line 1 contains the phrase 'his wife after him', and – according to my reading – the number 'sixteen'.[5]

אנתתה בתרה ח]הם[ ]מֹֿ וֹמֹהֹא[ ]oooo]בֹּגֹרֹ[ ]עֹֿש שת עשׂרה והואֿת 1

1. his wife after him … sixteen, and she/it was

According to *Jub.* 5.23, Noah completed embarking on the 'sixteenth day' of the second month, after which God closed the doors on the seventeenth. Only small portions of column 8 survive, so it is very difficult to identify what follows. Besides line 1, only the first words of lines 4 and 9 have previously been published:[6]

---

5. MQS read אנתתה בתרה ח]oon […]וֹ]סרה והואֿת (followed by *DSSR* and FGA³). My reading is based on photographs at the Ancient Biblical Manuscript Center (specifically, GAF_VII_970_A1 in the B1994 series for the end of the line, and 0324gen in the B1997 series for the beginning of the line). The first two words read by MQS are secure. My proposed reading שת עֹשׂרה is nearly certain; although the first letters of each word are partly lost, enough remains to be certain that both of these letters must be either *ayin* or *shin*. The last letters of the line appear to be a single word, as read by MQS; Fitzmyer (2004: 81) translates this 'and she was'. In support of this reading, the occurrences of the same spelling at 12.9; 20.17; 22.25 match the spacing almost exactly when superimposed as overlays. Also, the reading fits the context, since it could refer to the mention of Noah's wife at the beginning of the line. Alternatively, the subject could be another feminine noun, e.g., the ark ('and it was').

6. MQS, followed by FGA³ and *DSSR*.

4 עלמא
9 ובכול מש[

A few more words are visible for which I propose the following readings:[7]

17 אֹשׁתֹעֹי בֹּהֹ א[
19 וכשבועה וכתֹיבֹּיֹא oοο...............]
21 ופֹתֹלת שׁנֹיתֹהֹ עoοο[ ]...............]

17. he spoke with him ...[8]
19. and according to a vow and the writings ...[9]
21. and you perverted, you changed it ...[10]

Although this is not much to go on, I suggest that this section might be part of Noah preaching to the people, a popular tradition in early Jewish writings (e.g., Philo, *Quaest. in Gen.* 2.13; Jos. *Ant.* 1.74; *Sib. Or.* 1.147–198; 2 Pet. 2.5; *Gen. R.* 30.7; *Tanh.* Gen. 2.5 (on Gen. 6.9); *b. Sanh.* 108a–b).[11] If so, line 19 here would perhaps refer to God's resolve in Gen. 6.7 to destroy life as ordained, and line 21 could be a denunciation by Noah (although apparently to an individual).

Nothing has previously been translated of column 9, but my readings of a few fragmentary phrases allow hints of the general content.[12]

---

7.   These readings are based on ABMC photographs 0325 and 0326 in the B1997 series.

8.   For the first word, all but the final letter are reasonably certain. I read this as an Itpael perfect or imperative of שעי 'to talk, converse, relate' (*DJPA* 562; among the Dead Sea Scrolls, cf. 1QapGen 19:18; 4Q530 2ii+6–12 5; 4Q546 63). Because the last letter is obscured, it is not possible to identify whether this is first, second, or third person. Because of space considerations, I tentatively read a *yod* and hence third-person perfect or second-person imperative. On the other hand, there is a possible trace of a left foot to the last letter, and so possibly a *he* or *aleph* or even – at a stretch – a *tav*.

9.   The letters of the first word are reasonably certain. I read the noun שבועה 'oath' (cf. *DJPA* 533; 4Q546 7 2; *DSSC* 2:929). The last letters of the second word are very unclear, but it is difficult to find a plausible alternative. The word כתיבה for Scriptures is otherwise attested only in Babylonian Aramaic (see *DJPA* 272), but the singular passive participle כתיב is used of heavenly writings in other Aramaic texts from Qumran (e.g., 1QapGen 15.20; 4Q204 5 ii 27; see *DSSC* 2:859).

10. The reading of the first word is certain. I tentatively read this as *pael* perfect of פתל 'to pervert' (Jastrow 1255), 2nd person masculine, although it could alternatively be 1st person singular or 3rd person feminine. The word is not hitherto attested in Jewish Aramaic of this time period (according to *DJPA*, CAL, or *DSSC*), but is attested in Syriac (see *Thes. Syr.* 2:3343 and CAL) and Late Jewish Literary Aramaic (*Tg.* Prov. 2.15; see Jastrow 1255 and CAL). The Hebrew *niphal* occurs with the meaning 'perverted' in 1QS 10.24 and 4Q525 14 ii 28.

The second word is very uncertain. I read this as *peal* perfect 2ms from שני 'to change for the worse' (*DJPA* 560). The he could either be part of the 2ms (see 1QapGen 14.11, 15; 15.9; Fitzmyer 2004: 168, 169) or a 3rd person suffix: 'you changed it'. There is a similar phrase in the Enochic *Birth of Noah* text, with which 1QapGen seems to be related: ה[וֹן שני 'they perverted their [nature]' (4Q204 5 ii 18 [*DSSR* 3:555] = *1 En.* 106.14).

11. Of particular interest, Philo (*Quaest. in Gen.* 2.13) explains the seven days between the entry to the ark (Gen 7.4) and the start of the flood as a time to heed the announcement of the flood and repent. This assumes Noah preaching, and perhaps preaching from the ark during those seven days. See further Lewis 1978: 102 and n. 3, 135; Franxman 1979: 81–82; Feldman 1998b: 40–42; Dimant 1998: 132 and n. 42; Kugel 1998: 185–86.

12. These readings are based on the ABMC photograph B1997 0301. More can be read of these and other lines, but the readings are too uncertain as yet to help with understanding the narrative and so are not included here.

3 [לָךְ יָהֵב אנה שלטנא וֹ]
10 [oo]ךְ גוֹא תהוֹמא וֹ]

3. ... to you I am giving the dominion ...[13]
10. ... in the midst of the deep ...[14]

In line 3 is the phrase 'to you I am giving the dominion'. Thus, the section 9.2-8 seems to be a speech from God to Noah on the ark – unique to the *Genesis Apocryphon* – in which God alludes to dominion over animals from Gen. 1.28 (cf. Gen. 9.1-3). In any case, it is reasonably certain that the unleashing of the flood is described in 9.9–10.1. In 9.10 is a mention of 'the deep', and the word רבא at the beginning of 10.1 is probably part of the phrase 'the great [deep]' (cf. *Tg. Ps.-J.* Gen. 7.11). It would seem, then, that this part of the story corresponds to Gen. 7.11 (cf. *Jub.* 5.24-25, 29; *Book of Giants* 4Q206 4 i 16–20 = *1 Enoch* 3–4).

On board the ark, something occurs to Noah at night (1QapGen 10.2–3) – perhaps a vision – and Noah calls his family to sing, praise and bless God their Lord (1QapGen 10.8–10):

8. ... sing and praise![15] ... blessing ...
9. ... all ... and quiet ... all of you to your Lord ...
10. to the king of all ages forever and ever for all eternity. *vacat*

The ark comes to rest on one of the mountains of Hurarat (10.11-12), and Noah offers sacrifices on an altar to atone for all the earth – apparently while still on the ark (10.12-13)! He details the sacrificial procedures according to Torah regulations (10.13-17). After telling of God's acceptance of the sacrifice (10.18-?), Noah surveys the land from the door of the ark (11.1-10), then exits the ark and walks through the extent of the land (11.11-12). He blesses God (11.12-14), and God makes a covenant with him (11.15–12.6, a *vacat* marks end of section).[16] Then Noah descends the mountain with his children and 'the branch' (12.7-9), probably the vine shoot he plants in line 13, but possibly the branch returned by the dove. The current editions read here that Noah descends with his children and *grandchildren*, but this is incorrect both palaeographically and contextually.[17] The passage reads then:

8. [...] ... in the mountains of Hurarat, and afterwards I descended to the base of this mountain, I and my children and with the branch (ובנופא)
9. [...] ... for the desolation was great in the land.

13.   This reading is almost certainly correct. A similar phrase occurs in 1QapGen 21:10 (די אנה יהב לך) and superimposing these words fits the letters here perfectly. With regard to word order, the dative object usually follows the verb, but about 25% of the time precedes (Kutscher 1965: 33–34).

14.   The reading תהוֹמא is certain. I read the previous word as גוֹא 'midst' (see *DSSC* 2:806). This is the usual spelling in Aramaic texts from Qumran, although it is otherwise spelled גו in 1QapGen (*DSSC* 2:806). Such a variation is found in other texts, e.g., 4Q197 4 i 15 cf. 4 iii 1. A similar phrase occurs in a parallel context in the *Book of Dreams* (4Q206 4 i 17): the flood gates open בגוא ארעא.

15.   The verbs והללו ושבחו are read by MQS as perfects ('they sang and praised'), followed by DSSSE, DSSR, and FGA³. I read the verbs in line 8 as plural imperatives, which better accords with the 2nd plural address in the following line. For this section I follow the transcription of MQS and mostly the translation from FGA³ 83.

16.   See my proposed reconstruction of 1QapGen 11.16, p. 56 below.

17.   The last word of line 8 is ובנופא as a certain reading (based on ABMC photograph B1997 0304), and the reading ובני בנֹיֹ (GQ, followed by *ATTM 2*, *DSSR*, *DSSSE*, and FGA³) is impossible. Furthermore, line 9 specifies that Noah's grandchildren were born *after* the flood.

Noah then relates the birth of his grandchildren, who were born *after* the flood (12.9-12). He retells the story of the vineyard (12.13-27+) as the proper observance of a festival and laws about the use of produce according to the prescriptions of Torah, in a manner similar to that in *Jubilees* 7.1-6. Noah makes no mention of the shameful incident concerning his nakedness, but instead recalls his wine-induced slumber as the occasion for a lengthy revelatory dream and interpretation about the destiny of his descendants and eschatological judgment of the wicked (12.end?–15.end?). In the remaining discernible content dealing with Noah (15.end?–17.end?), he describes the allotment of land among his sons and grandsons, with special attention paid to geographic boundaries and close parallels to *Jubilees* 8–9, but deals with the sons in a different order.

Column 18 is unreadable. If it told the story of the Tower of Babel (Gen. 11.1-9) it could only have done so quite briefly (as does *Jub.* 10.18-26), but it is difficult to imagine how this would fit with the first-person narrative style that otherwise dominates 1QapGen. More likely, and more in keeping with the document as far as it is known, it jumped straight on to let Abram tell his story. It certainly must have begun with the story of Abram in Ur and his journey to Haran (Gen. 11.27–32; *Jubilees* 11–12), which was the source of considerable interest among early Jewish interpreters (see Kugel 1998: 244–71). Perhaps Abram's departure from Ur might have been set in the context of the story of the idolatrous Tower as in *Pseudo-Philo* (6–7).

In any case, by the beginning of column 19, Abram has made his way to Canaan and arrived at Bethel (1QapGen 18.?–19.6). From here until column 22 we can follow the story of Abram closely, as this material is well preserved. Abram tells that he built an altar at Bethel (19.7) and records his blessing to God (19.7-8). He notes that he had not as yet reached the 'holy mountains' – presumably meaning Jerusalem – and he continued south (19.8-9). He journeyed on to Hebron where he stayed two years (19.9-10). Adding that he had heard of grain in Egypt, Abram narrates the story of his departure to Egypt with Sarai and Lot to escape famine and his subsequent return and settlement at Hebron (1QapGen 19.10–21.22). This closely follows the Genesis narrative (Gen. 12.10–13.18) but with some considerable expansions. In telling his story, Abram incorporates numerous chronological details about his travels that correspond closely to *Jubilees* (B12, 23, 33, 95). Abram also takes pains to inform of specific geographic details, especially those having to do with the boundaries of the promised land (B15, 62, 64, 67, 69, 74, 77, 83, 89, 90). Most of the expansions have to do with the sensitive story of Abram and Sarai's sojourn in Egypt. Abram relates a dream that he interprets as divine guidance for his wife to pretend to be his sister in Egypt for his protection (19.14-19), after which Sarai weeps and fears that anyone might see her (19.21-23). In Egypt, she managed to escape notice for 5 years (19.23). Then Pharaoh's emissaries sought Abram out to consult his renowned wisdom and he instructed them from the book of Enoch (1QapGen 19.24–26).[18] Apparently, they caught sight of Sarai and became enraptured with her beauty. One of them, named Hirqanos (חרקנוש), sings praises of Sarai's matchless beauty and wisdom to Pharaoh in a lengthy poem reminiscent of the Song of Songs (1QapGen 19.end?–20.8).

Abram recounts that Pharaoh took Sarai by force, and relates Sarai's intercession for his life. Abram tells that he wept bitterly, and he narrates a lengthy prayer in which

18. See the corrected reading of 1QapGen 19:23-26, p. 87 below.

he lodged a complaint against Pharaoh and cried to God to protect Sarai (20.8-16). In response, God sent an evil spirit to inflict Pharaoh and his men, so that although Sarai lived two years in Pharaoh's household she was not touched (20.16-18). When Pharaoh's wise men failed to heal him, Pharaoh saw Abram in a dream, and sent Hirqanos to seek his help. Acting as intermediary, Lot revealed that Sarai is Abram's wife, and that if Sarai is returned then Abram will pray for Pharaoh (20.18-26). Several of these details are related to the story of Abram and Abimelek in Gen. 20.3, 7, 17-18. Pharaoh complied: he brought Sarai, rebuked Abram, and requested Abram to prayer for his healing. Abram exorcised the demon by praying and laying hands on Pharaoh. Pharaoh rewarded Abram handsomely, and with assurances that he had not touched her, returned Sarai with many gifts including Hagar, and expelled them from Egypt (20.26-32).

To the story of their return and resettlement in Canaan (1QapGen 20.33–21.22), 1QapGen adds several amplifications in comparison with Genesis 13:

- An explanation that Lot acquired his wealth and a wife in Egypt (20.34) and that Abram 'added greatly' to his wealth (21.5–6)
- Details of sacrifice and prayer at the altars at Bethel and Hebron (21.1-4, 20-22)
- Geographical details of his survey of the land (21.7-8, 10-12, 15-19)
- Comments that Abram was distressed at the parting with Lot, that Lot bought a house in Sodom (21.6-7), and that Abram invited the three Amorite brothers to a feast (21.21-22)

At the same time, he significantly abbreviates the dispute leading to Lot's separation (21.5-6) and omits mention of the wickedness of Sodom and its destruction.

With the story of the invading kings (Gen. 14.1-24), the *Genesis Apocryphon* abruptly shifts to third-person narration and quite literal translation of Genesis with small supplements (1QapGen 21.23–22.26). The most notable additions clarify that:

- the eastern kings had imposed tribute on the Canaanite kings (21.25-26)
- the king of Sodom escaped (21.32-33)
- Abram was informed of the movement of the kings by a former shepherd of his (22.1-3)
- Abram wept for his nephew (22.3-5)
- Salem is Jerusalem (22.13)
- Abram met with Melchizedek before the king of Sodom (22.12-14, 18-20)
- Abram returned both goods and captives (22.24-26)

The *Genesis Apocryphon* also presents the kings in a more consistent order than Genesis and translates some of their names and places.

A similar style of retelling continues in the story of Abram's vision (Gen. 15; 1QapGen 22.27-34). God begins his speech with a summary of Abram's travels that clarifies the chronological problems of Genesis in the same manner as *Jubilees*. God then instructs Abram to calculate the growth of his wealth, which he explicitly identifies as the reward of Gen. 15.1. Abram gratefully acknowledges God's blessing before complaining that he has no heir.

Unfortunately, the scroll breaks in the middle of this episode, at the end of a sheet. It is impossible to be certain how many sheets may have been lost from the end of the scroll. Whether the third-person narration continued on the lost following sheet(s) until the end of the work is impossible to determine, as is the nature of the retelling of that subsequent material. Also, it is uncertain whether the narrative continued through the Abram story and perhaps the other patriarchs, and how expansive the retelling may have been.

4. *Genre*

The *Genesis Apocryphon* is an Aramaic version of the story of Genesis (or at least the parts related to Noah and Abraham), and in places it has the character of a translation of Genesis similar to the style of the targums, especially in the story of Abraham. Because of this, some have called it an early example of the targum genre.[19] Nevertheless, as a whole it is not a targum, since most of it is a very free paraphrase and some large sections are only loosely inspired by the text of Genesis. The narrative of the *Genesis Apocryphon* is interpretative, that is to say it assumes a textual tradition of Genesis that it seeks to clarify, and it is the product of exegetical reflection on Genesis. In this, the *Genesis Apocryphon* shows numerous similarities to haggadic midrash, including similar exegetical techniques and even specific interpretations, leading some to identify its genre as midrash.[20] This, however, is misleading. One might refer to the activity of interpretation as midrash in a general sense, but since it does not make formal distinction between Scripture (as lemma) and commentary it is best not to call it an example of the *genre* midrash.

A distinctive feature that the *Genesis Apocryphon* shares with some other works such as *Pseudo-Philo* is that it offers an extended presentation of a scriptural text in a new narrative that seamlessly incorporates interpretation, clarification, harmonization, and supplementary traditions. It interprets by means of a new telling of the story. It recognizably follows the same general narrative order of Genesis, but has a new narrative framework (e.g., characters tell their story in the first person). Hence, many scholars have adopted Vermes's term rewritten Bible to designate the literary genre of the *Genesis Apocryphon* and similar works.[21] This too is somewhat misleading, even apart from the implicit anachronism of the term. Rewritten Bible (or better, Scripture) describes a formal feature that has to do with the process of producing the work, and hence can also refer to the phenomenon of such works, but it does not meaningfully describe what the new work is or how it functions.[22] In fact, a major difficulty in trying to determine a literary genre for the *Genesis Apocryphon* is that its function remains uncertain. It seems that such works must assume a context of relating scriptural texts with enhancements, to make the Scripture clearer, more systematic,

19. E.g. Black (1961: 193–95), Kuiper (1968). For a discussion of this and other views on the genre of the *Genesis Apocryphon*, see Fitzmyer (2004: 16–25).

20. E.g., Vermes (1973: 95–96, 124); also M. Black, A. Dupont-Sommer, M. Goshen-Gottstein, G. Lambert, R. Meyer, E. Vogt, A. G. Wright, F. Michelini Tocci, H. C. Kee (see the discussion and bibliography in Fitzmyer 2004: 18–19 and n. 28).

21. E.g., Alexander (1988), Evans (1988), White Crawford (1999), Bernstein (2001), Lange (2002a: 117–18). Although Segal (2005: 17) recognizes rewritten Bible as a genre, he excludes 1QapGen because it is written in a different language than its base text (Genesis).

22. See Brooke (2000f); also Nickelsburg (1984), Harrington (1986: 239), and Fisk (2000b: 947; 2001: 13–14 and n. 3).

more lively. But whether the context was school, synagogue, or home is unclear, as is whether the use was educational or liturgical, or for edification or apologetic purposes.

Because it assumes an authoritative scriptural tradition but does not seem intended to replace it – its language alone would distinguish it – many refer to the *Genesis Apocryphon* as parabiblical (or parascriptural).[23] This term is even less suitable as the name of a literary genre, though, since it describes still more generally in terms only of a perceived relationship to other writings (i.e., alongside and hence *not* Scripture). The term is best used as an umbrella for a wide range of texts of various genres generated centrifugally from Scripture, although I prefer to refer to the phenomenon less prejudicially (but also more awkwardly) as extending Scriptures. The *Genesis Apocryphon* is a significant example of this phenomenon, of the more specific type that can be described as rewriting or retelling Scripture. But it seems best not to regard either of these as specific literary genres. Indeed at this point I believe it best to refrain from attempting to determine a specific literary genre for the *Genesis Apocryphon*, particularly since the loss of both the beginning and end make it impossible to determine confidently the character of the work as a whole.

5. *Noah Motifs*

We can now examine some of the main motifs of the *Genesis Apocryphon*. I will focus especially on the Noah material since this has been so poorly preserved and has consequently received much less attention than the Abraham section.

a. *The Wayward Watchers and the Birth of Noah*
One of the most curious passages in the Hebrew Bible is the brief story in Gen. 6.1-4 about the 'sons of God' who mate with 'daughters of humans' and beget children. In the context of Genesis, it is intimately tied to the story of Noah and the flood, immediately following the report of the birth of Noah and his three sons (Gen. 5.28-32) and immediately preceding God's decision to destroy all living creatures on earth because of the wickedness of humans (Gen. 6.5-7). It seems to intend to provide the reason for the flood, but how? It bristles with riddles left unanswered by its tantalizing brevity. Who are the sons of God? Who are the Nephilim, and what is their relationship to the 'warriors of renown'? What does it mean that God's spirit will not 'abide' in humans forever but that their days will be 120 years? This can be understood as a limitation of lifespan (but problematically, people continue to live longer than that for a while), or as a time period before judgment (the flood). This seems to be a punishment related to the sons of God/daughters of humans incident, but how? Does it imply that humans enticed divine beings? In connection with the punishment is the statement 'for they are flesh'. The story then seems to be about divine–human miscegenation. If this is a story about angels raping human women, why does God express anger only at the rape victims, destroying humans and animals and leaving the angels apparently unpunished for their crime? When does this crime take place? What was so special about Noah at his birth that Lamech gave him a special name?

23. Fitzmyer (2004: 20) adopts Ginsberg's proposal (1967) of parabiblical as the literary genre.

It is evident that Gen. 6.1-4 is a myth fragment: it poorly fits its context, and it reads like an off-hand allusion to a well-known story, the point of which remains obscure without prior familiarity. The editor of Genesis seems little interested in the myth itself, other than as a general illustration of the increasing violence that infected the world and elicited God's decision to destroy all life on earth. But as part of Scripture, it is subsequently read for deep meaning in its new context, as the rich history of diverse interpretation attests (Alexander 1972; Kugel 1998: 179–83, 194–220). The problem seems to be the confusion of categories (as in the Levitical laws), but who are the 'sons of God': divine beings, or a particular class/race of humans?

As puzzling as this passage is to modern readers, it was one of the most important passages in Genesis during the Second Temple period, and was frequently retold and expanded. It was, particularly, the central passage for explaining the origin of evil and sin in the world that God had created (e.g., *1 Enoch* 6–7, 106–107; *Jub.* 4.15, 22; 5.1-11; 7.21-24, 27; 8.3; CD 2.17-19; 4Q180 7–9; cf. 1 Pet. 2.4; Jude 6).

In the *Genesis Apocryphon* Noah's birth comprises a long story, involving speeches by Lamech, Bitenosh, Methuselah, and Enoch, and before all of this, perhaps one of the Watchers. Altogether this occupies about a quarter of the extant text (1QapGen 0–5)! This material is almost completely extraneous to the Genesis story, but seems to be an expansion and adaptation of a similar story told in *1 Enoch* 106–107. In the *Genesis Apocryphon*, it serves loosely as an account of the birth of Noah from Gen. 5.28-29. It implicitly clarifies and fills gaps with regard to numerous elements left ambiguous in the Genesis story.

1. The sons of God are angels. The *Genesis Apocryphon* understands Gen. 6.1-4 as a story about an improper sexual union between angels and humans that produced a race of hybrid beings, as similarly in numerous other writings of the time period (esp. *1 Enoch* and *Jubilees*). The particular story-line here in the *Genesis Apocryphon* is closely related to that in *1 Enoch* 106–107 (4Q204 5 i–ii): Lamech fears that the strange child is 'from the angels' (*1 En.* 106.5-6, 12). Some of the language, however, is similar to *Jubilees* (4.15; 5.1; 7.21) and the *Book of Watchers* (*1 Enoch* 6–7 = 4Q201 1 iii; 4Q202 1 ii; 4Q204 1 ii), referring to them as 'Watchers', 'Holy Ones', and 'sons of heaven' (1QapGen 2.1, 16).

2. Lamech's wife was Bitenosh. Genesis does not name Lamech's wife, but here and in *Jub.* 4.28 she is identified by the name Bitenosh, literally 'daughter of man'. This serves as a pun connecting the story of Noah's birth with the sons of God story in Gen. 6.1-4.

3. The Nephilim are a hybrid semi-divine race, the offspring of angels and humans. Genesis 6.4 is ambiguous about the relationships among the Nephilim, the sons of God, their offspring, and the heroes of old. It is not clear whether the Nephilim should be understood as the race of offspring, or as an unrelated race mentioned only to contextualize the episode; that is, that the sons of God mated and had children in the distant past of great lore about mighty races of warriors. From Num. 13.32-33 one could gather that the Nephilim are a race of giants, but the word could also be read as 'fallen ones'. This ambiguity gave rise to many different interpretations, including the idea of 'fallen angels' (see Kugel 1998: 204–205).

1QapGen seems to understand the 'Nephilim' of Gen. 6.4 similarly to *Jubilees* (5.1, 7-10; 7.21-22; cf. CD 2.18-19) as the offspring of the angel–human union, a hybrid race of semi-divine giants. In 1QapGen 2.1, Noah's strange appearance causes Lamech to fear that he is 'from the Watchers' and 'belongs to the Nephilin'.

4. The descent of the Watchers happened 'in the days of Jared'. Genesis does not date the sons of God incident, although the order of Gen. 5.28–6.8 might imply that it took place between Noah's 500th and 600th year. Some traditions tended to date the incident earlier, around Noah's 480th year, or perhaps to the more distant past. The *Genesis Apocryphon* reflects a tradition that connects it to the time of Noah's great, great, grandfather Jared, that is attested in *1 En.* 6.6 (4Q201 1 iii 3–4); 106.13 (4Q204 5 ii 17–18); and *Jub.* 4.15 . Only the latter passage makes explicit the pun on which this is based: the word ירד on which the name is based means 'to descend', and this is apparently read as an allusion to the 'descent' of the angels. It is possible that this is secondary to the common tradition (based on Gen. 5.24) that Jared's son Enoch goes to live among the angels, thus creating a balance: angels descend to cohabit with humans, a human goes to live among angels. It should be noted that the 'days of Jared' is rather imprecise since Jared was among the longest living patriarchs, and overlapped with Noah. We will consider the complicated chronological problem further below.

5. Lamech receives revelation. In Gen. 5.28-29, Lamech names his son Noah, saying: 'Out of the ground that the Lord has cursed this one shall bring us relief from our work and from the toil of our hands'. In the overall canonical context, this relates to Noah's special role as deliverer *vis-à-vis* the judgment pronounced *after* the sons of God incident. But according to the flow of the narrative in Genesis, the sons of God incident appears to take place *during* Noah's lifetime: the story follows the narration of Noah's birth and the birth of his children (Gen. 5.28–29, 32), and the statement 'but Noah found favor in the sight of the Lord' (Gen. 6.8) implies that Noah was a contemporary. How could Lamech have known about impending disaster in the future for which Noah was the solution? Common to both the Enochic *Birth of Noah* story (*1 Enoch* 106–107; 4Q204 5 i 26–ii 30) and the *Genesis Apocryphon* (A8–9), Enoch reveals to Lamech the story of the Watchers and their judgment, and the role that Noah will play in the preservation of life. Thus, Lamech's naming of Noah is related to revelation about his future. If the apocalypse in 1QapGen 0–1 is by Lamech, then this would be a unique secondary addition to the story to explain why Lamech might suspect angelic parentage: he was already informed of the intercourse between the Watchers and women, but doesn't know the role of his son – this he learns only from his grandfather Enoch.

6. The angels and their offspring were punished. In Genesis, there is no mention of a punishment of the sons of God. Columns 0–1 of 1QapGen seem to be an apocalypse of God's anger toward the wayward angels, their imprisonment and ultimate judgment, and the destruction of their offspring. This motif that the angels and their monstrous offspring did not go unpunished is prominent in Jewish apocalyptic writings of the Second Temple period (e.g,. *1 En.* 9–10; 12.4-6; 14.1-7; 18.14-16; 21.1-10; 54.1-6; 55.3–56.4; 66; 67.4-12; 69.28; 88; 90.20-27; *Jub.* 5.6-11; 10.1-14; *T. Levi* 18.12; CD 2.16-21; 1Q27 1 i 5; Jude 6; 2 Pet. 2.4; *2 Bar.* 56.11-16).

7. This story is about the origin of evil. The Enochic traditions about the Watchers also emphasize that the angels introduced forbidden knowledge to humans about warfare, magic, and seduction that caused an epidemic of corruption and violence (e.g., *1 En.* 7–9; 10.8; 65; 69.6-12). Thus, humans and animals were destroyed because they became infected with impurity and sin by rebellious angels. This posits that evil originated effectively as an alien invasion which humans were powerless to resist, in

contrast to other traditions that emphasized the origin of sin as an exercise of free will rejecting God's law (as, e.g., emphasis on the Genesis 3 story; see Boccaccini 1998: 73–74). *Jubilees* has somewhat of a mediating view to avoid the possible conclusion that evil originates in the divine realm: the angels came to earth on a good mission, but were led astray on earth (*Jub.* 4.15; 7.20-28). The *Genesis Apocryphon* also seems to interpret the story about the Watchers as the origin of human sin (e.g., 'mystery of evil' in 1QapGen 1.2 ; cf. 1QH[a] 13.36; 1Q27 1.2; 2 Thess. 2.7). It is not clear whether it follows *1 Enoch* 7–9 with regard to an angelic rebellion in heaven, or *Jubilees* with regard to angelic straying on earth.

8. Noah was special from his birth. Lamech's naming of Noah in Gen. 5.29 implies that Noah was singled out for his unique destiny from birth. The *Genesis Apocryphon* reflects a tradition found also in *1 Enoch* 106–107 (4Q204 5 i 26–30) and a couple of other Noah writings (1Q19; 4Q534–536; see Puech 2001; Fitzmyer 2004: 122–23) that ascribe to Noah a fantastic appearance at birth and extraordinary accompanying phenomena. Nickelsburg has noted that these stories are important parallels to the birth narratives of Jesus: an extraordinary birth foreshadows the child's role in salvation, anxiety of the husband that he is not the father of the extraordinary child, a reassurance, and a special name (Nickelsburg 1998: 145–46).

Almost all of the exegetical elements with regard to this narrative in the *Genesis Apocryphon* are shared traditions that are not original to the author. The major distinctive contribution of the author, rather, is that he has fleshed out these traditions with intricate supplementary details to produce a compelling story of considerable length. Particularly prominent among the additional material are details reflecting intense interest in psychological and emotional states, and most remarkably in the woman's point of view (Nickelsburg 2003a). The same approach is displayed in the story of Abram and Sarai. There are two elements that might be considered exegetical and that have a good chance of being unique to the author: that the naming of Noah is the result of special revelation to Lamech, and certain details of the chronology which we will consider in detail next. In any case, the author shows a special interest in the motifs of revelation and working out details of chronology as is evident also in the Abram section.

b. *Chronology*
In the *Genesis Apocryphon* there are several intriguing features with regard to chronology in the Noah story.

1. The descent of the Watchers is dated 'in the days of Jared' (3.3)
2. Noah's children are married when he is 500 years old (6.10)
3. Lamech fears Noah is one of the Nephilim (2.1)
4. Shem is Noah's eldest child (12.10)

It will be easiest to begin with issues in Genesis and then describe how these are addressed in *1 Enoch, Jubilees,* and the *Genesis Apocryphon.* We will deal with two of the several complications with regard to chronology in the flood story in Genesis: the dating of the sons of God, and the order of Noah's sons.

In Genesis, the story of the 'sons of God' mating with the 'daughters of humans' (Gen. 6.1-4) is intimately tied to the story of Noah and the flood, immediately following the report of the birth of Noah and his three sons (Gen. 5.28-32) and immediately preceding God's decision to destroy all living creatures on earth because of the wickedness of humans. Thus, Gen. 5.28–6.10 has the following structure:

A1 birth of Noah – relief
A2 sons of Noah
    B1 sons of God
    B2 God's decision to destroy
A1 Noah found favor
A2 sons of Noah

But although there is an abundance of chronological details for dating Noah and the flood (problematic as it is), there are no concrete chronological data to relate the sons of God story to this chronology other than that the story appears (ambiguously) to provide the reason for the flood, and so presumably occurred sometime before the flood. It could, however, have been an incident in the distant past, alluded to in a flash-back. The structure of the story, however, suggests two possible frames in relation to the birth of Noah's sons and God's pronouncement of judgment. (1) Gen. 5.32 states: 'After Noah was five hundred years old, Noah became the father of Shem, Ham, and Japheth'. If Gen. 5.32 and Gen. 6.1-4 are read in chronological order, the sons of God incident would have happened sometime after Noah's 500th year, after the birth of his children. (2) The meaning of God's judgment that 'their days shall be one hundred twenty years' is ambiguous: it could refer to a reduced lifespan of humans, or to a period of 120 years before the flood. Since the flood is dated to Noah's 600th year, the latter interpretation could suggest that the sons of God incident took place shortly before Noah's 480th year. It is important to note that these two possible data provide conflicting dates: the one would suggest a date *after* Noah's 500th year and the other would suggest a date *before* Noah's 480th year. In general, subsequent interpreters pick one or the other for dating the sons of God incident, and interpret the other differently (see Kugel 1998: 212–14).

1 Enoch contains several important – and potentially divergent – traditions concerning Noah and the fall of the Watchers relevant to the treatment of this chronology in the *Genesis Apocryphon*. First, one tradition places the intercourse between the Watchers and women in the days of Noah's great-great grandfather Jared. This is attested in the *Book of Watchers* and related to a pun on ירד, 'to descend': the Watchers 'descended in the days of Jared' (*1 En.* 6.6 = 4Q201 1 iii 3–4; cf. *Jub.* 4.15). It is also attested in the story about the birth of Noah in *1 Enoch* 106–107 that is reflected in the *Genesis Apocryphon*: 'in the days of Jared, my father, they transgressed the word of the Lord …' (1 En. 106.13 = 4Q204 5 ii 17–18). But when in Jared's life is technically ambiguous because Jared is said to have lived long enough to overlap with Noah (962 years according to MT and LXX, and 847 years according to the Samaritan Pentateuch; Gen. 5.18-20). Although the chronologies differ, in each case Jared overlapped with Noah's life, as the table overleaf illustrates.

It would seem, however, that *1 En.* 106.13 implies that the incident occurred before the birth of Jared's son Enoch, who is telling the story; that is, why would Enoch say 'in the days of Jared, my father' for an event that occurred during his own lifetime? Possibly in line with this, in the *Dream Visions* Enoch says that he had visions about the sin of the Watchers in his youth, before his marriage (*1 En.* 83.2), and his subsequent prayer (*1 En.* 84.2-6) seems to assume the deed has been done. This tradition, however, remains ambiguous in *1 Enoch*: 'in the days of Jared' could indicate any time until Jared's death during Noah's lifetime.

Table 2. *Chronology of the Flood (dates* Anno Mundi *[AM]).*

	MT	SP	LXX	*Jubilees*	*LAB* 1	Jos. *Ant.* 1
Jared	460–1422	460–1307	960–1922	461–	950–1922	960–1929
Enoch	622–987	522–887	1122–1487	522–887	1122–1487	1122–1487
Methuselah	687–1656	587–1307	1287–2256	587–	1287–2256	1287–2256
Lamech	874–1651	654–1307	1454–2207	652–	1474–2241	1474–2181
Noah	1056–2006	707–1657	1642–2592	707–1657	1656–2606	1662–2612
-son born	1556	1207	2142	1207	1956	2162
Flood	1656	1307	2242	1307/8	2256	2262
					(3.6: 1652)	(8.61: 1662)

Second, there are also traditions attested in *1 Enoch* that associate the fall of the Watchers with Enoch's life. *1 En.* 12.1-6 and 87.3-4 place the fall of the Watchers after Enoch's first journeys but before his final removal to paradise (see Nickelsburg 2001: 233, 374; although cf. *1 En.* 83.2 which dates Enoch's visions before his marriage). This may in origin reflect a different tradition, and may have begun with speculation about Enoch: was there a connection between a human going to dwell with angels and angels going to dwell with humans? Also in the immediate context of the story of Noah's birth in *1 Enoch* 106–107, Lamech fears that Noah is 'from the angels' and that his strange birth portends something that will happen 'in his days on the earth' (*1 En.* 106.6). This might assume that the mating of the Watchers with women happened shortly before Noah's birth, so that Noah is feared to be a product of this unnatural union. It is noteworthy that according to the chronology of the Samaritan Pentateuch (as opposed to MT or LXX; see Table 2), there would be no conflict between these data, since Jared lives until the year of the flood in 1307, and Enoch overlaps 180 years with Noah. Thus, the sin of the Watchers could occur during Enoch's lifetime, during Jared's lifetime, and around the birth of Noah. If the chronology of the Samaritan Pentateuch is assumed, then Lamech's consultation of Enoch occurred during Enoch's first sojourn among the angels, not after his final removal to paradise.

Third, *1 En.* 93.3-4 seems to place the fall of the Watchers in the 'second week', after Enoch's removal to paradise but before Noah's deliverance from the flood (see Nickelsburg 2001: 443). Other passages may also date this incident to Noah's lifetime (see *1 En.* 65.1-10), and in this case, descriptions of the Watchers before Noah could be seen as revelatory visions of the future (cf. *1 En.* 64.1; 83.2).

Milik attempted to harmonize 'the days of Jared' with a time after Enoch by positing a dependance on the 'Enoch–'Irad' chronology of Gen. 4.18 (Milik 1976: 31). Given the ambiguity noted above, this is an unnecessary explanation. Some ancient interpreters understood 'the days of Jared' to mean late in his life, during the life of Noah. The rabbinic chronological text *Seder Olam* 1 shows a similar approach in its treatment of Peleg's name (cf. Gen. 10.25): 'the Split occurred during Peleg's last year'.

Another tradition relevant for the *Genesis Apocryphon* appears in a Noah fragment incorporated into the *Book of Similitudes*. *1 Enoch* 60.1 indicates that on the eve of the Feast of Booths in his 500th year, Noah saw a vision of the heavenly hosts and the divine judgment.[24] The date depends on Gen. 5.32, 'Noah was five hundred years old,

24. The manuscripts read 'Enoch' here, but as Charles notes (1912: 113) this text was originally

and Noah fathered Shem, Ham and Japheth', but there are no explicit clues as to the reason for associating a vision with the birth of Noah's children.

Jubilees is more specific in its interpretation of the chronology of this narrative. First, *Jubilees* similarly dates the descent of the Watchers to the 'days of Jared', but provides an explicit reasoning based on punning his name with יֶרֶד, 'to descend': 'He named him Jared because during his lifetime the angels of the Lord who were called Watchers descended to earth to teach mankind and to do what is just and upright upon the earth' (*Jub.* 4.15; *VBJ*). But notably, unlike in *1 Enoch*, this descent is not with malicious intent; it is a good mission that subsequently goes awry.[25] Second, *Jubilees* harmonizes this with another tradition drawn from interpreting the 120 years of Gen. 6.3 as time until the flood: that the sin of the Watchers occurred shortly before the 480th year of Noah's life (*Jub.* 5.7-9; 4Q252 1.1-3; see Kugel 1998: 212–13, 220). The relevant data here are that it dates the incident to the twenty-fifth Jubilee (=AM 1177; *Jub.* 5.1, cf. 4.33), and it regards the 120 years of Gen. 6.3 as a restriction on the life of the giant offspring of this perverse union (*Jub.* 5.7-10). But *Jubilees* also makes clear that the giant offspring are not destroyed in the flood, but kill each other off *before* the flood (VanderKam 1999: 160–61). Since the flood is dated to AM 1308 (*Jub.* 5.22-3, cf. 6.18), the sin of the Watchers must occur between AM 1177–87 at the outer limits.

Third, these two details are not necessarily in conflict since according to the chronology of the Samaritan Pentateuch, which *Jubilees* assumes, Jared lives until the year of the flood (AM 1307 according to SP, AM 1308 according to *Jub.* 5.22-3).[26]

Thus, the sin of the Watchers shortly before Noah's 480th year is still during Jared's life: in the chronology of the Samaritan Pentateuch, Jared dies when Noah is 600. This would not be the case with the chronologies of either the Masoretic Text (Jared dies when Noah is 366) or the Septuagint (Jared dies when Noah is 280). It is not clear, however, whether *Jubilees* imagines that the Watchers lusted after the women in the same year that they descended to teach or whether there is an intervening period.

Fourth, *Jubilees* adds precision to Gen. 5.32, indicating that Noah's first son (Shem) was born in his 500th year. Thus, although *Jubilees* follows the order of presentation of Genesis, narrating the birth of Noah's children (Gen. 5.32; *Jub.* 4.33) before the intercourse between the sons of God and the women (Gen. 6.1-3; *Jub.* 5.1), it necessarily regards these as not in chronological order: for *Jubilees*, Noah's children are born after the sin of the Watchers. This is puzzling because it departs from the usual tendency of *Jubilees* to arrange the text in chronological order (see Ruiten 2000: 193).

about Noah (*1 En.* 60.8 refers to Enoch as his 'grandfather'), and the mention of the 500th year alludes to Gen. 5.32.

25. Dimant argues that this is a secondary element to the tradition, and serves to negate any implication that evil invaded the earth from heaven; instead, it originated on earth (unpublished dissertation, as referred to by VanderKam 1999: 155).

26. *Jub.* 5.22–3 has the ark constructed in AM 1307 and only in AM 1308 does Noah enter the ark and then the flood start. This delay of one year *vis-à-vis* the chronology of SP may be so that the patriarchs (Jared, Methuselah, Lamech) die *before* entrance to the ark rather than being destroyed in the flood.

Table 3. *Chronology of the Flood in* Jubilees.[27]

Adam
Jared 461
Enoch 522
Enoch's sojourn 587
Methuselah 587
Lamech 652
Noah 707
Watchers sin 1177
Shem born 1207
Flood 1307

0 200 400 600 800 1000 1200 1400 1600 1800

Years AM

It is also difficult to know how to reconcile with this the description in *Jub.* 4.22 that during his first sojourn with the angels (AM 587–881), Enoch 'testified to the Watchers who had sinned with the daughters of men' (*VBJ*). According to the chronology of *Jubilees* (also SP), Noah's birth (AM 707; see *Jub.* 4.28) would have occurred during Enoch's first sojourn among the angels (AM 587–881; see *Jub.* 4.20-21). Therefore, this may be an allusion to the tradition in *1 En.* 106.13-17, according to which Enoch is consulted about the birth of Noah, and testifies to his vision about the sin of the Watchers.

Still, it is not clear whether this assumes that the sin of the Watchers occurred shortly before Noah's birth, or whether this is to be understood as a vision of the future. That is, is this detail incompatible with *Jub.* 5.1 that dates the sin of the Watchers between the 470th and 480th years of Noah's life (no earlier than AM 1177)? In any case, *Jubilees* attempts to add precision to the question of when the sin of the Watchers occurred, but not without some tension remaining. It appears that the key datum for *Jubilees* is the 120 years of Gen. 6.3, interpreted to apply to the giant offspring who are killed before the flood, but the author must assume that Gen. 5.28 and Gen. 6.1-3 are not in chronological order.

Against the background of these interpretative difficulties, it is possible to recognize in the fragments of the *Genesis Apocryphon* both continuity but also original interpretations which at the same time solve problems and create new ones. First, the *Genesis Apocryphon* dates the descent of the angels to the days of Noah's great-great

27. In the following chart, dates AM (*Anno Mundi*) are derived from the genealogies in the following passages: Gen. 5.3-32; 7.6; 9.28-29; *Jub.* 4.15-16, 20-21, 27-28, 33; 5.22; 10.16; *Ps. Philo* 1.2-22; 5.8; Jos. *Ant.* 1.83-88. The genealogies of *Ps. Philo* and Josephus are mostly in line with the Septuagint, but both elsewhere give a conflicting date for the flood that appears to be corrected toward the genealogies of MT (*Ps. Philo* 3.6: AM 1652; Jos. *Ant.* 8.61-62 AM 1662). The dates derived from *Ps. Philo* depend on (1) the assumption that it agreed with LXX concerning Adam's age at the birth of Seth, and (2) proposed emendations concerning the ages of Seth and Kenan at the births of their first sons (see Jacobson 1996: 1.286–87; Hendel 1998: 70–71).

grandfather Jared as in *1 Enoch* and *Jubilees*, with language very similar to *1 En.* 106.13: 'for in the days of Jared, my father' (1QapGen 3.3).

Second, according to 1QapGen 2.1, Lamech became afraid at Noah's birth because he thought that the 'conception was of the Watchers (מן עירין), and the seed was of the Holy Ones (ומן קדישין), and (that) it belonged to the Nephil[in] ([ין]'ולנפיל)'. It is most likely that the variation of prepositions (מן, ל) is deliberate and that Nephilim here are the giant offspring of the Watchers and women as in *Jub.* 7.21-2.[28] Thus, Lamech fears the supernatural features of Noah's birth as evidence that he is one of the Nephilim, a hybrid offspring of angels and women. If so, this would seem to assume that the inter-course of the Watchers with the women happened sometime before the birth of Noah. This would seem to reflect the type of traditions noted above that associate the sin of the Watchers with the time of Enoch's sojourn among the angels and/or shortly before the birth of Noah. Since like *Jubilees*, *Genesis Apocryphon* assumes the same chronol-ogy as the Samaritan Pentateuch, Noah's birth occurred during Enoch's first sojourn among the angels and this would be entirely possible (see Table 3).

Third, 1QapGen 6.9-12 emphasizes the completion of ten jubilees as an important time in Noah's life and associates with it both the marriage of his children and a vision.

> 9. ... *vacat* And when my days reached the number I had calculated
> 10. [ ] ten jubilees, then were my sons finished taking women for themselves as wives
> 11. [ ] the heavens in a vision. I saw and I was informed and made known about the doings of the sons of heaven, and what ...
> 12. [ ] the heavens. I hid this mystery in my heart and I revealed it to no one. *vacat*

This date almost certainly corresponds with Noah's 500th year in Gen. 5.32 (contra Bernstein 2005: 54), and probably reflects the same tradition as in *1 En.* 60.1 which also associates a vision of the angelic hosts and divine judgment with this date. But by specifying that Noah's children are *married* at this date, 1QapGen directly contradicts Gen. 5.32, which states that Noah's children are *born* when Noah is 500.

This is a very surprising and blatant departure from the narrative of Genesis. Given the author's usual care in following Genesis, the point probably has some important significance, but it is impossible to be certain because of the fragmentary nature of the text. The most likely explanation is that the author of the *Genesis Apocryphon* was trying to reconcile the literal order of Genesis (as defended by Philo, *Gig.* 1) with the dating of the Watchers episode assumed in *Jubilees*. If the latter (Gen. 6.1-4) occurred in or before Noah's 480th year, the birth of Noah's children (Gen. 5.32) must have been even earlier. If so, the author of the *Genesis Apocryphon* may have reasoned as follows:

> Gen. 5.32: birth of Noah's children, but sometime before Noah's 480th year
> Gen. 6.1: descent of sons of God (= Watchers), Noah's 480th year
> (not in Genesis): marriage of Noah's children, in his 500th year

If this inference is correct, that the *Genesis Apocryphon* dates the sin of the Watchers before year 480 of Noah's life, then Lamech's assumption that Noah at his birth is one of the Nephilim seems out of place. How would he know about the Nephilim 480

---

28. Fitzmyer (2004: 125) suggests that despite the variation of preposition, all three terms could be parallel (Watchers, Holy Ones, Nephilim), so that Lamech fears that Noah was the offspring of the Nephilim understood as wayward angels. This is unlikely.

years before their birth? It would seem that the *Genesis Apocryphon* is developed beyond the tradition in *1 Enoch* 106 on this point: there, Lamech is only scared that Noah looks angel-like; he does not know about hybrid offspring until Enoch reveals it. In the *Genesis Apocryphon*, it seems likely that Lamech learned some of this beforehand: 1QapGen columns 0–1 seem to be a revelation about the Watchers, and Lamech is the most likely recipient.

Thus, in the *Genesis Apocryphon*, Noah has a vision in his 500th year analogous to a vision by Lamech in connection with the birth of his son Noah (cf. Gen 5:28-29). Although the *Genesis Apocryphon* associates this date with the marriage of his sons, it is likely that lying behind this is a tradition that associated visions by Lamech and Noah at the birth of their first sons. If so, both the *Genesis Apocryphon* and the Noah fragment in *1 En.* 60:1 are secondary adaptations of this tradition, with somewhat awkward results.

With regard to Noah's children, the *Genesis Apocryphon* clarifies that Shem is Noah's eldest child (1QapGen 12.10). The data in Genesis on the order of Noah's three sons appear contradictory (see Kugel 1998: 220–21). Genesis 5.32 is a key text for the chronology of Noah's family: 'After Noah was five hundred years old, Noah became the father of Shem, Ham, and Japheth' (NRSV). But this text is unclear: does Noah's 500th year mark the birth of his first or last son? Also, it is not clear whether the order of the three sons in this passage (as also in Gen. 6.10; 9.18 and 10.1) is intended as a list from eldest to youngest. Three passages seem to contradict this order.

Genesis 10.21 is ambiguous: ‫ולשם ילד גם הוא אבי כל בני עבר אחי יפת הגדול‬. Most naturally it describes Japheth as the elder brother of Shem: 'And to Shem also were born (children) – (Shem) the father of all the sons of Eber (and) brother of Japheth the elder'. This is at any rate the way the Septuagint reads it: καὶ τῷ Σημ ἐγενήθη καὶ αὐτῷ πατρὶ πάντων τῶν υἱῶν Εβερ ἀδελφῷ Ιαφεθ τοῦ μείζονος. But many, presumably under the influence of the lists in the order Shem, Ham, and Japheth, translate '… Shem … the elder brother of Japheth' (e.g., NRSV, *Tanakh*). *Gen. R.* 37.7 notes the ambiguity of Gen. 10.21: it could mean either that Japhet or Shem is the eldest. But it reasons from Gen. 11.10 that Shem cannot be the eldest.

Genesis 11.10 indicates that 'Shem was one hundred years old when Arpachshad was born, two years after the flood' ‫שם בן מאת שנה ויולד את ארפכשד שנתים‬ ‫אחר המבול‬). According to this passage, Shem was one hundred years old in Noah's 602nd year. If so, Shem must have been born when Noah was 502. But Gen. 5.32 states that Noah became a father when he was 500 (‫ויהי נח בן חמש מאות שנה ויולד‬ ‫נח את שם את חם ואת יפת‬). Therefore Shem cannot have been his eldest, and consequently Gen. 10.21 must be read that Japheth is the eldest brother. This reasoning is explicitly described in *Gen. R.* 37.7 and *b. Sanh.* 69b.

Genesis 9.24 refers to Ham as Noah's youngest son (‫וייקץ נח מיינו וידע את אשר‬ ‫עשה לו בנו הקטן‬). Therefore, if one harmonizes these data, the order of Noah's sons must be Japheth, Shem, Ham. But they are never presented in this order in Genesis. As noted above, the three are usually listed in the order Shem, Ham, Japheth. The only alternative order is in the presentation of their descendants, starting with Japheth, then Ham and Shem (10.2-31).

So, the biblical data are confusing – and probably confused. I am not going to propose a solution to the problem of the chronology in Genesis (see Hendel 1998: 75–6), but I am interested in what ancient interpreters did with the problem. As early as Philo (*Quaest. in Gen.* 2.74-79), there is explicit recognition of the problem: Philo notes the discrepancy and explains that the order Japheth, Ham, Shem reflects moral quality not birth order. Rabbinic discussions also emphasize that the language of greater and lesser and the order may have to do with character rather than chronological order. For example, *Tanh.* (Buber) Gen. 2.19 (*Noah* 12, on Gen. 9.18).

> Was Shem really the oldest in that he comes first? Is it not also written (in Gen. 10.21): 'And unto Shem … the brother of Japheth, who was the oldest?' Why then did Shem precede Japheth? Because he was worthy (*kasher*) and virtuous for his creator. (Townsend 1989: 49)

Jubilees makes clear that the order of the sons is Shem, Ham, and Japhet.

> In its third year [1207] she gave birth to Shem for him; in its fifth year [1209] she gave birth to Ham for him; and in the first year during the sixth week [1212] she gave birth to Japheth for him. (*Jub.* 4.33; *VBJ*; dates are years AM)

It includes the problematic passage about the birth of Arpachshad being born two years after the flood, but omits the reference to Shem being a hundred years at the time: it would be impossible to harmonize the view of Shem as eldest son with the data that Shem was one hundred years old two years after the flood.

> These were Shem's sons: Elam, Asshur, Arpachshad (he was born two years after the flood), Aram, and Lud. (*Jub.* 7.18; *VBJ*)

Thus, Jubilees leaves a contradiction unresolved.

At first glance, the *Genesis Apocryphon* might be seen to simply follow *Jubilees*. Like *Jubilees*, it makes clear that Shem is the eldest son, and includes the passage about Arpachshad born two years after the flood, but omits the age of Shem at the time. That is, with regard to the question of the order of Noah's sons, it is in accord with *Jubilees*: it seems to show the same solution and same method.

On a closer inspection, however, it goes beyond *Jubilees* in trying to solve a further problem. Gen. 10.22 lists Shem's sons in the order Elam, Asshur, Arpachshad, Lod, and Aram. One might assume from this that Arpachshad is the third eldest son. Yet 10.21 and 24 assume that Arpachshad is the son of note, since he is the grandfather of Eber and it is through him that Shem can be regarded as the progenitor of the Hebrews. In the genealogy of Gen. 11.10-11 only Arpachshad is named among the children of Shem in a customary formula that implies he is the eldest ('When Shem was a hundred years old he fathered Arpachshad, two years after the flood. And after fathering Arpachshad Shem lived five hundred years and fathered other sons and daughters'). A potential problem if Arpachshad was not the first born is that it would assume children born on the ark. But Genesis does not mention grandchildren coming off the ark (Gen. 9.18; cf. 10.1).[29] The position of *Jubilees* on this question is not clear.

The *Genesis Apocryphon* shows three further interventions not in *Jubilees* that make clear its view that Arpachshad is the eldest child of Shem.

---

29. That all were chaste on the ark is a prominent motif in Jewish interpretation of the flood, e.g., Philo, *Quaest. in Gen.* 2.49; *Gen. Rab.* 31.12; 34.7; see Ginzberg 1937–67: 5:188, n. 54 and Lewis 1978: 146–47.

Table 4. *Shem's Genealogy.*

ApGen	Genesis	Jubilees
12.9 And there were born to [them] sons and dau]ghters after the flood.	10.1 These are the descendants of Noah's sons, Shem, Ham, and Japheth; children were born to them after the flood	
12.10-11 [To Shem, my] eldest [son] was born his first son Arpachshad two years after the flood. And [these are] all the sons of Shem, all of them: [11] [El]am and Asshur, Arpachshad, Lod, and Aram, and daughters: five women. *vacat*	10.21-22 To Shem also, the father of all the children of Eber, brother of Japheth the eldest, children were born. [22] The descendants of Shem: Elam, Asshur, Arpachshad, Lud, and Aram. 11.10-11 These are the descendants of Shem. When Shem was one hundred years old, he became the father of Arpachshad two years after the flood; [11] and Shem lived after the birth of Arpachshad five hundred years, and had other sons and daughters. (NRSV)	*Jub.* 7.18 These were Shem's sons: Elam, Asshur, Arpachshad (he was born two years after the flood), Aram, and Lud. *Jub.* 4.33 … In its third year [1207] she gave birth to Shem for him; in its fifth year [1209] she gave birth to Ham for him; and in the first year during the sixth week [1212] she gave birth to Japheth for him. (*VBJ*)

The three interventions are as follows.

1. It explicitly states that Arpachshad is Shem's eldest son
2. The phrase 'were born to them … after the flood' now serves to emphasize that *no* grandchildren were born before or during the flood
3. It also harmonizes Gen. 10.21-22 and 11.10-11 by directly quoting part from each (and omitting Shem's age at the birth of Arpachshad) to imply that they are not in conflict

These considerations make it likely that the author of the *Genesis Apocryphon* is working with both the text of Genesis and *Jubilees* (or at least traditions found in *Jubilees*) and seeking solutions to apparent tensions. He seems reluctant to diverge from either, but will when he feels compelled to. This suggests that *Jubilees* was of considerable authority for the author, and also, apparently, that he did not regard a precise text of Genesis to be sacrosanct. Both Genesis and *Jubilees* were revered traditions, but not to the degree that one could not correct the tradition where it seemed to be in error.

c. *The Character of Noah*
For the hero of one of the most captivating stories in the Western tradition, Noah is a remarkably flat and ambiguous character in Genesis. The most exciting moment in the development of his character in the Genesis narrative is when he gets drunk and lays about naked while he is disgraced by his son. Although he is described as a 'righteous man, blameless in his generation' who 'walked with God' and 'found favor in the sight of the Lord' (Gen. 6.8–9, 22), the Genesis account lacks anything about Noah's response to the events, other than statements that Noah did as instructed ('Noah did this; he did all that God commanded him', 6.22; 'and Noah did all that the Lord had commanded him', 7.5). Would not a righteous man have agonized over the

destruction of his fellow creatures, and pled with God on their behalf like Abram? Would not the man of God have spent much of the interminable year on the ark prostrate before his God, like Moses wrestling over the fate of humanity? If we expect such answers from Genesis, we are disappointed. In its crisp narrative, there is no mention of Noah praying to or blessing God. In fact, the only words Noah is recorded as having spoken in Genesis are to curse Canaan and to bless Shem and Japheth (which is perhaps indirect prayer: 'Blessed by the Lord my God be Shem, ... May God make space for Japheth', Gen. 9.26-27).

Of course, from the earliest time interpreters were transfixed by just the questions Genesis leaves tantalizing. We find the character of Noah developed in the ancient sources in two main directions. (1) One could find reasons to question Noah's character, and this becomes a prominent motif in the later rabbis: Noah was righteous only 'in his generation', that is, only in comparison with evil-doers that God was going to destroy; compared with Abraham and Moses he was not righteous . He was negligent in failing to pray. The description of Noah as a 'man of the earth' implies that he is a mundane rather than spiritually minded man. Moreover, some rabbis noted that 'the first to plant a vineyard' (Gen. 9:20) can also be read 'he profaned himself to plant a vineyard' (e.g., *Tanh.* [Buber] Gen. 2.20 (on Gen. 9.20); *Tanh.* Gen. 2.13 (on Gen. 9.20); *Gen. R.* 22.3; 30.9; 36.3).[30] The matter of the drunken sprawl cast a dark blot on Noah's character. (2) An opposite tendency, especially in the Greco-Roman period (and continued especially among later Christian commentators), was to depict Noah as a paragon of virtue. These writers tend to emphasize Noah's righteousness, and infer Noah as a preacher to his generation, a prophet anticipating Moses, and a man of fervent prayer (e.g., Wis. 10.4; Sir. 44.17; *1 En.* 67.1; *Jub.* 5.19; 10.17; *Sib. Or.* 1.125; Josephus, *Ant.* 1.75; Heb. 11.7; 2 Pet. 2.5; also *Gen. R.* 30.1; *b. Sanh.* 108a–b).[31] The *Genesis Apocryphon* is in this tradition, seeking to enhance the character of Noah. Noah's righteousness was foreshadowed in his extraordinary birth, and he was righteous and pursued truth from his youth (A13). Noah prominently prays and praises God on appropriate occasions (A22–24, 30, 38, 48). It seems possible that it also shows Noah preaching to the people before the flood (A27).

d. *Noah as Patriarch*
Throughout much of the Noah story, the *Genesis Apocryphon* seldom follows the narrative of Genesis closely, favoring instead a looser relationship with Genesis. It does, however, closely follow the Genesis narrative of Noah's exit from the ark, sacrifice, and covenant with God in columns 10–11. Examining this narrative will help illustrate the relationship of the *Genesis Apocryphon* to the biblical tradition, to *Jubilees*, and other traditions. It also provides some of the most reliable clues to interpretative concerns distinctive to the *Genesis Apocryphon*, since the two major interpretative motifs evident in the minutiae of the pericope about the covenant correspond to unique and deliberate reworkings of the larger narrative context.

30. See Lewis 1978: 151–52; Kugel 1998: 187.
31. See VanderKam 1980; Ginzberg 1937–67: 5:178–79, n. 28;. Kugel 1998: 185–87, 219–20.

We will start with a close examination of the covenant pericope (A39 = 1QapGen 11.15-17), and then relate our findings to features in the larger context. I restore line 16 somewhat differently than other editions.[32]

16 ‏[ואמר לי פושו] וסׄגׄוׄ̊ וׄמׄלׄו ארעא ושלט בכולהון בׄ[ב]רׄיהא ובמדבריהא ובכול די בהון

16. [And he said to me, 'Increase] and multiply and fill the earth and rule over them all: its f[ie]lds, its wildernesses, its mountains, and all that is in them.

The restoration of the beginning of the line is based on *Tg. Ps.-J.* Gen. 9.1, which fits well the space and the surviving letter traces: ‏ואמר להום פושו וסגו ומלו ית ארעא. It seems clear that the text at this point contains a parallel to Gen. 9.1: the wording 'the earth and rule over it' reflects Gen. 9:1 harmonized with Gen. 1:28.

In the following chart, a translation of 1QapGen is placed alongside the narrative of Genesis, as well as *Jubilees* and other scriptural passages. The text is broken into numbered sections (§) to facilitate comparison.[33]

Table 5. *God's Blessing on Noah (A39).*

	1QapGen 11	Genesis 9	Jubilees 6	Other
§1	[15] [And then the Lord] of the heavens [appeared] to me, and spoke with me and said to me	[1] God blessed Noah and his sons, and said to them,		Gen. 1.28 God blessed them, and said to them, Gen. 15.1 the word of the Lord came to Abram in a vision, saying
§2	'Do not fear, O Noah. I am with you and with your sons – to them as with you forever'.			Gen. 15.1 'Do not fear, Abram, I am your shield; your reward shall be very great'. Gen. 26.24 '… do not fear, for I am with you and will bless you and make your offspring numerous for my servant Abraham's sake'.

32. The transcription by MQS reads: ‏ooo○○○○○○○○○○○○ ארעא ושלט בכולהון ○○היא ‏ובמדבריהא ובטוריהא ובכול די בהון, followed by *DSSR* and *DSSSE*. FGA[3] also follows this, but reads ‏ימיהא, 'its seas' for the word after ‏בכולהון. The reading ‏ימיהא is too short for the space and the first letter looks like *bet*. It could possibly be ‏בׄ[יׄ]מׄיהא, although a *mem* does not well fit the ink traces. I read ‏בׄ[ב]רׄיהא ('its fields'; *DJPA* 110) which fits the space well (using ‏בריהא from the following word as an overlay). My reading is based on ABMC photo GAF X 1000 B (1994 series). For the term, see 1QapGen 13.8, and possibly 1QapGen 11.5.

33. Translations from Genesis are adapted from NRSV to facilitate comparison; translations from *Jubilees* are from *VBJ*.

	1QapGen 11	Genesis 9	Jubilees 6	Other
§3	[16] [And he said to me, 'Increase] and multiply and fill the earth	'Be fruitful and multiply, and fill the earth.	[5] 'Now you increase and multiply yourselves on the earth and become numerous upon it. Become a blessing within it.	Gen. 1.28 'Be fruitful and multiply, and fill the earth and subdue it;
§4a	<u>and rule over</u>	(LXX: and rule it.) [2] Fear and dread of you will be upon	I will put fear of you and dread of you on	<u>and rule over</u>
§4b	them all: its *f[ie]lds*, its wildernesses, its mountains and all that is in them.	every animal of the earth, and on every bird of the air, on every creeping thing on the ground, and on all the fish of the sea;	everything that is on the earth and in the sea.	the fish of the sea and over the birds of the air and over every living thing that moves upon the earth'.
§5	Behold, I [17] give to you and to your children everything for food of the greenery and the herbs of the land.	[3] into your hands they are delivered (SP, LXX: I have given it). Every moving thing that is alive, for you it will be for food; like the green herbs, I give you everything.	[6] I have now given you all the animals, all the cattle, everything that flies, everything that moves about on the earth, the fish in the waters, and everything for food. Like the green herbs I have given you everything to eat.	Gen. 1.29 God said, 'Behold, I have given you every herb yielding seed that is upon the face of all the earth, and every tree with seed in its fruit; you shall have them for food'.
§6	But, you shall not eat any blood.	[4] But, you shall not eat flesh with its life, that is, its blood.	[7] But, you are not to eat animate beings with their spirit – with the blood –	
§7		[5] For your own lifeblood I will surely require a reckoning: from every animal I will require it and from human beings, each one for the blood of another, I will require a reckoning for human life. [6] Whoever sheds the blood of a human, by a human shall that person's blood be shed; for in his own image God made humankind.	(because the vital force of all animate beings is in the blood) so that your blood with your vital forces may not be required from the hand of any man. From the hand of each one I will require the blood of man. [8] The person who sheds the blood of man will have his blood shed by man because he made mankind in the image of the Lord.	
§8		[7] And you, be fruitful and multiply, abound	[9] As for you – increase and become	

	1QapGen 11	Genesis 9	Jubilees 6	Other
		on the earth and multiply in it'. (originally probably 'and rule over it')	numerous on the earth'.	
§9	The fear of you and dread of you [18] ... forever ... [19]] I to you ... your children ...'			

At first glance, the version of this story in the *Genesis Apocryphon* might appear to be but a loose paraphrase of Genesis, with some free expansions and omissions. But on closer inspection, it appears that the author has followed the text of Genesis very closely, and his version is a relatively sophisticated interpretation of the Noah story reflecting distinctive theological ideas. Of the differences from Genesis, we can distinguish four types of material: (1) adaptations for the sake of the narrative, (2) readings reflecting a variant text of Genesis, (3) readings related to another retelling of Genesis, and (4) readings that represent deliberate exegetical activity.

1. *Narrative adaptations.* Throughout, there are minor adaptations for the sake of the narrative, most notably so that Noah speaks in the first person (1QapGen 11.15). This sort of material is in most cases unique to the *Genesis Apocryphon*, and represents the most conspicuous contribution of the author: he has produced a wonderfully colorful telling of the story by allowing the patriarchs to speak in their own voices. But this is (at least for the most part) not exegetically motivated; it belongs in the realm of the art of story-telling. It allows the author to explore psychological aspects of the story (Nickelsburg 1998: 143–44).

2. *Readings reflecting a variant text.* Two points in this narrative could possibly reflect a variant text of Genesis. (1) The addition of 'and rule over them' (§4a) finds a counterpart in LXX Gen. 9.1 'and rule it' (also reflected in Philo, *Quaest. in Gen.* 2.56), whereas this is lacking in all Hebrew texts of Gen. 9.1 (MT and SP). Also, the majority of commentators believe that Gen. 9.7 originally read 'and rule over it' (ורדו) rather than the redundant 'and become numerous upon it' (ורבו; e.g., Westermann 1984: 460, 469; Hendel 1998: 140). Thus, it is not impossible that the *Genesis Apocryphon* was following a text of Genesis 9 that included the phrase. Nevertheless, in the end it is more likely that the LXX and Philo reflect analogous attempts to highlight the correspondence of Gen. 9.1-7 with Gen. 1.26-30. At any rate, *Jubilees* betrays no knowledge of such a text (the reading of *Jub.* 6.5 'and become a blessing' presupposes וברכו, most likely read instead of ורבו), and such a variant alone could not explain the unique manner in which the *Genesis Apocryphon* has rewritten the episode. We will consider this matter further below under the fourth category.

(2) 'Behold, I give to you and to your children everything for food ...' (§5) has an active verb like SP and LXX of Gen. 9.2 ('into your hand I have delivered them)' rather than the passive verb of MT ('into your hand they are delivered'; see VanderKam 1989: 38).

MT Gen. 9.2: ... into your hand they are delivered (נִתָּנוּ)

SP/LXX: ... into your hand I have given them (נתתיו)

Jub. 6.6: I have now given you all the animals ... (= נתתי)

1QapGen 11.16–17: Behold, I give to you and to your children... (אנה יהב)

This could be one piece of evidence among others that 1QapGen used a Palestinian text of Genesis, and in any case would belong to the 'givens' for the author rather than the result of exegesis. However, it is more likely that the wording here in the *Genesis Apocryphon* is dependent on another retelling of Genesis, and thus belongs in the third category.

3. *Readings related to another retelling of Genesis.* The wording of the *Genesis Apocryphon* in §5 is best understood as dependent on, and abbreviating, the wording found in *Jub.* 6.6, 'I have now given you all the animals ...'. This is apparent when the larger passage is considered.

> MT Gen. 9.2–3: ... into your hand they are delivered. Every moving thing that is alive, for you it will be for food; like the green herbs, I give you everything.
> SP/LXX: ... into your hand I have given them. Every moving thing that is alive, for you it will be for food; like the green herbs, I give you everything.

> *Jub.* 6.6: I have now given you all the animals ... and *everything for food. Like the green herbs* I have given you everything to eat. (*VBJ*; =נתתי ... ואת־כל לאכלה כירק עשב)[34]

> 1QapGen 11.16–17: Behold, I give to you and to your children *everything for food of the greenery and the herbs* of the land. (והא אנה [י]הֹב לך ולבניך כֹּולֹא לֹמֹאֹכֹל בירקא ועשבא; MQS)

It seems that *Jubilees* reflects a Palestinian text of Genesis similar to that underlying SP and LXX (VanderKam 1977: 103–138). *Jubilees* 6.6 paraphrases this version 'I have now given you all the animals ... and everything for food. Like the green herbs I have given you everything for food'. In 1QapGen, the phrase 'everything for food of the greenery' (1QapGen 11.17) reflects the paraphrase of *Jub.* 6.6, which has reworked the construction of Genesis. The sections marked in italics above would be identical in Hebrew, with the exception of the preposition and conjunction:[35]

... כל לאכלה כירק עשב ... (*Jub.* 6.13)

... כל לאכלה בירק ועשב ... (1QapGen)

Similarly, the prohibition 'you shall not eat any blood' (1QapGen 11.17) does not correspond directly to Gen. 6.4 ('you shall not eat flesh ...') but to the developed prohibition of *Jub.* 6.13 '... not to eat any blood'.

It is very difficult to determine the relationship between the *Genesis Apocryphon* and *Jubilees*: which might have been first, and whether one directly influenced the other, or whether the similarities are due to common influence, either oral or literary. But these examples – and others – tend to favor use by the *Genesis Apocryphon* of a literary source with at least some of the *Jubilees* narrative.

Such use of *Jubilees* material can be exegetical, for example when the *Genesis Apocryphon* deliberately incorporates an interpretation to make a distinctive point, and there are numerous probable examples of this.[36] In this case, however, it more likely

---

34. This is a schematic retroversion for the purposes of the comparison only. No Hebrew fragment survives of this passage. Emphasis added to translation.

35. On the significance of the different preposition, see p. 60 below.

36. E.g., that the ark came to rest on 'one of the mountains' of Ararat, named Lubar and that Noah's sacrifice atoned for the earth (1QapGen 10.12-13 cf. *Jub.* 5.28).

belongs to the 'givens' for the author. As detailed below, the *Genesis Apocryphon* goes beyond *Jubilees* in making its own distinctive point quite at odds with *Jubilees*.

4. *Readings that represent deliberate exegetical activity.* This category most usefully reflects distinctive concerns on the part of the *Genesis Apocryphon*. Because the *Genesis Apocryphon* is so fragmentary and does significantly draw on other compositions, it is often difficult to assess which interpretative motifs reflect special interests of the author, and scholars have sometimes underestimated the creativity and independence of the author (cf. Vermes 1973: 122, 124). With regard to the pericope under discussion, the most significant differences from Genesis are due to deliberate and unique exegesis of the author of the *Genesis Apocryphon* relating to two main motifs in its reworking of the Noah narrative: harmonizing Genesis 9 with the creation mandate of Gen. 1.28-30, and harmonizing the account with the covenant with Abraham in Genesis 15. Each of these motifs is also the object of dramatic reworkings of the larger narrative by the author. In relation to both motifs, we find examples of pure exegesis – solving problems in the text – and seemingly also applied exegesis – interpreting the text in consideration of a practical concern external to the scriptural text (Vermes 1975b: 62). We will consider the two in turn.

e. *Noah's covenant and Genesis 1.28–30*
In *Jubilees*, the major focus of the pericope about Noah's covenant is the prohibition of eating blood from Gen. 9.4-7 (*Jub.* 6.7-8), which it significantly expands (*Jub.* 6.10-14). Although the *Genesis Apocryphon* reflects wording from this expansion, it otherwise omits any reference to the law of bloodshed. In fact, although both Genesis 9 and *Jubilees* 6 explicitly allow the eating of meat – with the proper restrictions regarding blood – the *Genesis Apocryphon* reworks the account by means of harmonizing with Gen. 1.28-29 apparently to nullify the concession to eating meat.

> Gen. 1.28-29: 'Be fruitful and multiply, and fill the earth and subdue it; and rule over the fish of the sea and over the birds of the air and over every living thing that moves upon the earth'. God said, 'See, I have given you every herb yielding seed that is upon the face of all the earth, and every tree with seed in its fruit; you shall have them for food'. (NRSV adapted)

> Gen. 9.1-3: 'Be fruitful and multiply, and fill the earth. Fear and dread of you will be upon every animal of the earth, and upon every bird of the sky, on every creeping thing on the ground, and on all the fish of the sea; into your hand they are delivered. Every creeping thing that is alive, for you it will be for food; like the green plants, I give you everything'. (NRSV adapted)

> *Jub.* 6.5-6: 'Now you increase and multiply yourselves on the earth and become numerous upon it. Become a blessing within it. I will put fear of you and dread of you on everything that is on the earth and in the sea. I have now given you all the animals, all the cattle, everything that flies, everything that moves about on the earth, the fish in the waters, and everything for food. Like the green herbs I have given you everything to eat'. (*VBJ*)

> 1QapGen 11.16-17: [... 'Increase] and multiply and fill the earth and rule over them all: its *f*[*ie*]*lds* (?), its wildernesses, its mountains and all that is in them. Behold, I give to you and to your children everything for food of the greenery and the herbs of the land.

Genesis 9.1-3 consciously recalls Gen. 1.28-30, repeating the mandate to be fruitful and multiply and fill the earth, and giving instructions regarding food. But there are distinct – and potentially ominous – differences. In place of 'subdue it and rule over ...',

Gen. 9.2 reads 'fear of you and the dread of you shall rest on' the animals. And whereas Gen. 1.30 had granted vegetation alone as food for all creatures, Gen. 9.2-3 allows the consumption of meat – reworking the language of Gen. 1.30 – with the restriction that the blood must not be eaten. The two changes are easily seen as related: 'fear and dread' could allude to a new adversarial relationship between humans and animals; thus 'dominion' could be understood to refer to a harmonious relationship now lost. These difficult passages inspired diverse interpretations (see below), but this reading of the text is one that is attested in ancient sources, and the *Genesis Apocryphon* adds a unique twist by means of several deliberate modifications. (1) By adding the phrase 'and rule over them all', it claims that the dominion was regained or renewed with Noah. (2) It omits the permission to eat meat. Instead of 'every moving thing that lives for you shall be for food like the green herbs', the *Genesis Apocryphon* reads 'everything for food *of the greenery and the herbs*'. For the phrase 'everything for food' the *Genesis Apocryphon* follows the wording of the paraphrase in *Jub.* 6.6, but by omitting mention of animals it conveys a different meaning than *Jubilees* and all known biblical versions. (3) This point is reinforced by a related modification. Instead of 'like' (preposition כ) the *Genesis Apocryphon* reads 'among' (preposition ב), limiting the 'everything for food' to vegetation, as in Gen. 1.29. Also possibly related might be the reading of two separate categories of plants – 'the greenery and the herbs' instead of 'green herbs' – perhaps to reflect the two types of plants mentioned in Gen. 1.29, 'herbage' and 'trees', or better to relate to 'everything'.

The narrative according to the *Genesis Apocryphon* asserts that with Noah there is a return to paradise conditions of Gen. 1.28-30: harmonious relations between humans and animals, and vegetation only for food. There is no evidence that the *Genesis Apocryphon* depended here on a different Hebrew text. Neither can one explain his departure from Genesis on the basis that the author was merely following *Jubilees* (or a related source) as he seems to do numerous times. For although the *Genesis Apocryphon* here reflects phrasing in common with *Jubilees*, his interpretation is radically different. Moreover, these changes at the micro level of details in the narrative correspond to arrangements of the narrative structure at the macro level that are unique to the *Genesis Apocryphon* (see further discussion below). This indicates that we are dealing with deliberate and distinctive interpretation on the part of the author.

It is impossible to prove what was in the mind of the author, but it seems likely that he read the syntax of Genesis 9 differently than the MT, with the effect that it represents a restatement of Genesis 1 (see table overleaf).

The author of the *Genesis Apocryphon* may have read 'every creeping thing that is alive' not as the subject of 'will be food for you' as in all known versions of Genesis 9 (esp. MT, SP, LXX), but as the object of the preceding phrase 'into your hand I have given'. Thus, he seems to have regarded this clause as a paraphrase of dominion over the animals in Gen. 1.28b. Moreover, by dislocating the passage about 'fear and dread' so that it follows the ban on eating blood (see Table 5 §9), he emphasized his view that 'fear and dread' are about adversarial relations between humans and animals, but not related to permission to eat animals. In this way, the author separates dominion over – as fulfillment of a divine mandate – from a negative consequence of the fall, namely animosity between humans and animals.

Table 6. *Genesis 9.1-3 in the* Genesis Apocryphon.

Gen. 9.1-3 (MT)	Gen. 9.1-3 as read by 1QapGen	
Be fruitful and multiply, and fill the earth.	Be fruitful and multiply, and fill the earth.	= Gen. 1.28a
Fear and dread of you will be upon every animal of the earth, and upon every bird of the sky, on every creeping thing on the ground, and on all the fish of the sea; into your hand they are delivered.	[Fear and dread of you] will be upon every animal of the earth, and upon every bird of the sky, on every creeping thing on the ground, and on all the fish of the sea.	
Every creeping thing that is alive	Into your hand I have delivered every creeping thing that is alive.	// Gen. 1.28b: dominion
for you it will be for food; like the green plants I give you everything.	For you will be for food among the greenery and herbs: I give you all (of them, i.e., plants).	// Gen. 1.29: vegetation alone for food.

That 'dominion' was an especially distinctive concern for the *Genesis Apocryphon* is evident from the manner in which the author introduced the motif into one or two other places in the narrative of the flood.

(1) Before the flood, God informs Noah of his plan to destroy the world and to save him, and probably alludes to the blessing of Gen. 9.1-2: '[*you shall rule*] over them, the earth and all that is upon it, the seas and the mountains …' (1QapGen 7.1, reconstruction adopted by Fitzmyer 2004: 78, 150). Perhaps it is the restoration of dominion that is the reward God says he is restoring to Noah in 1QapGen 7.5: 'glory, and my reward I am restoring to you' (יְקָר וֹאַגְרִי אנה משלם לך; MQS, FGA[3]). Noah rejoices at God's words (1QapGen 7.7).

(2) After Noah has entered the ark (1QapGen 8.1), and probably before the start of the flood (1QapGen 9.10), God again addresses Noah and alludes to the blessing of dominion: '… to you I give the dominion …' (לך יהב אנה שלטנא, 1QapGen 9.3).[37] The targums use the same root (שלט) to refer to the dominion granted to Adam in Gen. 1.28.

These promises of dominion, alluding to Gen. 9.1-3 but uttered to Noah *before the flood* are, to my knowledge, without precedent in any version of Genesis or any other early Jewish or Christian traditions.

What is the point of these unique additions for the *Genesis Apocryphon*? The broader concerns underlying these additions can be traced in numerous texts, although more often implicitly than explicitly (Jobling 1972b: 164–99): (1) what is the dominion granted humans in Gen. 1.26-28? (2) Was that dominion somehow lost, and if so is it regained? Different views are expressed by ancient interpreters who noticed that Gen. 9.1-3 consciously repeats to Noah God's commission to the first humans in Gen. 1.26-28, but with the difference that instead of 'dominion' over the animals as in 1.28, God now states that 'fear and dread' (military terms) will be upon the animals. Some strands of tradition emphasize a negative contrast between Adam in paradise and Noah: this

37. On this reading, see p. 38 above.

alludes in some way to the loss of a golden age, and with Noah a concession to a diminished era. An anonymous tradition cited in *Gen. R.* 34.12 asserts this uniquely: to Noah 'fear and dread returned, but dominion did not return. When did it return? In the days of Solomon, as it is written, For he had dominion over all the region (1 Kings 5.4)' (Freedman 1983: 1:278). More commonly the lost dominion is understood as having to do with harmonious relationships between humans and animals – animals as tame and obedient to humans, and/or even a universal vegetarianism – lost because of human sin,[38] experienced by the righteous,[39] but not restored generally until the messianic age.[40] Such views are probably related on the one hand to Greek philosophical views of loss of a golden age, and on the other hand to negative evaluations of Noah such as are common in later rabbinic texts.

Other strands of tradition emphasize Noah's similarity to Adam, reading Gen. 9.1-3 as a restatement of the promise to Adam (e.g, LXX Gen. 9.1), or a restoration of a lost dominion to Noah. Noah serves typologically as a second Adam, representing a new start and renewing the order of creation. For example, the rabbinic midrash *Genesis Rabbah* has the following tradition.

> The truth is that when the Holy One, blessed be He, created Adam, He gave him dominion over all things: the cow obeyed the ploughman, the furrow obeyed the ploughman. But when he sinned, He made them rebel against him: the cow did not obey the ploughman, nor did the furrow obey the ploughman. But when Noah arose, they submitted: ease is mentioned here ... (*Gen. R.* 25.2; attributed to R. Johanan, 3rd cent. CE Palestine)

Dominion here has to do with animals submitting to humans. The best expression of this view is Philo, who is especially valuable for our purposes because he dates to the first century CE. For Philo, Noah demonstrates dominion by the feat of gathering the animals into the ark, analogous to Adam naming the animals (Philo, *Quaest. in Gen.* 2.56; *Op. Mund.* 83–88; *Vit. Mos.* 2.61; see Jobling 1972a: 69, 81). Noah is 'the beginning of a second genesis of man, of equal honor with him who was first made in (His) image. And so he granted rule over earthly creatures in equal measure to the former and the latter' (Philo, *Quaest. in Gen.* 2.56, Loeb).

Our sources show great diversity, and it is notable that competing views are expressed within the same sources, especially Philo and *Genesis Rabbah*. But what is important for our purposes is the recognition that there was lively speculation that related human dominion to tameness of the beasts, that debated whether dominion was lost, and discussed the problems of wild beasts getting on the ark and cooperating with humans.

Against this background, by reading 'dominion' into Gen. 9.1–3 – using the same root (שלט) as the targums use at Gen. 1.28 – the *Genesis Apocryphon* is asserting that dominion over the animals *was* restored to Noah. Moreover, the author's unique rewriting of the scene reveals his intention. By having God grant dominion to Noah before the flood, it is evident that dominion is related to harmonious relations

---

38. Philo, *Op. Mund.* 148, *Quaest. in Gen.* 1.18; *LAE (Vit.)* 37–39; *LAE 9Apoc.)* 24.4; *4 Ezra* 6.54 cf. 7.10-12.

39. *Tg. Ps.-J.*, *Tg. Neof.* on Gen. 3.15; cf. *Num. R.* 11.3 [saying attributed to Simeon b. Yohai, 2nd cent. CE]; *PRK* 5.3; *PR* 15.3; *Sifre Deut.* 50 [saying attributed to R. Eleazar b. Azariah, 2nd cent. CE]; *b. Ber.* 33a; see Ginzberg 1937–67: 5.119 n. 113 and 5.188 n. 53.

40. Philo, *Praem. Poen.* 85–91; *Sib. Or.* 3.788–95; *2 Bar.* 73.6; *Gen. R.* 8.12.

between humans and animals, epitomized for Noah by gathering the animals on the ark. In this, the *Genesis Apocryphon* is very similar to the view expressed in *Gen. R.* 25.2 and in certain places in Philo.

We are dealing here with concerns of pure exegesis. The *Genesis Apocryphon* may here be wrestling with a question that receives much speculation in Jewish tradition: how did Noah get the animals on the ark? How did the animals coexist peaceably on the ark without the carnivores devouring the other animals? There were, after all, lions, tigers, and bears together with all their favorite prey arranged in a convenient smorgasbord. Would this not require a return to Edenic tranquility when there was peace among animals and animals willingly submitted to humans? It remains unclear whether this would be viewed as a permanent return of dominion – that is, taking the opposite view to that represented in *Gen. R.* 34.12 where dominion did not return in Noah's day – or whether this would be only a temporary dispensation of paradise conditions for the duration of the flood alone. Since both the *Genesis Apocryphon* and *Jubilees* attest the tradition of the flood as an analogue for eschatological judgment, and Noah for eschatological salvation and restoration, the interpretation here may also be related to the restoration of peace in visions of eschatological restoration (e.g., Isa. 11.6-9; 65.25).

It is also possible that there are concerns of applied exegesis involved. By removing the concession to eat meat, the *Genesis Apocryphon* seems to go further than any other known tradition in stressing Noah as a second Adam, restoring the vegetarian ideal of paradise. Is the author advocating vegetarianism? This is an intriguing possibility to ponder, but the texts are too fragmentary to be certain. In any case, it is likely that the dramatic innovations with regard to dominion and food are related, and are unique to this author. We will consider their possible significance and social context at the end of this chapter.

One other aspect of this paraphrase in *Genesis Apocryphon* is important to the motif of Noah as a new Adam (§4b): the realms of air, ground, and sea with their animals over which humans are to exercise dominion in Gen. 1.28 (cf. Gen. 9.2) become in the *Genesis Apocryphon* fields, wildernesses and mountains.

> Gen. 1.28: Be fruitful and multiply, and fill the earth and subdue it, and rule over the fish of the sea and over the birds of the air and over every living thing that moves upon the earth.

> Gen. 9.2: Be fruitful and multiply, and fill the earth.

> 1QapGen 11.16: [And he said to me, 'Increase] and multiply and fill the earth, and rule over them all: its ƒ[ie]*lds*, its wildernesses, its mountains and all that is in them.

This modification seems to be involved with two concerns of the *Genesis Apocryphon*. (1) The author again avoids mention of animals and shifts the focus to physical features of the land. (2) The motif of land introduces the other major concern for the *Genesis Apocryphon* in this narrative: Noah as parallel to Abraham. We consider this next, but there is one more passage to mention first that also may have to do with the motif of Noah as a new Adam.

According to my reading (see p. 38 above), after God makes a covenant with Noah, Noah and his sons descend the mountain curiously carrying a particular branch: 'in the mountains of Hurarat, and afterwards I descended to the base of this mountain, I and my children, and with the branch (ובנופא) ... for the desolation was

great in the land' (1QapGen 12.8-9). A possibility close at hand is that this might be
the olive twig returned by the dove (Gen. 8.11), although how this would factor into
the story is unclear and I am not aware of other traditions emphasizing retention of
this twig.[41] Much more likely is that this is a vine shoot for Noah to plant. This finds
support in the immediately following comment about the devastation in the land, and
the next thing Noah does is plant the vineyard (l. 13). Moreover, there are prominent
traditions speculating from where Noah obtained a vine to plant. Answers include
that he brought it with him (e.g., *Gen. R.* 36.3; *Tanh.* [Buber] Gen. 2.20 [on Gen. 9.20
Townsend 1989: 52]) or that he found a vine shoot (e.g., Philo, *Quaest. in Gen.* 2.67)
that had come from the Garden of Eden (*Tg. Ps.-J.* Gen. 9.20; *3 Bar.* 4.8-15; *PRE* 23).[42]
In the *Genesis Apocryphon*, the latter tradition seems more likely for two reasons:
(1) the definite 'the branch' suggests a particular and special item (cf. *3 Bar.* 4.8-15).
(2) The same term 'branch' figures prominently in Noah's vision in 1QapGen 14.16-
17, where Noah is a great tree that divides into three branches of descendants. I
suggest, then, that the *Genesis Apocryphon* here draws a parallel between Noah's
family (and hence, as a new Adam, humanity) planted anew in the land and the
tree/vine planted as a paradise image.

f. *Noah's covenant and Abraham's covenant*
With regard to Noah compared to Abraham, once again the significance of the *Genesis
Apocryphon*'s retelling of the passage is revealed by the distinctive reworking of the
larger narrative. Immediately before the pericope about God's covenant with Noah
(1QapGen 11.15-17), the *Genesis Apocryphon* adds three episodes that have no precedent in Genesis or *Jubilees*, or – to my knowledge – any other tradition. (1) Before
Noah exits the ark, the *Genesis Apocryphon* has Noah survey the land (1QapGen 11.1-
10):

> 1. ... I, Noah was in the door of the ark ... 2–8. ... 9. ... to the mountains and the wilder-
> nesses, to the thickets and ... 10. ... *vacat.*[43]

(2) Immediately upon exiting the ark, and before God's covenant with Noah, Noah
tours the land (1QapGen 11.11-12):

---

41.   There are traditions, however, speculating about where the olive leaf came from, whether
Israel, the Mount of Olives, or the Garden of Eden, e.g., *Tg. Ps.-J.* Gen. 8.11 and *Gen. R.* 33.6; see
Lewis 1978: 146; Ginzberg 1937–67: 5:185–6 n. 47; Bowker 1969: 170. Philo (*Quaest. in Gen.* 2.42)
and Josephus (*Ant.* 1.92) attest a tradition – following the LXX – that it was a branch and not just a
leaf. If it were the olive branch in view, possibly Noah plants it and this is related to his later dream
(1QapGen 13.13-17) in which a mighty olive tree grows, probably symbolizing Israel. Note that זיתא
is determinate, which puzzles Fitzmyer (2004: 165) since no olive tree has previously been introduced.
This could, however, be related to the previously mentioned branch, which was also determinate. Furthermore, if this were the connection, then most likely the tradition in view would be that the olive
leaf came from the land of Israel.

42.   Ginzberg (1937–67: 5:190–91 nn. 57 and 59) comments that *Tg. Ps.-J.* Gen. 9.20 and *PRE* 23
seem to reflect a view attested by Origen (on Gen. 9.20) that 'Noah's vine was the offshoot of the tree
of knowledge'; and one should add *3 Bar.* 4.8-15. Friedlander (1981: 170 n. 3) states concerning *Tg.
Ps.-J.*, '[a]pparently our Midrash wishes to connect the folly of Noah with the sin of Adam', as
explicitly in *3 Bar.* 4.8-15 and *Sifre Deut.* §323.

43.   L. 9 reads ○ooooo○אO וזדא לעובריא ודמדבריא לטוריא אooooo[(see MQS, FGA³). The
second complete word is probably a mistake for ומדבריא. Fitzmyer accidentally omits the anomalous
dalet from this word, but correctly reads the following as לעובריא (a test of overlaying letters from
nearby words fits the spacing and ink traces very well).

> [Then] I Noah went out and I walked in the land to its length and breadth ... [ ] ... luxuriance upon it in their leaves and in their fruit. And all the land was filled with grass, herbs, and grain.

(3) Noah then praises God (1QapGen 11.12-14):

> Then I blessed the Lord of [heaven] who performed wonders.[44] He is eternal, and to him belongs the praise. And again I praised (him) that he had mercy on the earth, and that he removed and destroyed from it all doers of violence and wickedness and deception, and (that) he delivered a righteous man . . . for his sake. *vacat*

When God instructs Noah to 'fill the earth' (1QapGen 11.16), the *Genesis Apocryphon* specifies 'fields ... wildernesses ... mountains' which directly recalls the language of Noah's survey and tour through the land (esp. 11.9). That is, it seems that the *Genesis Apocryphon* interprets 'fill the earth' as *taking possession of the boundaries of a specific promised land*. It is possible that the author found clues to this interpretation in the Genesis narrative itself, reading it along the following lines:

> Command/promise to fill/possess the earth/land (Gen. 9.1-17)
>   Story of sons = land dispute (Gen. 9.18-27)
> Fulfillment of possessing the land: nations dispersed (Gen. 10.1-32)

That is, Gen. 9.1 and 10.32 form an *inclusio* with regard to filling the earth, and this is interpreted in the light of the intervening story about the sons understood as a dispute over land boundaries. At any rate, this is how *Jubilees* understands Genesis 9–10. *Jubilees* 8.8-30 explicitly reads Gen. 9.26-27 as a dispute over territories after the flood. Noah settles the matter by revealing from a book the divinely appointed boundaries for the three sons (*Jub.* 8.11). Shem's portion includes the mountains of Ararat, as well as Eden, Mt. Sinai, and Mt. Zion, and is said to be a beautiful land (*Jub.* 8.21).

Although it is very fragmentary, the *Genesis Apocryphon* contains material that is very closely related to *Jubilees* at these points, especially with regard to descriptions of the territories of Noah's sons (1QapGen 16–17, cf. *Jub.* 8.10–9.13). Presumably, the land surveyed and toured by Noah in the *Genesis Apocryphon* is the allotment of Shem. It is again said to be 'pleasant' (*'dn*, 1QapGen 11.12), as *Jubilees* refers to both Shem's territory (*Jub.* 8.21) and the land surveyed by Abram (*Jub.* 13.2). Moreover, there are broader similarities to the description of Abram's view of the land from Bethel in *Jub.* 13.6-7: Abram notes the fruitfulness of the trees and water on the mountains, and then blesses God (cf. 1QapGen 11.9-14). Possibly, the idea of God showing Noah the land in 1QapGen was in part inspired by the motif in *Jubilees* of land allotments revealed in a book of Noah (*Jub.* 8.11).

But the *Genesis Apocryphon* goes its own way with the story, most obviously by having *Noah tour the land*. It reflects an original and close reading of Genesis that closely follows its structure.

---

44. I follow here the reading of MQS, although it is grammatically awkward. The suggestion by FGA[3] to read עֹבֵ֑ר in l. 13 is incorrect; the reading עֲבַד is certain (on the basis of ABMC photograph GAF_X_1000_B, 1994 series).

Table 7. *Noah tours the land.*

Genesis	1QapGen
Noah to go out ... to fill the earth (8.15-17)	Noah surveys land (11.1-10)
Noah goes out (8.18-19)	Noah tours land (11.11-12)
Noah sacrifices (8.20)	Noah praises God (11.12-14)
God's promises to Noah (8.21–9.17)	Noah promised land (11.15ff)

The three episodes which appear on first glance to be simple additions to the narrative are rather interpretative retellings of the narrative following the structure of Genesis but bringing out the meaning that the author finds inherent in Genesis. When in Gen. 8.16-17 God instructs Noah to 'go out of the ark' with the animals 'so that they may abound on the earth', the *Genesis Apocryphon* understands that God showed Noah the land. When Noah is said to go out of the ark (Gen. 8.18-19), the *Genesis Apocryphon* understands that Noah walked through the boundaries of a specific territory. The episode of Noah's sacrifice (Gen. 8.20) is especially interesting. Although the *Genesis Apocryphon* transplants the actual sacrifice to before Noah has left the ark (1QapGen 10.12-17), this episode is also retained after the exit from the ark as praise to God (1QapGen 11.12-14). When God then blesses Noah in Gen. 9.1 with fruitfulness so that they will 'fill the earth', the *Genesis Apocryphon* understands this as a covenant promise of land.

The author's model is Abraham. As the covenant with Abraham included a promise to possess a particular land, and Abraham was instructed to survey it and symbolically take possession by touring the boundaries, so also with Noah. Moreover, the description of Noah surveying and touring the land is specifically parallel to unique additions to the narrative in the *Genesis Apocryphon* about Abram that describe Abram carrying out God's instructions to survey and tour the promised land.

Table 8. *Noah and Abram Tour the Land.*

	Genesis	Jubilees	1QapGen
Noah surveys land	-----	-----	11.1-10
Noah tours land	-----	-----	11.11
Noah promised land	-----	-----	11.16
Abram promised land	13.17b	13.20b	21.10
Abram instructed to survey land	13.14–15	13.19–20a	21.10
Abram surveys land	-----	-----	21.10-12
Abram instructed to tour land	13.17a	13.21	21.13-14
Abram tours land	-----	-----	21.15-19

Thereby, for the *Genesis Apocryphon*, God's covenant with Noah is parallel to God's covenant with Abram: it includes promise of a specific land.

At several points, the author of the *Genesis Apocryphon* has harmonized his account of Genesis 9 to narratives about the covenant with Abram. The language in §1 and §2 (see Table 5) about the Lord of the heavens appearing to Noah and instructing him not to fear is extraneous to Genesis 9, but recalls the introduction to the covenant with Abram in Genesis 15 (as noted briefly by Bernstein 1999a: 209).

Table 9. *'Do not fear'.*

1QapGen 11.15	1QapGen 22.30	Gen 15.1	Gen. 26.24
(to Noah)	(to Abram)	(to Abram)	(to Isaac)
[And then the Lord] of the heavens [appeared] to me, and spoke with me and said to me,	After these things, God appeared to Abram in a vision, and said to him, …	After these things the word of the Lord came to Abram in a vision,	And that very night the Lord appeared to him and said, …
'Do not fear. O Noah, I am with you,	'Do not fear; I am with you, and I will be your [31] support and strength. I am a shield over you and a buckler for you against one stronger than you.	'Do not fear, Abram. I am your shield;	'Do not fear, for I am with you
and with your children that (it will be) to them as with you forever'.	Your wealth and your flocks [32] will increase greatly'.	your reward shall be very great'.	and will bless you and make your offspring numerous for my servant Abraham's sake'.

The *Genesis Apocryphon* uses the same paraphrase in both instances: 'Do not fear … I am with you' (1QapGen 11.15; 22.30). Incidentally, this paraphrase itself is tailored to anticipate God's reassurance to Isaac in Gen. 26.24: 'Do not fear, for I am with you and will bless you and make your offspring numerous for my servant Abraham's sake'. It seems, then, that the *Genesis Apocryphon* read 'God blessed Noah and his sons' (Gen. 9.1) as including Abraham and his descendants, and anticipating God's covenant with Israel. This point also probably lies behind another feature of the narrative: instead of addressing Noah and his three sons as in Genesis 9, in the *Genesis Apocryphon* God speaks only to Noah but announces that the message applies to sons as well (1QapGen 11.15 cf. Gen. 9.1; 1QapGen 11.17 [singular 'you and your children'] cf. Gen. 9.3 [plural 'you']). This allows 'sons' to have a wider connotation of 'descendants' than Noah's immediate children. It is likely that this is related to the motif to portray Noah as patriarch of Israel: in the *Genesis Apocryphon*, the promise to Noah's 'sons' has in mind his descendants through Abraham.

Throughout this narrative about Noah's covenant in the *Genesis Apocryphon* (pp. 54–67), we see techniques of harmonization, omission, rearrangement, expansion, and paraphrase, but all of the distinctive features of the rewriting. All derive from a close reading of Gen. 9.1-3 which finds in the story of Noah (1) restoration of paradise, and (2) a mediating link between paradise and Abraham, focused on possession of the promised land. Put another way, the *Genesis Apocryphon* portrays Noah as a new Adam and a proto-Abraham. This stands in marked contrast to a prominent view in rabbinic interpretation according to which the story of Noah is bittersweet: there is deliverance, but considerable loss. The rabbis tended to compare Noah unfavorably

with Abraham: he was a profane man, only the best of a degenerate lot, and the dominion was not restored under him (see Lewis 1978: 151–52, and p. 54 above). The
Genesis Apocryphon, on the other hand, highlights Noah's righteousness, and emphasizes that with Noah is a full restoration. In this way, it is in line with emphasis on
Noah's exceptional piety especially in Jewish interpretation in the Greco-Roman period
and Christian interpretation.

Since most of the features just described are unique to the *Genesis Apocryphon* –
and even contrary to the message of *Jubilees* which the *Genesis Apocryphon* otherwise
appears to follow – and they are expressed by interventions in both details and large-
scale structure, it is likely that we are dealing with distinctive concerns of the author.
These observations thus provide some implications for the purpose of the book: to
portray Noah and Abraham (1) as prophets, recipients of revelation concerning the
future of Israel, and transmitters of sacred tradition, and (2) as patriarchs who receive
the promise of land and observe divine law. In both cases, the *Genesis Apocryphon*
strives to connect Noah and Abraham to the promised land (even Jerusalem) and
sacrificial laws according to Torah. It may also provide some tiny weight of evidence
that it is better to view the book as consisting of a Noah cycle and an Abraham cycle,
rather than as intending a presentation of each of the patriarchs or a more general
rewriting of Genesis. This, however, remains uncertain.

g. *Observance of Torah*
In the Hebrew Bible, the laws incumbent on Israel as God's people are revealed to
Moses on Mount Sinai, including such matters as sacrifices, Sabbath and festivals,
and purity. But what about earlier patriarchs? Did they keep God's laws? What about
earlier sacrifices by Abel, Noah, Abraham? Did these follow divine law? The *Genesis
Apocryphon* shares one of the central concerns of *Jubilees*, to show the patriarchs
observing an eternal law, which according to *Jubilees* is inscribed on heavenly tablets. But whereas in *Jubilees* this is explicit by means of the framework of the Sinai
revelation and discussions of law, the *Genesis Apocryphon* makes the point only
implicitly by narrative. According to 1QapGen 6.1–5, Noah 'practiced truth' and
'walked in the paths of eternal truth' since birth. The subsequent narrative highlights
three main areas of this eternal law: the observance of laws of marriage, sacrifice
procedures, and the produce of fruit trees.

1. *Marriage*. Genesis provides little details about Noah's family: it identifies only
his father and three sons. The *Genesis Apocryphon* adds that Noah married his cousin,
named Imzera (אמזרע; 1QapGen 6.7), a detail also found in *Jub.* 4.33 (as ʾEmzaraʿ in
the Ethiopic). The name Imzera is apparently a pun on Noah and his wife as the pro-
genitors of a new human race: the name means 'mother of seed'. But the *Genesis
Apocryphon* also adds three unique elements (A15–16):

1.   Besides his three sons, Noah also had three daughters (who then presumably
      must have died in the flood)
2.   Noah arranged with his brother that their children should marry their cousins
3.   He did this 'according to the law of the eternal ordinance [which] the Most
      High [commanded] to humankind' (1QapGen 6.8-9)

The motif of patriarchs marrying close relatives is common in *Jubilees*: in its gene-alogical lists it regularly adds an identification of the wives as near kin, and from the fourth generation on (*Jub.* 4.15), often cousins. *Jubilees* also indicates that the eternal law of the heavenly tablets forbids intermarriage with Gentiles on pain of death (*Jub.* 30.7; cf. 20.3-6; 28.6-7).

There is a broader background to this. During the Persian and especially the Greek and Roman periods, many pious Jewish groups became alarmed that intermarriage with Gentiles would result in the dissolution of the Jewish people. The partial ban on intermarriage with certain peoples in the Mosaic law (Deut. 7.1–3) was interpreted as a universal ban (Ezra 9.10-12; Neh. 10.28-30; also Add. Esther C 14.15; Philo, *Spec. Leg.* 3.29; Jos. *Ant.* 8.191-2), on analogy with the requirement of strict endogamy for priests (Lev. 21.14). The examples of the patriarchs Abraham, Isaac, and Jacob who married near relatives were also seen by some as precedents (cf. Gen. 11.29; 20.12; 24.3-4, 15; 28.1-2). Tobit (3rd or 4th cent. BCE) shows both the view that strict endo-gamy was required by Mosaic law on all Israelites (Tob. 6.13), and an extension of the precedent from the patriarchs to include Noah (Tob. 4.12), reflecting a similar tradition as in *Jubilees* and the *Genesis Apocryphon*.

The *Genesis Apocryphon* reflects this broader tradition of concern for endogamy on the one hand, and on the other hand is more specifically related to *Jubilees*. How-ever, the *Genesis Apocryphon* reveals its own special interests. It does not share with *Jubilees* the genealogical lists clarifying the marriages of all the patriarchs. Instead, by focusing specifically on Noah and adding unique information about Noah arranging cousin marriages for his children, it emphasizes a parallel with Abraham, who arranged a cousin marriage for his son Isaac. Furthermore, the story is structured to stress Noah's life as a counteraction to the Watchers. In an envelope pattern, visions about the rebellion and illicit marriages of the Watchers (Enoch, A8; Noah, A17) frame the narrative that Noah followed the paths of truth and arranged marriages for himself and his children according to divine law (A13–16). The author of the *Genesis Apoc-ryphon* has taken some trouble to make this point, uniquely reworking the story to make the marriages of his sons the occasion for a vision about the Watchers (cf. Gen. 5.32). Thus, the marriages of the sons of Noah according to divine law counter the marriages of the sons of God contrary to divine law.

The special interest in the marriage of Noah may also be related to another motif in both the *Genesis Apocryphon* and *Jubilees*: Noah as priest.

2. *Sacrifice.* Without elaboration, Genesis mentions that on disembarking after the flood Noah built an altar to God and offered burnt offerings of every clean animal and bird (Gen. 8.20). What sort of sacrifice was this? Was it a sacrifice of thanksgiving, showing gratitude to God for saving him and his family? Or was the sacrifice to appease God or remove the guilt of sin? Ancient interpreters struggled with this question, often concluding that it was a sacrifice of thanksgiving (see Ruiten 2000: 224–25). One might also wonder whether Noah's sacrifices were in accordance with divine law, which in the biblical narrative was not revealed until Moses.

The *Genesis Apocryphon* addresses both of these questions in its narrative that is closely related to *Jubilees* (A32; cf. *Jub.* 6.1-3). Both explicitly state that Noah's sacri-fice is to atone for the land, and specifically show Noah meticulously carrying out the purification offerings for the congregation according to a distinctive interpretation of sacrificial law found also in the *Temple Scroll*. The two Torah prescriptions for this sacrifice differ: Leviticus 4.13-21 specifies a bull for a sin offering and the separate burning of fat and pouring out of blood, whereas Num. 15.22–26 specifies a bull for a burnt offering along with grain and drink offering, and a male goat for a sin offering. The rabbis harmonized the two, regarding Leviticus 4 as the general case and Numbers 15 as a special case (idolatry), whereas the *Temple Scroll* seems to reflect the opposite solution: Numbers 15 as the general case, and Leviticus 4 as a special case (Anderson 1992). The *Genesis Apocryphon* and *Jubilees* seem to reflect this same harmonization as well as another distinctive in common with the *Temple Scroll* sacrificial laws: that sin offerings are to be completed before burnt offerings (Yadin 1983: 1:146–148, cf. 1:89–91 and 2:58; also based on a harmonization with other Torah passages such as Lev. 5.8). Thus, as we can reconstruct from partial parallels in *Jubilees*, Noah's procedure in the *Genesis Apocryphon* is in three stages as follows:

1.   He sacrifices a sin offering (a goat for atonement, cf. Num. 15.24-25) followed by the other burnt offerings, burning the fat separate from the flesh (cf. Lev. 4.19)
2.   He pours out the blood at the base of the altar (cf. Lev. 4.18), and burns the flesh on the altar
3.   He offers turtledoves as a burnt offering, adding a meal offering with oil and frankincense (cf. Num. 15.24), and salt on all (as required on all offerings according to Lev. 2.13)

This is essentially the same as the procedure in *Jubilees* with the following differences. (1) The *Genesis Apocryphon* is more deliberate about the order of the procedure, specifying three distinct stages numbered 'first … second … third'. (2) The *Genesis Apocryphon* is more careful to reflect the scriptural precedents by mentioning the pouring out of blood and mentioning salt added to all the offerings, not just sacrifices from the herd. (3) The *Genesis Apocryphon* does not mention the sprinkling of wine, thus departing from the scriptural precedent which specifies a drink offering (Num. 15.24) and differing from *Jubilees*. The probable reason for this is that the *Genesis Apocryphon* anticipates his narrative: there can be no wine because Noah has not yet planted a vineyard! (4) Unlike *Jubilees* which delays Noah's exit from the ark so that this sacrifice can take place in the third month as the origin of the Festival of Weeks, the *Genesis Apocryphon* strangely has Noah offer this sacrifice before he leaves the ark! Having Noah sacrifice while on the ark is a serious disruption to the narrative in Genesis, and is completely unique. It must reflect a very important interest for the author, but because the text is so fragmentary it is not possible to discern what it might be. M. Bernstein (2005a: 59) suggests that 'the purification of the earth accomplished by Noah's sin-offerings had to be completed before Noah and the others descended from the ark', lest they be defiled upon disembarking.[45]

---

45.   As Dimant (1998: 138) has pointed out, *Jubilees* places Ararat within Shem's alottment, thereby perhaps regarding it as part of the 'prediluvian holyland'. This is also the case for the *Genesis Apocryphon*.

Considering the similarities and differences, it is most likely that the *Genesis Apocryphon* is dependent on *Jubilees* – or a narrative very similar to *Jubilees*, which the author adapts and improves with regard to his own interest.

Both the *Genesis Apocryphon* and *Jubilees* describe the sacrifice as an atonement for the land, a detail not found in Genesis. What is the basis of this interpretation? On the one hand, it recognizes a necessary relationship between Noah's sacrifice and God's promise not to destroy – Noah's sacrifice was not simply an act of gratitude for deliverance, but an ordained cultic act (the rabbis also found in this passage that Noah inferred God's provision for sacrifice). It seems also to have inferred the nature of mortal sin that elicited the destruction of all life (not explained in Gen. 6.5-7) from the laws concerning the shedding of blood that follow (Gen. 9.4-7): all creatures were guilty of bloodshed (see 1QapGen 6.19, 26 cf. *Jub.* 5.2-4; 7.23-25; also *1 En.* 9.1, 9). According to Num. 35.33, bloodshed pollutes the land, and can be expiated only by the blood of the one who shed it. Noah's sacrifices serve as a substitute for the blood of the murderers (van Ruiten 2000: 225–26). Also in both the *Genesis Apocryphon* and *Jubilees*, Noah is shown to be the prototypical priest, faithfully following sacrificial procedures of the eternal divine law.

3. *Fruit trees and festivals*. The story of Noah in Genesis (9.20-27) ends on a tragic and humiliating tone. The narrative teases with its brevity, with hints of the salacious. Closely following the Hebrew word order, it begins:

And he began (ויחל), Noah, a man of the earth, and he planted a vineyard.
And he drank from the wine and became drunk
and he was uncovered in the midst of his tent.

The Genesis story, interested in documenting 'firsts', undoubtedly meant to indicate that Noah was skilled in husbandry and the first to plant a vineyard. But the Hebrew verb typically translated 'he began' or 'he was the first' in this verse (√ חלל) can also mean 'to profane'. Thus, together with the expression 'man of the earth' (איש האדמה, Gen. 9.20), one could find hints of a slur on Noah's character: that in this episode he profaned himself.[46] The nuances that follow with regard to Noah's drunken nakedness and the episode with Ham easily cast a shadow of shame over the whole narrative. Some of the rabbis read the story in such a way, as we have already noted.

Both *Jubilees* and the *Genesis Apocryphon* greatly expand this story and transform it to show Noah observing the scriptural law governing the produce of fruit trees and piously keeping a festival with his family. Since the *Genesis Apocryphon* is very fragmentary but seems closely to correspond to *Jubilees*, it will be best to start with the latter.

---

46. E.g., *Gen. R.* 22.3; 36.3; *Tanh.* (Buber) 2.20 on Gen. 9.18ff. (Townsend 1989: 50); *Tanh. Yel.* Noah 13 (on Gen. 9.20; Berman 1996: 66). See Lewis 1978: 151–52.

Table 10. *Noah's Vineyard.*

Genesis 9	Jubilees 7 (VBJ)	1QapGen 12–15
	[1] During the seventh week, in its first year, in this jubilee [1317]	---
9 [20] Noah	Noah	[A46] 12 [13] I
	---	and all my sons
began,	---	began
a man of the earth,	---	to till the land
to plant a vineyard.	planted a vine	and I planted a large
	at the <u>mountain</u>	vineyard
	(whose name was <u>Lubar</u>,	on <u>Mount Lubar</u>
	one of the mountains of Ararat)	
	on which the ark had come to rest.	
	It <u>produced</u> fruit	[A47] and <u>by the fourth year</u>
	<u>in the fourth year</u> [1320]	it <u>produced</u> wine
		for me.
		[14] ... all ... *vacat*
	He guarded its fruit,	
	and picked it	
	that year during the seventh month.	
	[2] He made wine from it,	
	put it in a <u>container</u>,	
	and kept it until <u>the fifth year</u> [1321] –	
	until <u>the first day</u>	
	at the beginning of the <u>first month</u>.	
		[A48] And when the first festival came,
		on the first day of the first <u>festival</u>
		of the [first] month
		[15] ... of my vineyard,
		I opened this <u>vessel</u>
9 [21] He drank		and began to <u>drink</u> of it
some of the wine		on <u>the first day</u> of <u>the fifth year</u>
		[16] ...
		On this day I summoned my <u>sons</u> and grandsons and all our wives and their daughters and we gathered together and we went [17] [to the place of the altar?]... and I
		blessed the Lord of heaven, the Most High God, the Great Holy One who delivered us from our destruction
		[18] ... and to all ... *my household*
	[3] He joyfully celebrated	*I rejoiced*
	the day of this <u>festival</u>.	
	He made a burnt offering for the Lord –	and <u>fire</u> ...
	one young bull,	(see *Jub.* 7.5)
	one ram,	

Genesis 9	Jubilees 7 (VBJ)	1QapGen 12–15
	seven sheep each a year old,	
	and one kid –	
	that he might make atonement through it	
	for himself and his <u>sons</u>.	
	[4] First he prepared the kid.	
	He put some of its blood on the meat	
	(that was on) the altar which he had made.	
	He offered all the fat on the altar where he	
	made the burnt offering along with the bull,	
	the ram, and the sheep.	
	He offered all their meat on the altar.	
	[5] On it he placed their entire sacrifice mixed	
	with oil.	
	Afterwards he <u>sprinkled</u> <u>wine</u>	[19] and I <u>poured</u> on ... and
	in the <u>fire</u> that had been on the altar	the <u>wine</u> ...
	beforehand.	[20–26] ...
	He put frankincense on the altar	
	and offered a pleasant fragrance	
	that was pleasing before the Lord his God.	
	[6] He was very happy,	
	and he and his <u>sons</u>	
	happily <u>drank</u> some of this wine.	
		[27] ... every year and . . .
	[7] When evening came,	
	he went into his tent.	
and became drunk,	He lay down drunk and fell asleep.	
and he lay uncovered	He was uncovered	
in his tent	in his tent as he slept.	
[22] And Ham,	[8] Ham saw his father Noah naked and went	
the father of Canaan,	out and told his two brothers outside.	
saw the nakedness of		
his father,		
and told his two		
brothers outside.		
[23] Then Shem and	[9] Then Shem took some clothes, rose – he	
Japheth took a	and Japheth – and they put the clothes on	
garment,	their shoulders as they were facing	
laid it on both their	backwards.	
shoulders,		
and walked backward		
and covered the	They covered their father's shame as they	
nakedness of their	were facing backwards.	
father; their faces were		
turned away, and they		
did not see their		
father's nakedness.		
		[A49] 12 [7] – 14 [7] (dream
		visions)
		[A50] 14 [7] – 15 [20]
		(interpretation)
		[A51] 15 [21] ...
[24] When Noah awoke	[10] When Noah awakened	[Then I awoke,] Noah,
from his wine	from his <u>sleep</u>,	from my <u>sleep</u>,
		and the sun ... [22] ...
		[23] ... righteous ... [24–?] ...

Genesis 9	Jubilees 7 (VBJ)	1QapGen 12–15
and knew what	he realized everything that	
his youngest son	his youngest son	
had done to him,	had done to him.	
23–27 he said,	10 12 He cursed his son and said:	
(cursing of Canaan;	(cursing of Canaan;	
blessing of Shem and Japheth)	blessing of Shem and Japheth)	
28–29 (Death of Noah)		
	13–17 When Ham realized that his father had cursed his youngest son, it was displeasing to him ... He separated from his father ...	
	18–19 (sons of Shem and Japheth)	
	20–39 (Testament of Noah to sons)	
	– sins of Watchers	
	– sins of sons	
	– demons leading astray	
	– law about blood	
	– law about produce of fruit trees	

The main features of the rewritten story in *Jubilees* are as follows:

1. It adds a chronological framework, situating the story in the distinctive chronology of the book. Thus, Noah plants his vineyard in the first year of the seventh week of the twenty-seventh Jubilee; that is, AM 1317, about eight years after the flood.
2. It omits the ambiguous description of Noah as 'a man of the soil' who 'began'.
3. It specifies a location for the vineyard, on Mount Lubar.
4. It adds details to show Noah observing the scriptural law governing the produce of fruit trees in Lev. 19.23-25, according to a distinctive interpretation.
5. It adds details to show Noah observing a non-biblical festival, on the first day of the first month.
6. The story of Noah's drunkenness and subsequent cursing of Canaan is supplemented to highlight the leadership of Shem, and to prepare for the separation of the families.
7. There is a lengthy addition in which Noah gives a testament to his sons concerning the sins of the Watchers, the future sins of his sons and descendants, warning about demons leading astray, and admonishing to observe laws about blood and about the produce of fruit trees.

In this story, *Jubilees* seems primarily interested in issues of calendar, the law about fruit trees, and the festival on the first day of the first month.

Points 4 and 5 require some further explanation. First, Noah waits until the fourth year to harvest the grapes, and stores it in a fermenting container until the fifth year, when he sprinkles some as a drink offering, and drinks some with his family. In this way, *Jubilees* shows Noah observing the scriptural law about fruit trees in Lev. 19.23-25, according to which the produce of fruit trees planted in the land of Israel are 'forbidden' (literally, 'uncircumcised') the first three years, in the fourth year they are 'holy for praise' to the Lord (קדש הלולים), and in the fifth year they may be

eaten by the owner. But the biblical law is ambiguous. It leaves unclear exactly what
is to be done with the produce of the fourth year: can the owner eat it? That Noah is
here following a distinctive interpretation of Lev. 19.23-25 is made clear in a testament to his sons (*Jub.* 7.20-39) in which Noah instructs about the law concerning the
produce of fruit trees and attributes the practice to the authority of Enoch. Here *Jubilees* is explicit: the fourth year produce is offered as first fruits on the altar, and the
remainder belongs to the priests to consume before the altar. None of the fourth year
produce belongs to the owner.

This law appears to have been the subject of halakhic dispute in the Second Temple
period. The dominant rabbinic view – attested also by Josephus (*Ant.* 4.226–27) – is
that fourth-year produce should be treated like second tithe: it belongs to the owner to
be eaten in Jerusalem or converted to money spent on pilgrimage to Jerusalem (e.g.,
Sifre Num. 6; *m. Maaser Sheni* 5.2). In contrast, the view in *Jubilees* is shared by
4QMMT (B:62–63; DJD 10: 164–65) and 11QT^a 60.3-4 (Yadin 1983: 1:162–63), and
is also assumed by the *Genesis Apocryphon*. Somewhat similar views attributing the
fourth year produce to priests are attested by the Samaritans, Karaites, *Targum Ps-
Jonathan*, and some rabbis.

Why should Noah promulgate a law about the produce of fruit trees? This seems to
be based on a midrashic reading of Gen. 9.20 with Lev. 19.23-26, which juxtaposes a
law about fruit trees with a law against eating blood. *Jubilees* juxtaposes the two laws
both in its narrative about Noah, and in the testament Noah delivers to his sons.

Table 11. *Law About Fruit Trees.*

Genesis	Jubilees
Law about blood (Gen. 9.4-6)	Law about blood (*Jub.* 6.7-14)
Narrative about vineyard (Gen. 9.20)	Narrative about vineyard (*Jub.* 7.1-6)
Law about fruit trees (Lev. 19.23-25)	Law about blood (*Jub.* 7.23-33)
Law about blood (Lev. 19.26)	Law about fruit trees (*Jub.* 7.34-37)

The connection may also have been encouraged by the similarity between the
wording 'began (ויחל) … to plant a vineyard' (ויטע כרם, Gen. 9.20), and Deut. 20.6
'has anyone planted a vineyard (נטע כרם) but not yet enjoyed (חלל) its fruit?' That
is, Gen. 9.20 could be read as alluding to the law of releasing fruit for the owner's
use.

Some scholars have noticed that the narrative in *Jubilees* does not seem to match
the law (e.g., Kister 1992). In the narrative, Noah apparently drinks the fourth-year
wine as a priest, but oddly he waits until the beginning of the fifth year. Secondly,
Jubilees shows Noah observing a festival on the first day of the first month not in
Torah but attested in the *Temple Scroll* (11QT^a 14.9–18). The order of the sacrifices
in both of these texts shows that this festival is modeled on the scriptural Festival of
Trumpets on the first day of the seventh month in Num. 29.1, but with the sacrifice of
a kid first. This seems to represent a harmonization with other scriptural passages
(Lev. 8.14-18; Num. 8.12; Lev. 5.8; Lev. 19.19; Num. 6.16) that sin offerings are to
be completed before other offerings (Yadin 1983: 1:146–48, cf. 1:89–91 and 2:58).

Despite its fragmentary nature, it is clear that the rewriting in the *Genesis Apocryphon* is very closely related to *Jubilees*. They both similarly transform the vineyard

story to show Noah observing the law of fruit trees, and celebrating a festival on the first day of the first month. They both follow with a similarly expanded description of the division of the earth (*Jub.* 8.1–9.15; 1QapGen 15.?–18.?). Moreover, there are very particular details in common: the time element (fourth year, fifth year) for the harvest and consumption of wine, the setting on Mount Lubar, the vine 'producing' fruit (*Jubilees*)/wine (1QapGen), and Noah awakening from 'sleep' rather than 'wine'.

Several pieces of evidence suggest that *Jubilees* is either a source for the *Genesis Apocryphon*, or at least a fairly similar narrative served as a source for both of them. The pattern of material in common points to a close literary relationship, but certain features in the narrative of the *Genesis Apocryphon* look secondary in comparison to *Jubilees*. Most importantly, (1) the *Genesis Apocryphon* lacks the chronological framework of *Jubilees*. This means that the references to the fourth and fifth years in the *Genesis Apocryphon* are without a contextual referent. In *Jubilees*, the first, fourth, and fifth years are years in the seventh week of the twenty-seventh Jubilee, according to the distinctive chronology of *Jubilees*. In the *Genesis Apocryphon*, by default they can only refer to the years since Noah planted the vineyard. (2) The law of fruit trees is less well integrated into the narrative about Noah in the *Genesis Apocryphon*. The *Genesis Apocryphon* lacks both the motivating midrashic framework and the corresponding law. The story is also less coherent: there is no mention of storage of the wine, and possibly no antecedent for 'this container'. Most strikingly, Noah drinks first *before* sprinkling wine as an offering, and so does not so closely adhere to law. This seems to betray little particular interest in the law as such, in contrast to *Jubilees*.

These features, then, seem to indicate the use of traditional material. The author's interests are rather to be found in places where there are distinctive additions, omissions, and changes. (1) The *Genesis Apocryphon* is more interested in the festival, but still, not necessarily its particularities. It seems likely that the *Genesis Apocryphon* did not include the detailed description of the order of sacrifices (it would probably have to fit in the latter half of line 12.18, before the reference to pouring in line 19). But the author adds that Noah waited until 'the first festival', that Noah's grandsons and all of their wives and daughters participated, that they went together (presumably to the altar), and he adds a blessing to God. If there is a law attached to this pericope, it is the observance of this festival 'every year' (1QapGen 12.27). Thus, the *Genesis Apocryphon* does seem to have some special interest in the festival, but more in the fact that Noah is observing a festival with his whole family.

(2) Unlike *Jubilees*, the *Genesis Apocryphon* interprets the beginning of Gen. 9.20, and it does so in a way that suggests a common tradition with the Aramaic targums. Both the *Genesis Apocryphon* and the targums render the first part of the sentence using the same Aramaic verbs (פלח √, צרי √) as Noah beginning to work the earth, avoiding any negative overtones. For the *Genesis Apocryphon*, this may also highlight Noah as a second Adam, who was also to 'work the ground' (Gen. 2.15; 3.23).

(3) The *Genesis Apocryphon* probably omits the mention of the drunkenness of Noah, Ham's offense, and the cursing of Canaan. It seems unlikely that these topics could be dealt with in the gap at the bottom of col. 12 and the top of col. 13. There are about fourteen lost lines, and in these must fit the beginning of the vision about the cedar and willows, of which the explanation occupies about ten lines (see 1QapGen 14.9-18). (4) Instead, the sleep of Noah becomes an occasion for a dream vision, which is narrated at great length (almost three columns).

Thus, it seems that the author's interest in this narrative is primarily in renovating Noah's character, showing him piously observing a festival, and this festival as occasion for a vision. The vision is the true focus of the story for the *Genesis Apocryphon*. On the one hand, it corresponds to Noah's testament in *Jubilees*. On the other hand, in the larger context of the *Genesis Apocryphon* it associates Noah with Abraham as recipient and transmitter of revelation through dreams.

h. *Revelation*

The *Genesis Apocryphon* prominently emphasizes the notion of antediluvian revelation in a succession of at least four dreams or visions by Enoch, Noah, and perhaps Lamech (A1, A8–9, A17–18, A49–50). Unfortunately, the apocalyptic passages are extremely poorly preserved, but one can gain a sense of their importance to the *Genesis Apocryphon* by the statistic that including their interpretations, these occupy up to about seven of approximately seventeen surviving columns of the *Genesis Apocryphon* before the Abraham cycle. There is a rich tradition focusing on Enoch as the recipient of revelation about proper calendar, astronomy, the sins of the Watchers and the dissemination of forbidden knowledge on earth, and eschatological judgment.[47] This lies at the heart of the extensive Enochic literature, and influenced other writings such as *Jubilees* (4.19, 21-22), *Testament of the Twelve Patriarchs* (*T. Sim.* 5.4; *T. Levi* 10.5, cf. 14.1; 16.1; *T. Naph.* 4.11; *T. Benj.* 9.1) and *Pseudo-Philo* (3.9-10).

At least one of the apocalypses in the *Genesis Apocryphon* is attributed to Enoch (A8), and seems to be expanded and adapted from *1 Enoch* 106–107: in response to Lamech's anxiety over his son Noah, Enoch reveals the sins of the Watchers, the corruption of the earth and the flood, and eschatological judgmnent. The apocalypse at the beginning of what survives of the *Genesis Apocryphon* (A1) seems to describe the binding of the Watchers and the destruction of their offspring, and the corruption of the earth by forbidden knowledge. This may also be by Enoch, but it is possible that this was attributed to Lamech, who seems to have the narrative voice in the first part. If so, this would be a unique element, and would apparently reflect a reading of Lamech's naming of Noah (Gen. 5.28-29) as a revelation (cf. Philo, *Quaest. in Gen.* 1.87, which understands Lamech's comment at Noah's birth as prophecy). It would also associate a series of apocalypses by each of the patriarchs in succession, since there are also dream visions attributed to Abraham (B17–18, B94–97).

By surviving the flood, Noah is a key transitional figure: he is the one through whom antediluvian wisdom and revelation – mainly from Enoch – is preserved and transmitted in books to Abraham and eventually Levi (e.g., *Jub.* 7.20-39; 21.10; *T. Levi* 10.12; cf. 14.1; 16.1; *2 En.* 33.12; see Stone 1999). *Jubilees* attributes five areas of special knowledge to Noah transmitted through books:

1. Priestly laws about sacrifice and blood (*Jub.* 6; 7.28-33; cf. 21.10; *ALD* 10.10)
2. Laws about the produce of fruit trees (*Jub.* 6; 7.35-37; cf. 21.10)
3. The sins of the Watchers (*Jub.* 7.20-27)
4. The division of land among Noah's descendants (*Jub.* 8.10-12)
5. Demons and healing (*Jub.* 10.12-14)

---

47. For recent studies, see VanderKam 1995; Boccaccini 1998; Nickelsburg 1999; Reed 2005.

In the first three cases, *Jubilees* explicitly portrays Noah as transmitting knowledge from Enoch (*Jub.* 7.38-39; cf. 4.25). In the fourth case, the source of the book with the land boundaries is unclear. Only the knowledge about demons and healing is explicitly stated to be direct revelation to Noah, through angels.

The *Genesis Apocryphon* reflects this motif of Noah as transmitter of knowledge through books: it assumes the book of division of land (A52), and refers to Abraham teaching from the 'book of the words of Enoch' (B24), which must have been passed through Noah. But the *Genesis Apocryphon* is especially interested in the motif of Noah as a recipient of divine revelation himself (Bernstein 1999a: 217–18 n. 51, 225–26 notes the motif of secret knowledge to Noah in 4Q253 and 4Q418 201–27). It makes of the instructions about blood a visionary scene ('And then the Lord] of the heavens [appeared] to me, and spoke with me …', 1QapGen 11.15; cf. 22.27; see Fitzmyer 2004: 156). Most significantly, however, the *Genesis Apocryphon* attributes two substantial apocalypses to Noah. The first (A17–18) seems to be related to a Noah fragment awkwardly incorporated into the Book of Parables (*1 En.* 60.1-6, 7-10, 24-25).[48] In both, Noah has a vision in his 500th year about the impending divine judgment, he sees a large company of angels, and is assisted by a great angel who interprets the vision.

In the second passage (A49–50), the story of Noah's drunkenness is transformed into a revelatory dream vision (his awaking from the dream [A51] corresponds to Gen. 9.24a). The nature of the vision is unclear, but the language and images are standard fare of Jewish apocalyptic (see esp. Daniel 2, 4; *1 Enoch* 65–68; 85–90; *2 Baruch* 36–40; see Fitzmyer 2004: 164–70):

1. Language of superiors (gold and silver; sun, moon and stars) destroying inferiors (breaking stones and ceramic pots; chopping down trees; 1QapGen 13.9-11). This probably alludes to the rape and violence wrought by the evil angels on earth.
2. Releasing of waters (1QapGen 13.11-12). This probably alludes to the flood.
3. An olive tree that grows tall and glorious, but is buffeted by the four winds of heaven until it is broken and its leaves and fruit are scattered (1QapGen 13.13-17). This alludes to Israel and its dispersion (cf. Jer. 11.16-17).
4. A great cedar tree on a mountain which sprouts three shoots (1QapGen 14.9-17); this represents Noah as patriarch with his three sons, one of whom will bring forth 'an upright planting'.
5. 'They will turn aside, the majority of them will be evil' (1QapGen 15.9); this probably refers to the future apostasy of Israel.
6. A man from the south with a sickle and fire (1QapGen 15.10-13); this represents judgment, but it is unclear whether the agent is an angel or an enemy nation, and whether the recipient is Israel or the wicked nations.

It is likely that the vision is related to fragments of a second Noachic apocalypse incorporated into the Book of Parables in garbled form (*1 En.* 65.1–69.1). In both, Noah narrates in the first person, and he describes visions which are then interpreted. The visions concern the sin of the Watchers and their punishment, the flood, the

---

48. All manuscripts now refer to Enoch, but it clearly applied originally to Noah: the 500 years is from Gen. 5.32; *1 En.* 60.8 alludes to Enoch as the visionary's great-grandfather.

preservation of Noah and his sons and their promise of a righteous lineage, the future sins of Israel, and eschatological judgment.

These two Noah visions are not evidence of direct relationship between the Book of Parables and the *Genesis Apocryphon*, but probably of a common source – possibly but not necessarily a Book of Noah. The brief report in *1 En.* 10.1-3 of an angel dispatched to Noah to reveal the pending judgment, Noah's deliverance, and the destiny of his descendants could be either a summary of such a common source, or a source of the tradition. In any case, the *Genesis Apocryphon* reworks the material for its own interests. The 500th year becomes associated with the marriage rather than birth of his children (cf. Gen. 5.32; *Jub.* 4.33) so that Noah can serve as a counter to the Watchers. Noah's drunken slumber is renovated as a dream vision which highlights Noah as a proto-Abraham: the promise of righteous descendants recalls the promise to Abraham (1QapGen 14.12-13), and Noah's vision has similarities to a vision also attributed to Abraham in the *Genesis Apocryphon* (cedar tree, awaking from sleep 1QapGen 19.14-17). Overall, it seems likely that with the heading 'book of the words of Noah' (A12), the *Genesis Apocryphon* seeks to supply the book that according to *Jubilees* is transmitted by Noah, but it claims a large degree of Noachic revelation: a full third of these twelve columns (5.29–17.end?) is occupied by the two apocalypses of Noah (6.11-22; 12.end–15.20) and the visionary instruction about blood (11.15–12.6). Due to the fragmentary nature, it is not clear whether the *Genesis Apocryphon* had any counterpart to Noachic revelation about exorcism and healing.

i. *Geography*
The *Genesis Apocryphon* shows a special interest in geographical details. The most obvious of these are additions taken over from *Jubilees*, or possibly a common source.

1.   Noah's ark landed on 'one of' the mountains of Ararat (Hurarat in 1QapGen), identified as Mt Lubar (A31, cf. A46)
2.   Noah built his altar and planted his vineyard on Mt Lubar (A32; A46)
3.   The boundaries of land for Noah's sons and descendants are specified in detail, as ordained in a book (A52–58)

In the last point, the details of land boundaries seem to harmonize an idealized view of the nations from Genesis with a contemporary Hellenistic view of world geography based on the Ionian world map: the world divided into three parts separated by rivers, and focusing on a central sacred place.[49] Shem's portion is central (Asia), and is the pleasant land of blessing that includes the sacred places: Eden, Mt. Sinai, and Mt. Zion at the center of the world. Thus, it includes the land later possessed by the tribes of Israel. Japheth's portion is the cold region (Europe) to the north of the River Tina (= ancient Tanais, modern Don). Ham's is the hot region (Africa) to the south of River Gihon (from Gen. 2.13, identified with the Nile). The *Genesis Apocryphon* seems to follow basically the same geography as *Jubilees*, with a few differences of detail, and a different order of presentation: the *Genesis Apocryphon* presents the three regions first in order from North to South, and then in order of the priority of the sons (Shem, Japheth, Ham). This distribution of land among Noah's descendants highlights (a) that

49.   Alexander 1982; Scott 2002: 28–43; on the geography of *Jubilees*, see also Hölscher 1949; Frey 1997.

the placement of peoples – especially the land of Israel – was eternally pre-ordained on heavenly tablets, and (b) that Noah prefigures Abraham's promise of land and Moses' allotment of the promised land among the tribes of Israel (Scott 2002: 33).

There are also details unique to the *Genesis Apocryphon*. (1) Enoch lives with the angels in Parvaim. Here, the *Genesis Apocryphon* uses the scriptural name of a distant place renowned for gold (2 Chron. 3.6) as a designation for the mythical dwelling place of the righteous at the ends of the earth (cf. *1 En.* 106.8; 60.23; 65.2; Fitzmyer 2004: 137). (2) From the ark, Noah surveys the land, and then travels through it (A35, A37). Here it is clear that the author's interest is not just land in general, but the boundaries of a specific land. In this case, the territory of Shem represents the land of God's chosen people. In this way, the *Genesis Apocryphon* again highlights Noah as a proto-Abraham.

j. *Characterization*

A considerable amount of unique expansion in the Noah cycle of the *Genesis Apocryphon* concerns characterization. To the story of the birth of Noah from *1 Enoch* 106–107, the *Genesis Apocryphon* adds exploration of the emotions and psychology of the characters (Nickelsburg 1998: 143–44). The raw and realistic emotion of Bitenosh as she defends her faithfulness to Lamech (A5) is both touching and almost unparalleled in ancient Jewish writings. We may also note the greater inclusion of women and family in the scenes (e.g., 1QapGen 6.7-8, 10; 10.1; 11.15; 12.8, 13, 16).

6. *Abraham Motifs*

The *Genesis Apocryphon* is most famous for its remarkable retelling of Abram and Sarai's sojourn in Egypt. This is in good measure due to the delightful character of its narrative, especially the inclusion of a dream vision which provides divine warrant for Abram's ruse of passing off Sarai as his sister, and the addition of a long, lingering poem in praise of Sarai's beauty. But it is also due to the fact that columns 19–22 represent the best preserved section of the manuscript. This part, corresponding to Gen. 12.8–15.5, was translated almost in its entirety in the *editio princeps* (Avigad and Yadin 1956).

a. *Character and Piety of Abraham*

For the patriarch chosen by God to be father of the Israelite people, a man called 'righteous' and 'friend of God', Genesis is remarkably frank in telling stories that sound scandalous. One story in particular reveals behavior unexpected in such a pious person: the story of Abram and Sarai's journey to Egypt told in Genesis 12. Abram resorts to deceit to save his own skin, and shows a shocking lack of concern for Sarai. He accepts payment as Sarai is taken into Pharaoh's harem. Is the mother of the chosen people – including the priestly tribe – defiled? Does the famed wealth of the father of the Jewish faith come from pimping his wife? In the end, it is Pharaoh who rebukes Abram and sends him away! But Abram pulls the same stunt again when he settles in Abimelek's land in the Negeb (Genesis 20). Abraham introduces Sarah as his sister, and the story is similar, although there are several details that ameliorate some of the more scandalous implications this time around. Whereas Genesis 12 does nothing to alleviate the assumption that Pharaoh had sexual relations with Sarai, in

Genesis 20 we are explicitly told that Abimelek did not sleep with her. God himself warns Abimelek that Sarai is Abram's wife and that he will die unless he returns her. Abimelek defends his innocence, and God agrees with him. Abimelek rebukes Abram, but this time Abram ventures a defense and prays for healing for Abimelek.

These stories that present the patriarch in a shockingly unsavory light (as similarly the Hagar–Ishmael stories in Genesis 16, 21) quite naturally attracted a great deal of 'spin doctoring' in the various retellings of Genesis to stress the uprightness of Abram's character and the purity of Sarai. In fact, scholars have pointed out that the second occurrences of these stories probably reflect early retellings that became enshrined in Scripture.

When the *Genesis Apocryphon* retells the story of Sarai and Abram in Egypt, it combines elements from both accounts, and adds many details besides. In the following table, italics indicate significant differences from Genesis 12.

Table 12. *Abram and Sarai in Egypt.*

Gen. 12: Egypt	1QapGen: Egypt	Gen. 20: Abimelek
Famine in Canaan	[B13] Famine in Canaan	
	[B14] *Abram hears about grain in Egypt*	
Abram journeys to Egypt	[B15] Abram journeys to Egypt	Journey to Gerar in the Negeb, the kingdom of Abimelek
	Details about boundaries	
On the eve of entering Egypt	[B16] On the eve of entering Egypt	
	[B17] *Abram has a dream about a cedar tree and a palm tree: the palm speaks in defense of the cedar and saves it from being cut down*	
	[B18] *Abram interprets the dream:*	
Abram warns of danger:	[B19] Abram warns of danger:	
because of her beauty	[because of her beauty]	
the Egyptians will kill Abram and take Sarai	the Egyptians will kill Abram and take Sarai	
Abram instructs Sarai:	[B20] Abram instructs Sarai:	[Abram had instructed her at the start of their travels:
	'[On]*ly this is the whole favor*	'This is the kindness
	[*that you must do for me*]*:*	you must do me:
	in every place [*we reach,*	at every place to which we come,
'say	say] *about me,*	say of me,
you are my sister	"*he is my brother*"	"He is my brother"'.]
so that it will go well with me	*and I will live under your protection*	
and my life will be spared	and my life will be spared	
on your account'	on your account'	
	[B21] *Sarai weeps*	
	Sarai fears lest anyone should see her	
Egyptians see Sarai's beauty	---	

Gen. 12: Egypt	1QapGen: Egypt	Gen. 20: Abimelek
	[B22] *Abram dwells five years in Egypt*	
	[B23] *Three Egyptian nobles, the chief named Hirqanos, seek Abram's wisdom and give him gifts*	
	[B24] *Abram teaches from the book of Enoch*	
	[B25] *Banquet?*	
Pharaoh's nobles see Sarai	[…]	
they report Sarai's beauty	[B26] they report Sarai's beauty *and wisdom*	
to Pharaoh	to Pharaoh *with an extended and detailed poem*	
Sarai taken to Pharaoh	[B27] Sarai taken to Pharaoh *Pharaoh admires Sarai's beauty*	Abimelek takes Sarah
	Pharaoh takes Sarai as wife	
	[B28] *Pharaoh seeks to kill Abram.*	
	Sarai says: 'He is my brother'	
Abram prospers	Abram is *spared*	
'because of her'	'because of her'	
Abram receives many gifts	---	
	[B29] *Abram and Lot weep because Sarai was taken by force*	
	[B30] *Abram prays for God to strike Pharaoh so that he cannot defile Sarai*	
God sends an affliction on	[B31] God sends an *evil spirit*	[God had afflicted Abimelek
Pharaoh and his household	to afflict Pharaoh and his	and made the women of his
because of Sarai	household	household barren]
	[B32] *Pharaoh was not able to approach Sarai*	[Abimelek had not slept with Sarah]
	[B33] *Sarai is with Pharaoh for two years* (cf. *Jub.* 13:11, 16)	
	[B34] *Pharaoh calls wisemen, wizards, and physicians, but the evil spirit afflicts them as well*	
	[B35] *Hirqanos requests Abram to come and pray for Pharaoh*	
	[B36] *Pharaoh saw Abram in a dream*	God speaks to Abimelek in a dream,
	[B37] *Lot reveals that Sarai is Abram's wife and must be sent back before Pharaoh can be healed*	and warns him that he will die for taking Abraham's wife
	[B38] *Hirqanos reports to Pharaoh*	

Gen. 12: Egypt	1QapGen: Egypt	Gen. 20: Abimelek
		Abimelek defends himself: I am innocent … they told me she is his sister
		God agrees that he is innocent, and will spare him if he restores Sarah to Abraham
Pharaoh rebukes Abram and tells him to take Sarai and leave	[B39] Pharaoh rebukes Abram and tells him to take Sarai and leave *all the provinces of Egypt* [B40] *Pharaoh asks Abram to pray for him*	Abimelek rebukes Abraham
		Abraham explains: you would have killed me; she is my half-sister; we have always used this story in our travels Abimelek gives gifts to Abraham and Sarah to prevent revenge
	[B41] *Abram lays hands on Pharaoh and prays for him*	Abraham prays for Abimelek
	The evil spirit departs [B42] *Pharaoh gives gifts to Abram*	God heals Abimelek
	[B43] *Pharaoh swears an oath that Sarai was not touched* [B44] *Pharaoh returns Sarai* [B45] *Pharaoh gives gifts to Sarai, including Hagar*	
Pharaoh expels Abram	[B46] Abram and Sarai escorted out of Egypt	

This is an extremely important text for the history of interpretation since it shares numerous similarities with later rabbinic interpretation of the biblical narrative. Here we will deal only with those features that relate to renovating the character of Abram and the purity of Sarai.

1. It was not Abram's plan. Rather, it was authorized by God through a dream. This dream about the cedar and the palm is unique to the *Genesis Apocryphon*.
2. Sarai seeks to avoid attention of other men, and is successful for five years.
3. Abram is sought out as a wise teacher, and instructs the Egyptian nobles.
4. Pharaoh takes Sarai by force. Thus, the narrative shows that Abram was powerless to stop the abduction, puts all the blame on Pharaoh, and removes the hint in Genesis 12 that Abram accepted the new situation and welcomed the wealth he received.
5. Abram weeps and prays for God to judge Pharaoh for taking Sarai by force, and to prevent Pharaoh from defiling Sarai. The weeping and praying is a standard feature in all subsequent retellings of the story.
6. Abram does not receive any wealth when Sarai is taken to Pharaoh's house.

7.   The evil spirit that afflicted Pharaoh and his household apparently made them impotent. In any case, no one was able to even approach Sarai let alone have sexual intercourse with her.

8.   Pharaoh's rebuke on Abram is considerably softened by his respectful request that Abram pray for his healing.

9.   Abram prays for Pharaoh and he is healed.

10.   Pharaoh gives gifts to Abram after the healing. Thus, Abram does not owe his wealth to the deception, as in Genesis 12, but to the pious act of praying for God's healing.

There are two concerns in all of this. First, to defend the integrity of Abram: he did not lie, he is not guilty of deception for profit, he did everything in his power to protect his wife. The concern here is to show Abram, as the father of the Israelites, as a model of piety and wisdom. Second, to defend Sarai's purity: she was the model of the chaste wife who sought to avoid the attention of other men, and she did not have sexual relations with Pharaoh nor was even touched by any of the Egyptians. The concern here is that Sarai is the mother of the Israelites. According to the Torah (Deut. 24.4), a wife cannot return to her first husband after having a second husband. If Sarai and Pharaoh consummated a marriage, then Isaac would be an unlawful child. Furthermore, she is the mother ultimately of the future priestly line, which has very strict requirements on marriage (cf. Lev. 21.7).

Both of these concerns are common in other retellings of Genesis as the following examples illustrate. *Jubilees* (13.10-15) omits mention of Abram's instruction for Sarai to say she is his sister and emphasizes instead forceful abduction by Pharaoh. Philo (*Abr.* 91–98) omits any mention of the deception, and describes Pharaoh as cruel and forcefully abducting Sarai. Throughout, Abram exhibits nobility and piety and both Abram and Sarai pray for God to help. Philo shows his special concern for the purity of the priestly line and the prophets that would descend from Abram and Sarai, stressing that God struck Pharaoh to keep Abram's marriage inviolate, 'that marriage from which was to issue not a family of a few sons and daughters, but a whole nation, and that the nation dearest of all to God, which … has received the gift of priesthood and prophecy on behalf of all mankind'. Josephus (*Ant.* 1.154-7) explains that Abram's deception was necessary because of the Egyptians' 'frenzy for women', and Abram prays for Sarai. *Targums Neofiti* and *Ps-Jonathan* both try to justify Abraham's deception, and after the episode with Abimelek, Abimelek offers proof that he has not violated Sarah.

The *Genesis Apocryphon* also enhances the character of Abram in his dealings with his nephew Lot. Genesis implies mutual conflict not only between the shepherds, but between Abram and Lot as well, and that the separation was Abram's idea: 'Then Abram said to Lot, "Let there be no strife *between you and me*, and between your herders and my herders … *Separate yourself from me* … thus they *separated from each other*"' (Gen. 13.5-11 NRSV, emphasis mine). The *Genesis Apocryphon* considerably abbreviates this account (B54), omitting any hint that Abram had anything to do with the separation by succinctly narrating: 'Lot separated from me on account of the behavior of our shepherds', and adding a brief note that Abram was distressed that his nephew had separated from him. In this it is similar to *Jub.* 13.17-18, but the *Genesis Apocryphon* also adds that Lot took all his herds with him and that Abram, like a generous uncle, gave many more to his nephew as a parting gift. It also shows Abram weeping for Lot when he is later kidnapped (cf. Josephus, *Ant.* 1.176).

The *Genesis Apocryphon* emphasizes the piety of Abram beyond Genesis by adding accounts of Abram praying to God (B30, 41), and supplying his prayers (B9, 30), and adding explicit mention of sacrifices and offerings (B51–52, 71). It particularly highlights Abram as grateful to God. When Abram returns safely to Bethel from Egypt, the *Genesis Apocryphon* adds to the brief notice in Genesis ('there Abram called on the name of the Lord', Gen. 13.4) that Abram rebuilt the altar, offered sacrifices and offerings, that he praised the name of God, blessed God, and 'gave thanks there before God for all the flocks and good things that he had given me, because he had treated me well, and because he had returned me to this land in peace', B51–53). In place of the seemingly ungrateful response of Abram to God's promise of 'great reward' – 'what will you give me, for I continue to be childless?' (Gen. 15.2) – the *Genesis Apocryphon* shows Abram humbly and gratefully acknowledging God's many blessings: 'My Lord God, my wealth and (my) flocks are vast (indeed); but why do I have all these things, (seeing that) when I die I shall depart (from this life) bereft (and) without children?' (Fitzmyer 2004: 111).

Similar to the author's treatment of the story of the Watchers, the story of Abram and Sarai in the *Genesis Apocryphon* is composed almost entirely out of shared traditions, in this case particularly with *Jubilees*. The author's main contribution has to do with embellishing details, once again especially to highlight emotional aspects and to create a lively narrative.

b. *The Beauty and Purity of Sarai*
Genesis does not describe how the Egyptian officials came to meet Abram and Sarai, but mentions only their fascination with Sarai (12.14-15), and that they give gifts to Abram because of Sarai (12.16). One could read this as implying that Sarai's beauty was renowned, and Egyptian officials came to marvel at her famed beauty. Such seems to be the understanding of Josephus (*Ant.* 1.163): 'On their arrival in Egypt all fell out as Abraham had suspected: his wife's beauty was noised abroad, insomuch that Pharaothes, the king of the Egyptians, not content with the reports of her, was fired with a desire to see her and on the point of laying hands on her'.

That Sarai's beauty surpassed that of all women – derived from Gen. 12.11-15 – is a common topos in Jewish traditions (e.g., Philo, *Abr.* 91–98), but the most remarkable expression is found in the *Genesis Apocryphon* (B26). It includes an extended poem in the style of the Song of Songs, reported by the nobles to Pharaoh, describing Sarai's physical beauty as well as her wisdom and domestic skill. The poem concludes, 'Above all women her beauty is greatest; her beauty is far above them all. Together with all this beauty there is much wisdom in her, and whatever she does with her hands is perfect' (1QapGen 20.6-8).

On the one hand, we might be tempted to find this large expansion devoted to Sarai's beauty rather curious and whimsical, but it should be noted that the author has perceptively emphasized the same point stressed in Genesis by chiastic structure (opposite).

The narrative focus of the story is apparent: the praise of Sarai's beauty, and Sarai taken to Pharaoh. Together they provide a joint focus. Positively, it plays up the motif that the patriarchal wife is the most beautiful woman, and that the patriarchs attract the attention of foreign kings. Negatively, it specifies danger to the patriarchs and to the entire promise: will Sarai's dignity and purity be marred? If she is made fertile, will it be Pharaoh's child?

A. Abram builds an altar at Bethel and calls on God's name (12.8)
  B. Abram travels by stages from Bethel to the Negeb (12.9)
    C. Famine was severe in the land (12.10)
      D. Abram travels from the Negeb to Egypt (12.10)
        E. Danger: 'you are a beautiful woman' and 'they will kill me' (12.11-12)
          F. Abram instructs Sarai 'say you are my sister' (12.13)
            G1. 'That it may go well with me because of you' (12.13)
            G2. And I might live (12.13)
                H1. The Egyptians praise Sarai's beauty to Pharaoh (12.15a)
                H2. Sarai is taken to Pharaoh (12.15b)
            G1. It went well with Abram because of her (12.16)
            G2. But the Lord afflicted Pharaoh because of Sarai (12.17)
          F. Pharaoh rebukes Abram 'why did you say, "she is my sister"'? (12.19)
        E. Protection: Pharaoh put men in charge of him (12.20)
      D. Abram travels from Egypt to the Negeb (13.1)
    C. Abram was very rich in cattle, silver, and gold (13.2)
  B. Abram travels by stages from the Negeb to Bethel (13.3)
A. Abram returns to altar at Bethel and calls on God's name (13.4)

The focus on Sarai's beauty raises a serious problem in the narrative: why would a virtuous woman be so visible that her beauty would quickly be common knowledge? The potential embarrassment is apparent in Josephus's account mentioned above. Was Sarai wantonly flaunting her beauty? If she were a humble and chaste wife keeping herself to her home, how would her beauty have become known?[50] One tradition reflected in latter rabbinic writings addresses the problem by positing that Abram tried to smuggle Sarai into Egypt hidden in a casket, but the customs guards discovered her in a search of Abram's belongings (e.g., *Gen. R.* 40.5 on Gen. 12.14). The *Genesis Apocryphon* reflects reasoning along these lines, but provides a far more satisfying solution (B21–22). As also in *Jub.* 13.11-12, the *Genesis Apocryphon* indicates that Abram and Sarai dwelt five years in Egypt without incident – apparently Sarai kept a low profile as a virtuous woman would be expected to (cf. 1 Pet. 3.3-6). The rewritten narrative in 1QapGen 19.19-23 intentionally avoids any hint that Sarai might be exposed to public gaze, for example by leaving out both Gen. 12.12 and 14. The former might imply that Abram expected the Egyptians to see her ('and when they Egyptians see you ...'), and the latter suggests that Sarai was publicly visible from their first entrance into Egypt ('When Abram entered Egypt the Egyptians saw that the woman was very beautiful'). Moreover, the *Genesis Apocryphon* adds that when she heard about the danger from lustful Egyptians 'Sarai [no longer wished] to go toward Zoan [with me, because she feared gr]eatly within her, lest any[one] should see her' (19.22-23). What draws attention to the couple is instead Abram gaining renown as a sage without peer, to which we turn in the next section.

It is possible that the presentation of Sarai in the *Genesis Apocryphon* may reflect a midrash on the ideal Israelite wife from Prov. 31.10–31 combined with Song of Songs, inspired by Gen. 12.11 ('I know well that you are a beautiful woman'). The report of the nobles about Sarai's beauty is in the form of the Song of Songs, and what is said of her corresponds to the characteristics of the ideal Israelite wife in Prov. 31.10-31.

---

50. On the ideal of a woman's domain restricted to the home, and avoiding the gaze of other men, see *4 Macc.* 18.6-7; Philo, *Spec. Leg.* 3.169; *Flacc.* 89; cf. Sarah as model of the unadorned, virtuous wife in 1 Pet. 3.1.

1.   She brings benefit to her husband (Prov. 31.11-12; 1QapGen 19.20; 20.10)
2.   She is skilled with her hands and works hard (Prov. 31.13-22; 1QapGen 20.7-8)
3.   Her husband is prominent in public (Prov. 31.23; 1QapGen 19.24-25)
4.   She keeps to the household (Prov. 31.27; 1QapGen 19.23)
5.   She is wise (Prov. 31.26; 1QapGen 20.7)
6.   She surpasses all women (Prov. 31.29; 1QapGen 20.7)
7.   She is especially beautiful (Song of Songs; 1QapGen 20.2-7; cf. Prov. 31.30)

Likewise it is also possible that the use of a cedar and date palm to symbolize the patriarch and his wife in Abram's dream (B17) may involve a midrash on the Song of Songs, where these two trees represent the lover and his beloved (Song 5.15; 7.7-8) and Ps. 92.13-15 [Eng. 92.12-14] where these two trees characterize the righteous who 'still produce fruit in old age'.[51]

c. *The Wisdom of Abram*
1QapGen provides an ingenious and highly significant solution to the question of how Sarai comes to the attention of Pharaoh's nobles, but it has been obscured by a couple errors of transcription that have been replicated since the *editio princeps*. The following translation of the crucial passage by Fitzmyer well reflects the original transcription by Avigad and Yadin, followed with only minor variations by all other translations known to me. I have indicated the disputed words by underlining.

> [I stayed there for five years], and after those five years three of the *nobles* of Egyp[t came] to me [   ] of *Pharaoh* Zoan concerning [my] words and concerning my wife. They gave [me many gifts and as]ked of m[e] kindness, wisdom, and truth. So I read before them the [book] of the words of Enoch. (1QapGen 19.23–25; Fitzmyer 1971)

In his recent revised edition (FGA[3]), Fitzmyer corrected the first underlined word to 'at the end of', and changed the third underlined word to 'knowledge' (still incorrect), but the critical second error remains. By this reading, Pharaoh's nobles are attracted by the fame of both Abram's wisdom *and* Sarai's beauty.

This reading, however, is incorrect. The three disputed words should be read: 'at the end of', 'my wisdom' , and 'writing'.[52] Thus,

ולסוף חמש שניא אלן   23

24 [אתו] תלתת גברין מן רברבי מֹצרי[ן   ]ת פֹרֹר[ו] צען על מלי ועל חֹכמתי והווא יהבין

25 ל]י   [הֹן סֹפֹרא ֹאֹחכמֹתֹא וקושטא וקרית קודמיהון לכֹתֹב מלי חֹנֹוֹך

23. ... And **at the end of** these five years

24. [came] three men of the nobles of Egyp[t ...] of Phara[oh] Zoa[n] on account of my words and **my wisdom**. They gave

25. [*to me great gifts and sought for me to teach?*] **to them writing** (or 'reading'), wisdom, and truth. And I read before them the [book] of the words of [*En*]och.

51. See discussion and references in Gevirtz 1992: 237–39.
52. This reading is based on ABMC photograph GAF_19_970_A, 1994 series.

In support of this reading, a similar list of terms is found in the *Aramaic Levi Docu-ment*.[53]

ראש כל עובדיכון יהוי קושטא ועד עלמ[א] י[הו]י קאים עמכון צדקתא <u>וקוש</u>[טא

וכען בני <u>ספר</u> ומוסר <u>וחוכמה</u> אפי/י ל_ביכון ותהוי הוכמתא עמכון ליקר עלם

'Let the chief of all your deeds be truth, and fore[ver] m[ay it b]e established with you. Justice and **tru[th**] ... And now, my children, teach reading and **writing**, and instruction, and **wisdom** to your children, and may wisdom be with you for etermal glory'.[54]

With these corrections, the passage makes clear that the focus is Abram's wisdom (the reference to Abram's 'words' was previously ambiguous). The nobles do not come to see Abram's wife, but come bringing gifts to hear Abram's words and his wisdom, presumably because he already has a famous reputation as a wise man (perhaps modeled on the Solomon and Queen of Sheba story, 1 Kgs 4.29-30; 10.1-13; Fitzmyer 2004: 191). Apparently while feasting with Abram, however, they catch a glimpse of Sarai, and depart more captivated with his wife.

The motif of Abram as a wise teacher is extra with regard to Genesis and *Jubilees*, but it is common in Jewish tradition from the Second Temple period on (see Wacholder 1964: 54). Josephus reflects a very similar tradition that Abraham conferred with and taught the Egyptian intellectuals:

> Abraham consorted with the most learned of the Egyptians, whence his virtue and repu-tation became still more conspicuous ... Thus gaining their admiration at these meetings as a man of extreme sagacity ... he introduced them to arithmetic and transmitted to them the laws of astronomy. For before the coming of Abraham the Egyptians were ignorant of these sciences, which thus traveled from the Chaldaeans into Egypt, whence they passed to the Greeks. (Josephus, *Ant.* 1.165-66)

The *Genesis Apocryphon* makes a similar point about Abram's superiority in the account of the healing of Pharaoh (B34–42). All the wise men, magicians, and healers of Egypt fail and flee, and Pharaoh must turn to Abram for healing. This episode resonates both with Moses' triumph over the wise men, sorcerers, and magicians of Egypt (Exod. 7.11, 22; 8.7, 18) and Daniel as the wise counselor who can interpret the king's dream where his enchanters, magicians, and sorcerers fail.

In the *Genesis Apocryphon*, the motif of Abram's wisdom accomplishes two things. (1) It provides an explanation for how Sarai came to the attention of the officials, thus defending her purity (cf. Josephus). (2) It promotes Abram as a sage of divine mys-teries.

d. *Revelation*

In addition to the motif of Abram as wise, the *Genesis Apocryphon* emphasizes Abram as a recipient and transmitter of divine revelation. On the one hand, Abram is the one entrusted with the records of revelation from before the flood (cf. *Jub.* 12.25-27).

---

53. This was kindly pointed out to me by Robert Kugler.

54. Kugler 1996: 119–120 cites this as *Ar. Levi* (Cairo Geniza; Cambridge e 3b–f 23) 85–88 with overlaps in 4QLevi[a] ar (4Q213) 6 i–ii 7–9. The reference according to DJD 22 is 4QLevi[a] ar is 1 i 7–9 (Stone and Greenfield 1996: 9); for a critical text of the Geniza fragments see *ALD* 13.3–4, 15–16 in Greenfield, Stone and Eshel 2004: 102–107, 207–209.

Abram reads to the Egyptian nobles from a 'book of the words of Enoch' (B24).[55] On the other hand, Abram is also a direct recipient of revelation. Beyond the vision mentioned in Gen. 15.1 (B94), the *Genesis Apocryphon* adds a dream (B17) and a 'vision of the night' (B61), neither of which have a counterpart in *Jubilees*. The revelatory language is similar to that in Daniel ('dreamed a dream'; 'saw a dream'; 'behold'; 'vision of the night'; 1QapGen 19.14; 21.8; Dan. 2.1, 19, 43; 4.15; 7.7).

The dream added to the story of Abram and Sarai's sojourn in Egypt (B17, cf. Gen. 12.11-13) is unique to the *Genesis Apocryphon* and especially noteworthy (see Gevirtz 1992). It is a 'symbolic dream' comparable to those interpreted by Joseph (Genesis 40–41) and Daniel (Daniel 2, 4), but here, Abram interprets his own dream (B18). Thus, in addition to justifying Abram's ruse, the addition of this dream portrays Abram as both recipient of revelation and interpreter of dreams like Joseph and Daniel. The additions should probably be regarded as exegetical: encouraged by the reference to Abram as a prophet in Gen. 20.7 and the analogy of a vision in Gen. 15.1, the author may have inferred that Abram's statement 'I know' in Gen. 12.11 and the notice of divine speech to Abram in Gen. 13.15 also imply visions.

Unlike in the Noah cycle where the *Genesis Apocryphon* adds extensive visions completely extraneous to the Genesis story, the added dreams of Abram are directly related to the narrative of Genesis (the imminent danger in Egypt, and the covenant of Genesis 15) – at least in what survives. Nevertheless, the Noah and Abram sections are tied together by appeal to Enochic revelation. If Abram is renowned as learned in divine mysteries transmitted from Enoch, it raises the question whether in what is lost there might also have been revelations of the future history of Israel and/or eschatological judgment attributed to Abram (cf. *2 Baruch* 57 which associates revelation about divine law and eschatology to Abram's time). This remains unknown, but it is clear that the motif of revelation is one of the major concerns of the author of the *Genesis Apocryphon*.

e. *Abram as Patriarch*

Abram functions in greatly expanded roles in the *Genesis Apocryphon*. First, as we have noted, he is portrayed as a renowned teacher of wisdom (1QapGen 19.24-25; cf. 20.19-21). Second, although Abram is not explicitly called a prophet as he is in Gen. 20.7, this passage has influenced the enhanced presentation of Abram as a prophet who heals and receives revelation (B34–42; B17, 24, 61, 94). Third, it also seems that the *Genesis Apocryphon* intends to show Abram as priest. Genesis records that Abram built altars at Bethel and Hebron and called on the name of the Lord at the altar at Bethel before and after the sojourn to Egypt (Gen. 12.8; 13.3-4; 13.18). There is no explicit mention of sacrifice in these three instances. *Jubilees* expands the two accounts with the altar at Bethel (*Jub.* 13.9, 16), explicitly mentioning that Abram offered burnt offerings and describing his praise to God. The *Genesis Apocryphon* is closely related to the account in *Jubilees* with some significant verbal overlaps in the two accounts, but also some significant differences.

---

55. The motif of Abraham as revealing Enochic knowledge to the Egyptians is also found in Ps-Eupolemus; Wacholder (1974: 288–90) posits some type of contact between Enochite works (*Enoch, Jubilees*, and especially the *Genesis Apocryphon* on this point) and Ps-Eupolemus, who he believes was a Samaritan priest.

Table 13. *Abram as Priest.*

1.	Genesis Apocryphon	Genesis (NRSV)	Jubilees (VBJ, modified)
B8	19 [7] and I built there an altar and I called there on [the name] of Go[d]	12 [8b] and there he built an altar to the Lord and invoked the name of the Lord	13 [8] ... he had initially built the altar on this mountain – he called on the name of the Lord:
B9	19 [7-8] and said, '**You are** [my] Go[d, the et]er[nal God ...] ... eternal Lord ...'		'**You my God, are the eternal God**'.
			13 [9] He offered to the Lord a sacrifice on the altar so that he would be with him and not abandon him throughout his entire lifetime.
B10	19 [8] Until now I had not (or you have not) reached the holy mountains;		

2.	Genesis Apocryphon	Genesis (NRSV)	Jubilees (VBJ, modified)
	20 [34]–21 [1] ... until I reached Bethel, the place where I (had) built the altar,	13 [3-4] ... Bethel ... to the place where he had made an altar at the first;	(13 [15]) He went to the place where he had first pitched his tent – at the location of the altar, with Ai on the east and Bethel on the west.
B51	21 [1] and I built it once again.		
B52	21 [2] I **offered upon it burnt offerings** and a meal offering to **God Most High**,		Jub 13 [16] He **offered upon it a burnt offering** and called on the name of the Lord: 'You, Lord, **Most High God**, are my God forever and ever'.
B53	21 [2-4] and I called there on the name of the Lord of the ages, and I praised the **name of God**, and I **blessed** [3] God. I gave thanks there before God for all the flocks and the good things which he had given me, because he had done good to me, and because **he had brought me back** [4] **to this land in peace.** *vacat*	13 [4] and there Abram called on the name of the Lord.	Jub 13 [15-16] He **blessed** the Lord his God **who had brought him back in peace.** [16] During this forty-first jubilee ... he returned to this place. He offered upon it a burnt offering and called on the **name of the Lord** ...

3.	Genesis Apocryphon	Genesis (NRSV)	Jubilees
B70	21 [20] I built there an altar	13 [8b] and there he built an altar to the Lord.	
B71	21 [20] and on it I offered a holocaust and a meal offering to God Most High. Cf. 21:1–4		

To the second account (B51–53), the *Genesis Apocryphon* adds 'and a meal offering' to the burnt offering mentioned in *Jubilees*. In the third account (B70–71), the *Genesis Apocryphon* also adds the mention of Abram offering 'a burnt offering and a meal offering' that is not in *Jubilees*. This suggests that the *Genesis Apocryphon* has a special interest in explicitly showing Abram offering burnt offerings together with meal offerings.

This makes it all the more interesting that in the first account (B8–10) where the *Genesis Apocryphon* again closely corresponds to *Jubilees*, the *Genesis Apocryphon* lacks the mention of burnt offering added in *Jubilees* – Abram merely praises God there. Instead, the *Genesis Apocryphon* has a unique, enigmatic addition: 'Until now I had not reached the holy mountains' so he continued to the south. Probably this is meant as a reference to Jerusalem, some twenty miles to the south of Bethel, which Abram is shown as visiting later (Salem identified as Jerusalem; on this passage *Gen. R.* 39.15 similarly comments that Abram 'drew a course and journeyed toward the [future] site of the Temple'). In comparison with *Jubilees*, this note in the *Genesis Apocryphon* also seems to function in some unclear way to explain why Abram did not offer sacrifices at an altar he just built, but only praise: perhaps having to do with deference to Jerusalem in some way. Only after returning from Egypt – implicitly having at least passed through Jerusalem – does Abram rebuild the altar at Bethel and for the first time offer sacrifices. Perhaps the sense of disjuncture is a result from the use of another source not fully integrated. In any case, although the *Genesis Apocryphon* does not provide the extensive sacrificial details as with regard to Noah's sacrifices, it seems that the author does exhibit a special interest similarly to portray Abram as priest and sensitive to priestly concerns.

Fourth, with less certainty, there are possible hints that the *Genesis Apocryphon* may seek to incorporate royal overtones as well into its presentation of Abram. The motif of Abraham as king is attested already in the LXX of Gen. 23.6 ('a king from God among us'), and expounded by Philo (*Quaest. in Gen.* 4.76) and Josephus (*Ant.* 1.159); it is also found in later rabbinic sources (e.g., *Gen. R.* 55.1). In the *Genesis Apocryphon*, the possible reflections of such a motif are enhancements to the narrative of Genesis to the effect that Abram hosts a covenant meal to solemnize an alliance with three neighboring prominent men, and leads forth an army of 318 select men to battle the Mesopotamian kings. Furthermore, the king of Sodom respectfully addresses Abram as 'my lord' (B72, 85, 91; cf. Gen. 14.21).

This tendency seems to be reinforced by allusions to the exploits of key figures. Like Jacob, he takes his family to Egypt during a time of famine because he 'heard there was grain in Egypt' (1QapGen. 19.10; almost a literal translation of Gen. 42.2). Like Moses only he can bring relief from plagues on Egypt (see 1QapGen 20.16-21, 24–25, 28–29), and in the end he plunders Egypt. Like Joseph and Daniel he interprets dreams and shows himself superior to the king's advisers. Like Solomon he is renowned for his great wisdom so that dignitaries come to learn from him and bestow gifts on him. Thus, as patriarch of all Israel, Abram prefigures all the leading roles and figures of Israel: priests, prophets, kings, sages, and scribes.

f. *Chronology and Calendar*
The *Genesis Apocryphon* shows special concern to work out the chronology of Abram's travels and especially the length of his stay in Egypt. This is reflected in four passages.

1.   Before going to Egypt, Abram settled in Hebron at the time it was built, and stayed there two years (B12). This passage is virtually identical to *Jub*. 13.10.

2.   Abram and Sarai dwelled in Egypt for five years before Pharaoh abducted Sarai, which happened at the time when Zoan was built (B22). The chronological point is the same as *Jub*. 13.11–12, but the *Genesis Apocryphon* works it into its additional story about three Egyptian nobles coming to be taught by Abram.

3.   Sarai lived in Pharaoh's palace for two years (B33). There is no passage corresponding to this in *Jubilees*, but the two-year period is assumed in its chronological notes (they enter Egypt in AM 1956, live there five years before Sarai is abducted, and return to Canaan seven years after entering Egypt in AM 1963; *Jub*. 13.11-12, 16).

4.   God recounts Abram's travels: 'See, ten years have passed since the day that you departed from Haran: you spent two here, seven in Egypt, and one since you returned from Egypt' (B95). There is no corresponding passage in *Jubilees*, but it reflects the same chronology in its dating of events (cf. *Jub*. 13.8, 10-12, 15-16; 14.1).

In what survives of the Abram cycle, there is no indication that the *Genesis Apocryphon* shares the special interest of *Jubilees* in religious calendar (that is, there is no apparent concern to associate Abram's sacrifices with particular festivals) or the larger chronological framework of systematically dating all events. It is interested more basically in issues of solving chronological problems, and it agrees with the solution in *Jubilees* to a famous problem in biblical chronology (Wacholder 1964): how long did Abram spend in Egypt? One tendency was to minimize the amount of time Abram spent in Egypt – and Sarai in Pharaoh's house! – to a very short period, and this is the predominant view found in the later rabbis. A dominant view during the Hellenistic period was to emphasize a lengthy stay in Egypt, during which Abram instructed the Egyptians. One reading of the scriptural data supports the former view: from Gen. 12.4 and 16.16 one can gather that it was ten years between Abram's departure from Haran until the conception of Isaac, which according to Gen. 16.3 was 'after Abram had lived ten years in the land of Canaan'. This would allow no more than a few months in Egypt. But Gen. 16.3 is ambiguous: it could mean ten years after Abram had first entered Canaan, allowing the view that a lengthy stay in Egypt is included in the ten years.

The solution represented in *Jubilees* and the *Genesis Apocryphon* follows the latter view, and works out the details in relation to other scriptural data. On the analogy of the Jacob story (probably encouraged by the similar phrase 'for the famine was severe in the land' Gen. 12.10 cf. 43.1) it was inferred that the famine in Canaan also lasted seven years, and that this involved two years of family separation and five years together (Gen. 45.6; the parallel between the two stories is also attested in later rabbinic writings, without deriving the chronology from it, e.g., *Gen. R.* 40.6 and *Tanh.* Gen. 3.12 on Gen. 14.1). One other scriptural datum was pulled in: that Hebron was built seven years before Zoan in Egypt (Num. 13.22). By associating the seizure of Sarai with the construction of Zoan (apparently by means of the polemic against the 'princes of Zoan' from Isa. 19.11-13) is posited a two-year stay of Abram in Hebron.

All of this reflects a highly creative approach to the chronological details in Genesis. Even though the commonalities with *Jubilees* reveal that the solution is not original to the *Genesis Apocryphon*, the unique features of this work – especially the summary by God which may betray polemical concern – indicate that the author is vitally interested in the matter.

g. *Geography*

A special concern for geographic details, and especially land boundaries, is one of the features that ties together the Noah and Abram cycles in the *Genesis Apocryphon*.[56] First, whereas the *Genesis Apocryphon* seems to have followed *Jubilees* with regard to the land allotments among Noah's descendents (A52–58), it now uniquely applies these to Abram. Thus, the *Genesis Apocryphon* assumes the Nile as the boundary to Egypt, the 'land of the sons of Ham' (B15). Whereas Genesis merely includes God's instruction to Abram to look over the land and to walk through it (Gen. 13.14-15, 17), the *Genesis Apocryphon* adds narrations about Abram carrying these out. Betraying local knowledge, the author uniquely specifies that Abram went north of Bethel and climbed Ramath-Hazor – the highest peak in the area – to survey the land (B64). The land he views follows the description of the land promised to Abram in Gen. 15.18 ('from the river of Egypt to … the river Euphrates'). Then Abram walks through the land (B67), symbolically taking possession of it. The boundaries are those of the territory allotted to Arpachshad (*Jub.* 9.4; 1QapGen 17.11-15): from the Nile northward along the Mediterranean coast to the Taurus mountains in the north, then east to the Euphrates, and south-east along the Euphrates to the Persian Gulf, then along the coast of the Arabian Peninsula clockwise to the Gulf of Aqaba, and then south around Sinai back to the Nile.

Second, both in this narrative and the narrative about the war of the kings (particularly 1QapGen 21.23-30; 22.4-5, 22.7-10), the author logically works out practical matters of geography (e.g., moving Abram to the highest peak in the area -- Ramath-Hazor – from which to survey the land; the route of the kings and Abram's pursuit) and contemporary identifications of geography ('Gihon River' = the Nile; the 'Taurus mountains' as an east–west border; 'Red Sea' = the Persian Gulf and Indian Ocean; 'Reed Sea' = the present-day Red Sea and/or Gulf of Aqaba; Shinar as Babylon; Ellasar as Cappadocia (Alexander 1988: 105–106).

Third, the author explicitly identifies Salem with Jerusalem, and the Vale of Shaveh with the Valley of Beth Ha-Kerem near Jerusalem (1QapGen 22.13-14, cf. Gen. 14.17-18). This reflects a special concern to associate Abram with Jerusalem (see also 1QapGen 19.8, 'until now I had not reached the holy mountains'), a motif common in early Jewish writings. It is possible that this is anti-Samaritan polemic, but not necessarily.

h. *Characterization*

As in the Noah cycle, 1QapGen fleshes out the characters of Abram and Sarai with tender details about emotions and inner psychology (Nickelsburg 1998: 148, 155–56): Abram was 'alarmed' by his dream and Sarai 'wept' at his words and was afraid that anyone should see her (B18, 21). Abram 'wept bitterly' over the seizure of Sarai, 'in sorrow … as tears ran down' his face he 'begged for mercy' from God and lodged a complaint against Pharaoh (Fitzmyer 2004: 202 notes the legal connotations to this),

---

56. See Fitzmyer 2004: 171–78, 180–83, 221–28; also Scott 1997; 2002.

then 'wept and was silent' (B29, 39). He was 'grieved' over the parting of Lot and 'wept' over his capture, then 'gathered his courage' to rescue him (B60, 84, 85). That the nobles extolled Sarai's beauty in a poem, and Pharaoh 'desired her greatly' and 'marvelled at all her beauty' (B26, 27) also exhibits this psychological interest in a manner that borders on the erotic, as also in Bitenosh's reference to orgasmic pleasure with Lamech in defence of her faithfulness (1QapGen 2.9-10; Nickelsburg 1998: 148).

7. Relationship to Genesis

What did the text of Genesis that the author regarded as Scripture look like? How did the author treat the scriptural text? How much of the story of Genesis is represented, and in what order? These questions can reveal information not only about the purpose of the *Genesis Apocryphon*, but also about the nature and status of Genesis at the time.

Compared with Genesis, the *Genesis Apocryphon* is mostly a relatively free paraphrase that is often expansive but sometimes abbreviated. At times, however, one finds in the *Genesis Apocryphon* short passages of fairly literal translation of the Hebrew text of Genesis in a style similar to that of the Aramaic targums (see Fitzmyer 2004: 38–45, and especially the list p. 39). In these cases, it shows agreements with the SP and the LXX in some places where these differ from the MT (see the analysis in VanderKam 1978; 1977: 278–79). For example, against the spelling of Ararat (אררט) in the MT, it is spelled with a *he* in SP (הררט), 1QapGen 10.12 (הוררט), and 4QGenComm[a] (4Q252) 1.10, and this spelling seems to be assumed by the LXX as well (see also 1QIsa[a] 37.38). As VanderKam has argued, what was Scripture for the author of 1QapGen was probably an old Palestinian text of Genesis that is characterized by harmonistic expansions and editorial work, similar to what served as the basis of the SP.

In its retelling, the *Genesis Apocryphon* leaves out little of the content of Genesis (see Table 1). There are a few omissions in the Noah story: there is no mention of the sending out of the birds from the ark (Gen. 8.6-12, cf. 1QapGen 10.11-13) as also in *Jubilees*, and it includes none of the mini narratives interspersed in the genealogies (e.g., of Nimrod, Gen. 10.8-12); it also probably omits mention of Noah's drunkenness and Ham's shameful behavior (Gen. 9.21-27; cf. 1QapGen 12.13), and the story of the Tower of Babel (Gen. 11.1-9). Almost nothing is missing from the Abraham story, although there are small omissions such as the statement that the Egyptians saw Sarai when they entered Egypt (Gen. 12.14); the *Genesis Apocryphon* instead emphasizes that Sarai escaped notice for five years (1QapGen 19.19-23).

Moreover, from what is extant, the *Genesis Apocryphon* almost invariably follows the order of Genesis. All of the close to 70 fairly literal translations from Genesis occur in the same sequence as in Genesis.[57] Even where the *Genesis Apocryphon* engages in elaborate reworking of Genesis, it also generally follows the order of Genesis. This is most clearly seen in the story of Abraham. It contains much additional material, including a lengthy description of Sarai's beauty and dreams by Abram, but the story unfolds in precisely the order of the Genesis narrative with only a couple of minor cases of dislocation for the purpose of narrative anticipation: Lot's wealth is

---

57. See Table 1, and see the list of most occurrences in Fitzmyer 2004: 39; to these add 1QapGen 6.23; 11.11, 18; 12.1, 9, 10, and probably omit 21.21.

introduced earlier to clarify that it was gained in Egypt, along with a wife [see A47–50]; and Abram's Amorite friends are introduced before the story of the war of the kings to prepare for their assistance of Abram in rescuing Lot [see A73 and A74–86].

The story of Noah is much more fragmentary and includes some very extended additions, but similarly there seem to be few exceptions from a tendency to follow the order of the narrative in Genesis. The *Genesis Apocryphon* relates the story of the sons of God episode (A1, cf. Gen. 6.1-3) before that of the birth of Noah (A2, cf. Gen. 5.28-29). Also, the *Genesis Apocryphon* harmonizes the two references to the birth of Noah's sons (A15), and probably also the two references to God's decision to destroy humanity (A20).

Another example of dislocation is really a case of harmonization. The genealogy of Noah's sons in Genesis 10 is harmonized with the genealogy of Shem in Genesis 11, and presented before the story of Noah's vineyard (A42–45, cf. Gen. 9.20). This is to present the genealogy at the point when Noah's sons and future progeny are introduced in Gen. 9.18-19, and the order of sons is rearranged to harmonize with Gen. 9.18 (Shem, Ham, Japheth), which reflects the author's understanding of the birth order of the sons. The author thus avoids reduplication, and achieves a better narrative progression. He solves awkwardness in the narrative of Genesis by separating genealogies from the division of the land, and clarifies what he regards as the correct order of Noah's sons. There are similarities with *Jubilees* in these matters, but also independence.

One dislocation (A32, 34) is remarkable, because it is one of very few cases in the *Genesis Apocryphon* where the story-line of Genesis itself is radically changed. The *Genesis Apocryphon* rearranges the events after the flood so that Noah builds an altar and offers sacrifices (A32–34) *before* he exits from the ark (A35), in contradiction of Genesis 8 and *Jubilees* 6, and all known traditions. The text is too fragmentary to be certain of the purpose of this rearrangement, but given the usual practice of the *Genesis Apocryphon*, it is reasonable to assume that such departure reflects special interest of the author (see p. 70 above).

With regard to the relationship to Genesis, it is necessary to distinguish between the Noah and Abram sections: these treat Genesis in a somewhat different manner. Although there is a roughly similar amount of material surviving from each section, there are very few examples of translation of Genesis in the Noah story (Fitzmyer, 2004: 39, lists 1QapGen 10.12 and 12.13; to this should be added 6.23; 11.11, 18; 12.1, 9, 10), but many in the Abraham section (Fitzmyer lists 63, although a few of these do not qualify). The Abraham section in general stays much closer to Genesis than the Noah section. Furthermore, the use of the divine names is sharply different between the Noah and Abraham sections (see p. 97 below). We should, however, subdivide each of these and distinguish four sections in the *Genesis Apocryphon* that relate somewhat differently to the scriptural text.

1.   The birth of Noah. This extensive story is completely extraneous to Genesis. It is really an expansive rewriting of *1 Enoch* 106–107, only loosely connected to the brief notice in Gen. 5.28-29 and the story of the sons of God in Gen. 6.1-5. Covering over five columns in 1QapGen, it is about 3000% longer than the related text in Genesis. There is no translation of Genesis.

2.   The book of Noah. This follows Genesis 6–11 generally in order but with some rearrangement and additions derived from Genesis, some significant

omissions, as well as minor and substantial haggadic additions both by the author and from other sources, specifically *Jubilees*. Covering about twelve columns in 1QapGen, it represents an expansion of about 250–300% in relation to Genesis. There are eight brief passages that are translations from Genesis.

3. Abram up to the settlement in Canaan. This section follows Genesis 12–13 quite closely and with more translation from Genesis (about 22 short passages). It includes some minor additions derived from other scriptural passages, some abbreviation, as well as minor and substantial haggadic additions both by the author and from other sources, specifically *Jubilees*. Covering about four columns in 1QapGen, it represents an expansion of about 350–400% in relation to Genesis.

4. Abram and the war with the kings to the covenant. This section follows Gen. 14.1–15.4 (where it is cut off) very closely, leaving out almost nothing and including about 40 passages that are translations from Genesis. There are no substantial haggadic expansions, so that this section – a little over a column surviving in 1QapGen – represents an expansion of only about 130–40% in relation to Genesis. It is also set apart from the other sections by its abrupt switch to narration in the third person instead of first person by the various patriarchs. Fitzmyer (2004: 229) conjectures that perhaps the strange content of these chapters explains the lack of expansion, but this seems unlikely. There was certainly a rich body of tradition already surrounding the mysterious Melchizedek story (e.g., 11QMelchizedek) that could easily have found a home here.

Taken together, the different character of these four sections strongly indicates different uses of source material. We need to consider this next.

8. *Relationship to Other Ancient Texts and Traditions*

One of the most vexing puzzles with regard to the *Genesis Apocryphon* is sorting out its relationship to other ancient texts. There are especially striking similarities with *1 Enoch* and *Jubilees*. The question is whether these are to be explained by direct textual relations, use of common textual sources, or more general common traditions.

a. 1 Enoch

The story of the birth of Noah and the Watchers in the *Genesis Apocryphon* (A2–11) tells essentially the same story as told in *1 Enoch* 106–7, and with the same structure: that Noah at birth exhibited extraordinary traits, causing Lamech to fear that his son was sired by the Watchers, but his grandfather Enoch reveals the truth about both the Watchers and Noah. Actual verbal similarities are minor but significant (refer to Table 1 for references):

*   'Lamech was frightened' that Noah's birth was 'from the Watchers ... Holy Ones' (A4)
*   'I Lamech ran to Methuselah my father' (A6)
*   'And when Methuselah heard' (A7)

- Enoch revealed that the sin of the angels took place 'in the days of Jared, my father' (A8)
- Enoch reassured 'in truth not in lies' that Noah is Lamech's son (A8)
- Enoch told Methuselah 'Go, tell your son Lamech' (A9)
- Enoch described Noah: 'his eyes shone like the su[n]' (A9)
- Enoch revealed a 'mystery' (A9)
- 'And when Methuselah heard' Enoch's message he related it to Lamech (A10)
- The message was communicated 'in secret' (A10)

But there are also the following main differences: in the *Genesis Apocryphon*, the story is narrated by Lamech rather than Enoch, and it is overall several times longer, due especially to a great expansion of Enoch's oracle and the addition of an emotional exchange between Lamech and Bitenosh, and a conclusion by Lamech. These differences seem to be related to special interests of the author of the *Genesis Apocryphon* also evidenced in the Abraham cycle: to let patriarchs speak in their own voice and to explore emotional responses (see Nickelsburg 1998). There is also a minor detail shared with *Jubilees*: Lamech's wife was named Bitenosh (*Jub.* 4.28). As Nickelsburg has argued, there is no need to posit a source other than *1 Enoch*, adapted and expanded by means of other traditions and the author's own special interests (Nickelsburg 1998: 155, 157–58; 2001: 76).

Beyond the birth of Noah story, the *Genesis Apocryphon* also shares with *1 Enoch* the motif that Noah had a vision in his 500th year (*1 En.* 60.1; cf. 1QapGen 6.9-22), although the content is different: in *1 Enoch* it is about eschatological judgment, and in the *Genesis Apocryphon* it is about the sin of the Watchers. This looks secondary in *1 Enoch*, because it is adapted to Enoch, and may well point to the use of a common source.

Another feature pointing to the use of common source material with *1 Enoch* in the Noah section is the peculiar use of divine titles. The divine titles in the Noah cycle correspond to a remarkable degree to those favored in *1 Enoch*, especially 'Great Holy One' (5× in 1QapGen; 4× in the *Book of Watchers*, 1× in the *Dream Visions*, 3× in the *Epistle of Enoch*; see Nickelsburg 2001: 42–43). In the Abraham cycle, however, there is almost a completely different pattern of divine titles. Two features are especially notable. (1) The term אלהא ('God') is used frequently in the Abraham cycle (8×) in place of YHWH in Genesis, but it is never used in the Noah cycle. (2) The title 'God Most High' from the Melchizedek episode in Genesis 14.18-22 is prominent in the Abram cycle (9×) but rare (1×) in the Noah cycle.

b. Jubilees

More difficult is the matter of the relationship between the *Genesis Apocryphon* and *Jubilees*. There are especially close similarities between the *Genesis Apocryphon* and *Jubilees* with regard to major additions in the Noah story (refer to Table 1 for references):

- Noah's sacrifice after the flood is said to be for atonement, and the procedures are detailed, drawn from Levitical laws of sacrifice (A33)
- Noah observes the law about fruit trees, according to a distinctive interpretation (A47)

- Noah divides land among his sons (A52–55), and Noah's sons divide land among their sons (A56–58). In both cases, boundaries are described, and many details are similar: e.g., the Tina River, mountains of Asshur, etc.

These often involve significant patterns of verbal similarities. There are also numerous minor similarities of detail and wording (see also the analysis by VanderKam 1977: 142–98, 278–79):

- Lamech's wife is named Bitenosh (A5)
- Noah's wife is named Imzera (A14)
- 'Creeping things' (Gen. 6.7) is translated as 'wild beasts' (A20)
- Noah enters the ark on the sixteenth day of the second month (A26; cf. Gen. 7.7, 10-11, 13)
- The ark lands on 'one of the mountains' of Hurarat (A31), specified in *Jubilees* (5.28) to be Mount Lubar. This identification is not found in any biblical version or the targums, although the term occurs in two other Qumran texts, *Pseudo-Daniel* (4Q244 8 3) and the *Book of Giants* (6Q8 26 1) (Fitzmyer 2004: 161). The *Genesis Apocryphon* looks secondary to the narrative of *Jubilees*, because it later introduces Mount Lubar as the location where Noah plants his vineyard – as also in *Jubilees* (1QapGen 12.13 cf. *Jub.* 7.1) – but without the context of *Jubilees* that Noah stays at the mountain where the ark rests, and is buried there (*Jub.* 7.17; 10.15).
- Noah's sacrifice after the flood atones for the earth (A32)
- The wording of the instructions about food: 'I give to you … everything for food' (A39)
- Shem is the eldest son (A43)
- Arpachshad 'was born (passive) … two years after the flood' (A43)
- Omission of Shem's age (A43)
- Noah planted a vineyard on Mount Lubar (A46)
- 'And Shem … divided among his sons, and … first … for Elam' (A56)
- 'And Japheth divided … among his sons … first … for Gomer' (A57)

In the Abraham material, there are no major additions in common between the *Genesis Apocryphon* and *Jubilees*, but there are again numerous minor similarities in detail and wording.

- Abram's prayer: 'You are my God, the eternal God' (B9)
- Abram traveled 'south' (B11)
- Abram 'reached Hebron' and 'dwelt there two years'; 'At that time Hebron was built' (B12)
- Lot is specified as the son of Abram's brother (B47)
- On the altar at Bethel, Abram 'offered upon it burnt offerings … to God Most High' (B52)
- Abram 'blessed God' who 'had brought (him) back … in peace' (B53)
- 'Lot parted from' Abram (B54)
- Lot 'dwelt' 'in Sodom' (B58)
- Abram was distressed that his nephew Lot 'had separated from him' (B60)
- God instructed Abram to look from 'the place where you are dwelling' (B63)

- God promised Abram that his 'descendants will be innumerable' (B65)
- 'The king of Sodom … fled' (B79)
- A survivor told Abram 'that his nephew Lot … had been captured' (B82)
- The king of Sodom 'approached' Abram, addressed him as 'lord Abram' and requested he return the captives 'whom you rescued' (B91)

There are also some more general but distinctive motifs in common:

- Abram was in Egypt five years before Pharaoh took Sarai (B22)
- Abram was renowned for his wisdom (B23)
- Abram studied and transmitted the 'book of the words of Enoch' (B24)
- Sarai was with Pharaoh two years (B33)
- Abram's tour of the land is similar to the description of Shem's boundaries (B67)
- the chronology of Abram's travels (B95)

But there are some very significant differences. Besides material in one and not in the other, there are a number of places where features that have a point in *Jubilees* are found in the *Genesis Apocryphon*, but without a meaningful context. (1) The *Genesis Apocryphon* includes numerous chronological details in common with *Jubilees*, in both the Noah and Abraham stories, but lacks the larger chronological framework which is such an integral part of *Jubilees*. (2) In 1QapGen 11.17, the wording 'I give to you … everything for food of the greenery' seems secondary to the condensed paraphrase in *Jubilees*, but with the change of a preposition to make a very different point: the *Genesis Apocryphon* omits the permission to eat meat. (3) Both have stories showing Noah observing the law of fruit trees, but whereas it is well integrated in *Jubilees*, with an implicit midrash on Gen. 9.20 and an explicit discussion of the law, the *Genesis Apocryphon* lacks these features and shows little interest in the law, focusing instead on the festival of the first day of the first month. Other aspects of this narrative appear to confirm the secondary nature of this story in the *Genesis Apocryphon*. The time references ('fourth', 'fifth' years) depend on the *Jubilees* chronological scheme of jubilees and weeks of years, which is lacking from the *Genesis Apocryphon* (*Jub.* 7.1-2 cf. 1QapGen 12.13-15). Also, it seems unlikely that there was an antecedent for 'this container' mentioned in 1QapGen 12.15; there does not seem to be room for a prior introduction of the container as in *Jub.* 7.2. (4) Both have extended accounts of the division of land boundaries among Noah's sons and grandsons which are additional to Genesis, but *Jubilees* otherwise follows the order of Genesis and has counterparts to the table of nations in Gen. 10.1-32 and the genealogy of Gen. 11.10-17 (see Ruiten 2000: 307–309, 313–30, 367). The *Genesis Apocryphon* in comparison, looks secondary, lacking the parts of *Jubilees* that correspond to the table of nations and genealogy of Genesis 10, 11 and retaining only the parts that are additional to Genesis.

In these examples, in comparison with *Jubilees*, the version in the *Genesis Apocryphon* looks secondary. We can thus safely rule out the possibility that the *Genesis Apocryphon* was a source for *Jubilees*. On the other hand, García Martínez argues that the *Genesis Apocryphon* cannot be dependent on *Jubilees*, but rather on a common source, a 'Book of Noah' (García Martínez 1992: 40–41; see below). Two of his examples concern the combination in the Noah story of the *Genesis Apocryphon* of features found in *Jubilees* and in Noah materials in *1 Enoch*. Stronger is his argument that 'Mt

Asshur' in *Jub.* 8.21 must be a mistake from an Aramaic original 'Mt Taurus' which is preserved in 1QapGen (17.10):

טור אשור > טור אתור > טור תורא

We could add a further example. Although both similarly detail Noah's sacrifice after the flood to correspond to Levitical sacrificial law and emphasize that it was to atone for the earth, in *Jubilees* this is combined with delaying Noah's departure from the ark until the third month to show Noah keeping the Festival of Weeks as a covenant festival, an important motif for the author. The *Genesis Apocryphon* lacks the connection with the Festival of Weeks, and drastically departs from all known tradition to show Noah offering the sacrifices before exiting the ark, so this cannot take place in the third month. Also, whereas *Jubilees* mentions the sprinkling of wine as typical of burnt offerings (see Num. 28–29), the *Genesis Apocryphon* omits this, apparently out of consideration that Noah has yet to plant a vineyard (1QapGen 12.13). It should be noted that *Jubilees* looks like it is adapting a source here for its own interests: the sacrifices do not correspond to biblical descriptions of the Festival of Weeks. This could suggest a common source or tradition used independently by both *Jubilees* and the *Genesis Apocryphon*. We will consider next a possible Book of Noah source.

c. *Book of Noah*
It is possible that a 'Book (or books) of Noah' existed, as has been long conjectured. Possible evidence includes Noah materials in common between *1 Enoch* and *Jubilees*, and a handful of Noah texts in the Dead Sea Scrolls (*Noah* [1Q19]; *Birth of Noah*[a-c] [4Q534–6]; the *Genesis Apocryphon*), as well as several references to books attributed to or associated with Noah (*ALD* 10.10; *Jub.* 8.12; 10.13; 21.10; 1QapGen 5.29; and some medieval texts including the *Sefer Asaf ha-Rofe*, *Sefer ha-Razim*, *Sefer Raziel*, and the *Book of Asatir*; see García Martínez 1992; Stone 1999: 136–41; Werman 1999; Nickelsburg 2001: 541–42; Puech 2001; Stone 2006).

Nevertheless, the following cautions are in order. First, it is probable that one should distinguish between the birth of Noah traditions and the book of Noah traditions. Birth of Noah material is never referred to as a subject of a 'Book of Noah'. Moreover, in the *Genesis Apocryphon*, the introduction to the 'book of Noah' (A12) comes after the birth of Noah story, which is narrated in the voice of Lamech. The book of Noah is narrated in the first person by Noah.

Second, the ancient references to a book or books of Noah allude to different content. Some refer to various priestly purity laws. The *Aramaic Levi Document* (c. latter 3rd cent. BCE or early 2nd cent. BCE) mentions a 'book of Noah' as a source of instruction about priestly laws, transmitted through Abraham and Isaac to Levi (*ALD* 10.1–10 [preserved only in Greek]; cf. 5.8; Greenfield, Stone and Eshel 2004: 91). Topics include purity laws, sexual sin, sacrificial procedures, and the treatment of blood. *Jubilees* 21.1-24 seems to be based on this text; it describes Abraham instructing Isaac about priestly law from a 'book of my ancestors, in the words of Enoch and the words of Noah' with very similar content (including the following blessing). Another set of traditions associates various esoteric teachings with Noah. *Jubilees* 10.13 mentions several books written by Noah and passed on to Shem, including one containing angelic instruction about medicine and evil spirits. The medieval references to a 'book of Noah' seem to be dependent on *Jubilees*, mentioning remedies and healing (*Book of Asaf*) and magic, incantations and astrological mysteries (*Sefer Ha-Raziel, Sefer Raziel*). Different again, *Jub*. 8.12 alludes to a book of Noah outlining division of the land (see Scott 2002: 35–36).

Some have argued that these various traditions are too disparate to derive from a single 'book of Noah' (e.g., Dimant 1998; Bernstein 1999a: 226–31), but Stone (2006) has recently defended the likelihood of an actual book of Noah source including these topics but probably not the birth of Noah material. He notes that there is no compelling reason that a single book of Noah – or several different Noah books – could not address such disparate topics. Indeed, in 1QapGen 5.29, the heading '[A copy of] the book of the words of Noah' (Steiner 1995) comes after the story about the birth of Noah and introduces an account of the early life of Noah, the Watchers, the flood, Noah's covenant with God, sacrifices, laws about blood and fruit trees, vision about eschatological judgment, and division of the land among Noah's sons. This corresponds rather well to the various topics attributed in other sources to a book of Noah.

Third, it does need to be admitted that it is possible to explain these various descriptions without the existence of an actual text or texts regarded as a 'Book of Noah'. There may be nothing more than traditions that Noah transmitted ancient revelation in the form of books, developed in different ways by various writings. In fact, the descriptions in *Jubilees* may be dependent on the tradition referred to in the *Aramaic Levi Document*, which it used as a source (VanderKam 2001: 138), and the *Genesis Apocryphon* and the medieval references could be dependent on *Jubilees*.

In summary, the matter is still uncertain, although the balance of likelihood favors the existence of an ancient book(s) of Noah that would date to the third or fourth centuries BCE (Stone 2006). There is no definitive evidence, however, that the *Genesis Apocryphon* was dependent on a textual Noah source beyond *1 Enoch* (primarily 106–107 for the birth of Noah) and a *Jubilees* narrative, supplemented with the author's own interpretation and haggadic expansion of Genesis (see Fitzmyer 2004: 20–22). Particularly the pattern of similarities to distinctive features in the narrative of *Jubilees* – especially chronology and geography – in both the Noah and Abraham sections strongly suggests that the *Genesis Apocryphon* was dependent on *Jubilees* or a common source(s) with a narrative close to parts of *Jubilees*; perhaps a proto-*Jubilees* narrative without the laws.

9. *Methods*

In summarizing methods employed by the author of the *Genesis Apocryphon*, one can distinguish broadly between techniques of rewriting Genesis and free composition. In rewriting, the author modifies an existing narrative, in this case the story of Genesis. One type of modification consists of simple additions, which are mostly relatively small. Most of the time, such additions are of details that might be regarded as implicit in the narrative of Genesis, either by inference or anticipation. Sometimes, additions are drawn from other traditions that presumably have achieved a level of authority for the author. A smaller number of additions appear to be utterly novel, but these are almost always by way of analogy with other scriptural stories that have some similarity or point of contact.

A second type of modification consists of omissions from the story to produce a condensed version. Sometimes the omissions are very small, for example a single word, while other times whole episodes are left out. In many cases, the omissions would seem to be motivated by a desire to streamline the narrative by removing redundancies or material that could be seen as a distraction to the focus of the author. In other cases, omissions seem to exclude material that could be deemed offensive or troubling. With such omissions (e.g., the story of Noah's drunkenness) it is not clear whether the author is asserting his view that this story does not belong in the scriptural story, or is rather de-emphasizing or re-interpreting.

A third type of modification entails various types of rearrangement to juxtapose material that is deemed to belong together, or to produce some sort of harmonization. We noted a couple of significant instances of rearranging the narrative in direct contradiction to the narrative of Genesis (e.g., sacrifice before leaving ark), but the text is too fragmentary to be certain of the purpose.

Many of the modifications can best be described as substitution: the author substitutes a new version of the narrative that incorporates additional details, omits, and/or rearranges material. Examples include updating of names and places, hybrid quotation (e.g., a sister–wife story that combines details from Genesis 12 and 20; a single genealogy of Shem drawing on Gen. 10.21-22 and 11.10-11), synthesis of biblical data with other traditions, and instances of contradicting Genesis (sacrifice before leaving ark; dominion).

It is questionable whether any significant amount of material in the *Genesis Apocryphon* can be considered completely free composition. For most of the material additional to Genesis, the author did not work with a blank slate, but reworked traditions from other sources with similar techniques of rewriting as used on Genesis and/or drew on analogies from elsewhere in Scripture. For example, the extensive story of the birth of Noah closely corresponds to *1 Enoch* 106–107; the long song about Sarai's beauty draws on Song of Songs and the ideal wife in Proverbs 31.

10. *The* Genesis Apocryphon *as a Book*

Without knowing how much is lost from the beginning and end of the *Genesis Apocryphon*, and what it contained, it is impossible to make confident judgments about the nature and purpose of the work as a whole (Schuller 2003: 209). Moreover, such rewritten texts are repositories for various traditions not all of which are of special interest to the author, and this is certainly the case with the *Genesis Apocryphon* and its use of sources. Nevertheless, we may reliably detect particular concerns of the author in two ways. First, because the Noah and Abram sections exhibit different character and use of sources, common treatment of the Noah and Abram material – especially the expansions and additions – points to matters of special interest to the author (see especially Nickelsburg 1998). Second, where minute details of the rewriting correspond to unique structuring of the larger context of the narrative, the author reveals part of his particular *Tendenz*. I will consider the material isolated by these two criteria under three categories: readability, praxis, and authority.

First, under the rubric of readability I loosely refer to modifications for the sake of the story, to make the narrative more coherent and more vivid, and to remove obstacles to understanding its message (see the discussions by Alexander 1988: 104–107 and Bernstein 1996). Thus, as we have noted, the author is interested in clarifying chronological, genealogical, and geographical details, especially identifying names and boundaries of the land. He clarifies obscure details and ambiguous passages using logical inference. For example, where Gen. 13.3-4 mentions that Abram returned 'to the place where he had made an altar at the first', the *Genesis Apocryphon* infers that this implies a second construction, and so paraphrases 'the place where I had built the altar, and I built it once again' (1QapGen 21.1-2). Also, Gen. 14.10 says that the kings of Sodom and Gomorrah fled from the Mesopotamian kings and fell into bitumen pits (14.10), but in v. 21, the king of Sodom greets Abram after his victory! The *Genesis Apocryphon* modifies the text to clarify: the king of Sodom flees, and the king of Gomorrah falls into a pit (1QapGen 21.32-33). Moreover, it makes plain that Melchizedek blessed Abram, whereas in Genesis it is ambiguous who is blessing whom (B90). Also, the *Genesis Apocryphon* clarifies that the tithe Abram gave to Melchizedek was only from the Mesopotamian kings; it did not include any of the goods belonging to the king of Sodom, which Abram is said to return in full (1QapGen 22.17, 24-26; Vermes 1973: 108–109).

The author introduces information to anticipate details assumed later in the narrative of Genesis. For example, the mention of Hagar as an Egyptian in Gen. 16.1 implies to the author that she must have been acquired in Egypt, and so he adds to the end of the story about Abram and Sarai in Egypt that Pharaoh gave Hagar to Sarai (1QapGen 20.31-32). The *Genesis Apocryphon* also adds a brief narrative about Abram making an alliance with three of his neighbors Aner, Eshkol, and Mamre (B73) to anticipate their abrupt mention in Gen. 14.13, and also adds a notice that they accompany Abram to rescue Lot (B86) to anticipate their right to a share of the plunder in Gen. 14.24.

Many of these are common and natural interpretations and best qualify as examples of 'pure' exegesis, although that category can be misleading: for example it is very likely that there is also ideological interest in the descriptions of boundaries of the land. It is also clear from *Jubilees* that matters of chronology can be intimately bound up with practical matters related to legal dispute such as the calendar, but it is unclear how much this is a special concern of the *Genesis Apocryphon*.

Distinctive to the *Genesis Apocryphon* are two further enhancements of the story found in both parts: first-person narration and details about psychological and emotional states. Bernstein is probably correct that the purpose of the former is to make the story vivid rather than to assert authority as in *Jubilees* (Bernstein 1999: 15–17). The psychological detail is unique to the *Genesis Apocryphon* and in marked contrast to the reserved tone of the narrative in Genesis, in which Noah is a flat character and Abram appears stoic and impassive – even when carrying out the instruction to kill his son! This effort to explore the inner life of the characters, for example what Abram and Sarai must have been feeling, gives the *Genesis Apocryphon* a reflective or even homiletical character (see below). The addition of prayers (A30, 38, B9, 53) and motivation (A16, B10) is also part of this, but reveals that the interest is not merely abstract: there is a concern to portray exemplary characters for emulation. This overlaps somewhat with the next category.

Second, the *Genesis Apocryphon* shows concern about certain matters of praxis.[58] Nickelsburg has argued that the anxiety about wives and strangers reflects a concern

---

58. It is necessary to qualify the early assessment by Nickelsburg (1981, 265) when he states that 'unlike *Jubilees* and the *Testaments*, the extant sections indicate little interest in halakhic matters or

about proper marriage (1998: 152–54) and my own analysis of the contrast drawn
between the illicit marriage of the Watchers and the lawful marriage of Noah's children supports this. At the level of the story, the concern is to assert the purity of the
patriarchal lineage by providing proper genealogies that include the wives. There is
also a practical concern here, but unfortunately, it is not possible to identify the precise
nature of the issue or its social context (Schuller 2003: 206–209). At the very least,
these marriages are to be exemplary, and it is probably also safe to say that the author
shared the strong polemical view of *Jubilees* against intermarriage with foreigners
(esp. *Jub.* 30.7; cf. 20.4; VanderKam 2001: 107–108, 114–18). It is less clear whether
the consistent practice of lineage endogamy – especially patrilineal parallel cousin
marriage (father's brother's child, still the preferred marriage among Bedouin) –
applied to the patriarchs represents a polemical preference for the author or is merely
representative of endogamous marriage. In any case, the stories are for warning and
emulation. I believe that this is the point of the intense focus on the psychological
states of Bitenosh and Sarai. This focus is not applied to all characters – for example
Noah's wife or Lot – but specifically with these two women in stories about the threat
of miscegenation. The presentation of these women warns of the danger to women of
intercourse with Gentiles and models the proper attitude of the chaste and pious wife:
fear of foreign men, and devotion to husband and home (note especially the striking
reference to the sexual pleasure of Bitenosh with her husband). Noah serves as an
example of the pious parent who carefully arranges proper matches for his children.

We have also seen that the *Genesis Apocryphon* endorses particular positions with
regard to sacrifice (sin offering before other sacrifices), the produce of fruit trees
(fourth-year produce treated like priests' portion), and the festival on the first day of
the first month. These are also attested in the *Temple Scroll*, and were apparently the
subject of polemics. The *Genesis Apocryphon* is not simply dependent on *Jubilees* for
these, but shows independent interest in the matters. The unique placement of Noah's
sacrifice on the ark is almost certainly related to views about purity of the land that
were important to the author, but are now unclear.

Also unique is the author's emphasis on dominion and food in the remarkable
reworking of the covenant with Noah. If it is the case that the intent is to advocate
vegetarianism, this would certainly be a distinctive polemical view in ancient
Judaism.[59] It would not be without analogy, however, in certain contexts. A vegetarian diet seems to have been typical for pious Jews in a Gentile context where the
concern was to avoid eating meat sacrificed to idols (Dan. 1.12-13; 10.3; 2 Esd. 9.24;
16.68; *4 Macc.* 5.2; Rom. 14.21; 1 Cor. 8.7-13; 10.25-29; Josephus, *Life* 14; cf. Tob.
1.10-11; Jdt. 10.5; 12.1-2; 1 Macc. 1.62-63; 2 Macc. 5.27; 6.8, 21; *4 Macc.* 5.8, 14,
26; 6.15; 10.1).

The concern over boundaries of the land also may have practical considerations
behind them, although it is not possible to be certain. One could imagine such possibilities as legal dispute over the extent of the territory to which the law of fruit trees
applies, polemic against assimilationists who introduce 'customs strange to the land'
(1 Macc. 1.44), or apologetic related to territorial expansion under the Hasmonaeans

---

moral exhortation'. These concerns may be less prominent and explicit in the *Genesis Apocryphon*,
but concern for them is part of the author's purpose in writing.

59. On the vegetarian ideal (rather than practice) in ancient Judaism, see Rendsburg 2005.

(1 Macc. 15.33). At any rate, the sanctity of the land is part of a theological viewpoint that has eschatological implications – independence in a renewed nation (e.g., Bar. 2.34; 2 Esd. 9.7-8) – with inescapable political overtones during the Hellenistic period. It has also been suggested that the emphasis on the special sanctity of Jerusalem might be part of an anti-Samaritan polemic, but this is very speculative.

Third, several features relate to questions of authority. The topics mentioned just above assert the existence of an eternal divine law kept by the patriarchs before Moses. The *Genesis Apocryphon* emphasizes antediluvian revelation received by Enoch and Noah, recorded in books that are transmitted through Abram. That revelation concerns both observance of eternal divine law, and eschatology. There is a prominent emphasis on 'truth' (1QapGen 6.1-6, 23; 15.20; 19.25). This conglomeration of motifs, along with the elevation of Noah as priest, a new Adam and Torah-observant patriarch is related in some way to what Boccaccini describes as 'Enochic Judaism' (Boccaccini 1998: 12–13, 68–79) and what Stone describes as a 'priestly-Noachic tradition' (Stone 1999). Reconstructing the social setting of this tradition has proven elusive – the origins are variously dated in the fourth or third centuries BCE – but the essential features seem to be alienation from the priestly establishment and temple, and a fundamentally different worldview that posited the origin of evil as a supernatural invasion rather than resulting from human choice. Although it is impossible to determine the specific setting of the *Genesis Apocryphon*, it has been influenced by such traditions at least, and its rewriting of Genesis is probably related in part to competing claims to Scripture and the legitimate authority to interpret it, such as the polemic reflected in *1 En.* 99.2 and 104.10-13.

Thus, authority is grounded in both antiquity and revelation. In the context of Second Temple Judaism, appeal to the antiquity of laws is an apologetic concern, and appeal to revelation for ultimate authority – as especially in apocalyptic movements represented by the Enochic literature, *Jubilees*, the Dead Sea Scrolls, and early Christianity – is a polemical position. It represents rejection of other bases of authority such as universal wisdom or Greek reason, to which those with greater assimilation to surrounding culture might appeal. It also differs from the type of exegetical authority as ultimately championed by the rabbinic movement. There is no indication, however, that the *Genesis Apocryphon* is in any way directed at non-Jews, or even Jews of a different persuasion. It seems rather to be a popular religious writing for internal use.

Although there are no clear clues to an overall agenda such as with *Jubilees*, there does seem to be coherence among the major concerns reflected in the narrative of the *Genesis Apocryphon*. The author seems especially sensitive to matters of marriage and food. The tone is considerably less strident than *Jubilees*, however. Instead of heavy-handed coercion to behavior change (e.g., *Jub.* 7.27-29; 30.7; 50.6-13), the *Genesis Apocryphon* seems focused more on inculcating affective attitudes: pride with regard to Jewish traditions and laws; in women a fear of foreign men; in parents a sense of responsibility with regard to proper marriage for their children; (possibly) vegetarianism as an ideal. One gets the impression that a sense of threat is less immediate, and that the author addresses a pious community that is relatively segregated and seeks to reinforce boundaries and nurture devotion to a life of piety and study.

In the Hellenistic period, the figures of Noah and Abram were readily embraced as universal figures and therefore of interest to Jews seeking to accommodate Judaism to the broader Hellenistic culture: Abraham could be presented as a bringer of culture, and Noah associated with other ancient deluge myths (e.g., *Ps.-Eupolemus, 3 Sib. Or.*). The *Genesis Apocryphon*, however, like Ben Sira, *Jubilees*, and others, empha- sizes an utterly particularist presentation of these patriarchs: they are patriarchs of a people set apart, and exemplars of rigorous Torah observance (Hengel 1974: 1: 152).

11. *Summary*

The *Genesis Apocryphon* retells the stories of Noah and Abraham from Genesis, for the most part carefully following the scriptural narrative but generously combining traditions from other sources, particularly Enochic literature and *Jubilees*. Although the use of different sources is reflected in some unevenness in the story, the author is not a slave to his sources. He shows himself to be a very close reader of the scriptural text and a sophisticated exegete (Bernstein 1996: 43, 56–57), and presents several novel interpretations by reworking both large structure and minute details. The work reflects a 'holistic approach' toward the text of Genesis: 'the author thinks ahead, and does not (as often happens in rabbinic midrash) treat the Bible atomistically as a series of discrete statements' (Alexander 1988: 107). Despite his high regard for both Genesis and his *Jubilees* source, he occasionally contradicts both to make his own point.

Chapter 3

REWORKED PENTATEUCH

1. *Description of the Manuscripts*

Five fragmentary Hebrew manuscripts are called *Reworked Pentateuch* (=4QRP) because they share the feature of presenting – apparently – the entire Pentateuch as a running text in a single scroll, but reworked with some rearrangement, exegetical additions, and subtractions. These are: 4Q158 (=4QRP^a) originally published by J. Allegro (1968) as 'Biblical Paraphrase', and 4Q364–367 (=4QRP^{b-e}) originally edited by J. Strugnell and published by E. Tov and S. White Crawford (1994). If indeed each of these manuscripts covered the entire Pentateuch – no evidence survives for Genesis 1–20; Leviticus 1–10; Numbers 18–26 or Deuteronomy 21–34, and only 4Q365 contains parts from all five books of the Pentateuch – these would have been by far the longest scrolls recovered at Qumran, approximately 22–27 meters long (Tov and White Crawford 1994: 187–92). That is about three times the length of the Great Isaiah Scroll (1QIsa^a, approximately 8.75 m.).

In terms of palaeographic dating, the manuscripts range from mid to late Hasmonaean (4Q367) and late Hasmonaean (4Q364, 365, 366; Tov and White Crawford 1994: 201, 260–61, 336–37, 346) to early Herodian (4Q158; Strugnell 1970: 168). That is, all would seem to have been copied during the first century BCE. Nevertheless, there appear to be two different scribal traditions represented, which could indicate that they were copied in different places: three of the manuscripts (4Q158, 4Q364 and 4Q365) evidence the full spelling and other scribal features characteristic of what Tov has described as the 'Qumran scribal school', whereas the other two are closer to the 'Masoretic tradition' (Tov, *et al.* 1994: 188–89, 202–203, 261, 337, 346).

4Q158 has 14 fragments remaining (and 1 small unidentified fragment). These cover parts of Exodus 4, 19–22 and 30 – and possibly Genesis 47 – with harmonizing and interpretative insertions and juxtapositions from Gen 17.7; 32.25-32; Exod. 3.12; 6.2-3; Deut.5.24-31; 18.18-20 (see Segal 1998). It shows an arrangement similar to the Samaritan Pentateuch (SP), with parallel passages from Deuteronomy 5 interspersed in the Mount Sinai theophany of Exodus 20:

> Deut. 5.24-27/Exod. 20.19b-22a/Deut. 5.28-29/Deut. 18.18-20, 22
> Exod. 20.12, 16, 17/Deut. 5.30, 31/Exod. 20.22b–21.10

Segal (1998: 47–48, 52–53) suggests that two other juxtapositions are due to thematic association: Exod. 4.24-26/Gen. 32.25-33/Exod. 4.27-28 and Exod. 3.12/Exod. 24.4-6. There are also several additions not found in any known edition of Genesis: some unidentified content before Gen. 32.25 (frg. 1-2 1-2), an addition of the angel's blessing to Jacob following Gen. 32.30 (frg. 1-2 7b-10a; probably also in 4Q364 5b ii 13ff; see Segal 1998: 59–60), a description of the people following MOses' instructions to return to their tents (frg. 7–8 5and a section about the redemption of Israelites from Egypt (cf. Exodus 15) on fragment 14 (although there is some question if this belongs to the same text).

4Q364 consists of 32 fragments (and 35 small unidentified fragments) covering parts of Genesis (25–48), Exodus (21–26), Numbers (14, 33) and Deuteronomy (9–11; 14). Like the Samaritan Pentateuch, it has a longer form of Gen. 30.36, inserts Num. 20.17-18 before Deut. 2.8-14, and has other minor details in common, mostly spelling. It also includes three additions not attested in known editions of Genesis: an expansion about Jacob's departure preceding Gen. 28.6 (cf. *Jubilees* 27), an addition with wording from Exod. 19.17 preceding Exod. 24.12, and an addition about God speaking with Moses between Exod. 24.18 and 25.1. Throughout the manuscript, the Tetragrammaton is uniquely preceded by two vertical dots (like a colon), perhaps as a reminder not to pronounce the divine name (White Crawford 2000a: 776).

4Q365 is the most extensively preserved manuscript with 38 fragments (and 24 small unidentified fragments) that attest parts of every book of the Pentateuch: Genesis 21.9-10, Exodus 8–39; Leviticus 11–26; Numbers 1–27; and Deuteronomy 2 and 19. Fragment 26a–b shows that Numbers began immediately following the end of Leviticus, with one blank line separating the two. There are two rearrangements to juxtapose Num. 4.47-49 and 7.1, and Num. 27.11 and 36.1-2. There are also two large additions in comparison with known scriptural texts: a Song of Miriam before Exod. 15.22 and descriptions of festivals of oil and wood after Lev. 24.2a – festivals associated with Mosaic law also in the *Temple Scroll* (4Q365 23 9–11; 11QT^a 23–24). It also shares with the *Temple Scroll* an otherwise unique order of the Israelite tribes (4Q365 23 9–10; 11QT^a 24.10–16; Tov and White Crawford 1994: 295). The text is otherwise similar to SP in minor details.

4Q366 is extant in only five fragments, with parts of Exodus 21–22; Leviticus 24–25; Numbers 29–30 and Deuteronomy 14 and 16. Lev. 24.20-22 and 25.39-43 are juxtaposed, as are Num. 29.32–30.1 and Deut. 16.13-14 concerning Sukkoth, which are followed by an otherwise unattested and unidentified addition (4 ii).

4Q367 is the least well preserved manuscript with only three fragments (and one small unidentified fragment) containing only small parts of Leviticus: 11.47–13.1; 15.14-15 juxtaposed with 19.1-15; and 20.13 juxtaposed with 27.30-34. Lev. 19.5-8 is omitted, replaced by a small gap. There is also a small gap left as a paragraph break between 20.13 and 27.30; at several other points on fragment 3 the copyist left gaps to avoid a defect in the leather. Before Lev. 20.13 there seems to be an addition otherwise unknown.

According to the editors (Tov and White Crawford 1994: 319–33), five further fragments originally grouped with 4Q365 on the basis of the same scribal hand are more likely to belong to a copy of the *Temple Scroll* (4Q365^a 4QTemple?) since they do not contain running 'biblical text' and the content shows similarity to the *Temple Scroll*.[1] This is not a compelling argument, though. The content of 4QRP is only fragmentarily known, and there are in it other examples of lengthy additions unattested in known editions of Scripture as well as significant similarities to the *Temple Scroll*. Moreover, the content of these disputed fragments is not much different from the addition about festival sacrifices which is joined to Leviticus 23 on 4Q365 23 (see below).

---

1.   Swanson (2004) also regards 4Q365^a as a separate work, but as an interpretative rewriting rather than a copy of the *Temple Scroll*.

Other evidence – palaeography, orthography, scribal practice – favors the identification of these fragments as belonging with 4Q365.[2] Additionally, the physical evidence of similar diagonal creases on fragments 6, 12, and 23 of 4Q365 and fragment 2 and 3 of 4Q365a suggests that all of these are from the same scroll (the damage patterns are especially comparable between 4Q365a 2 and 4Q365 12 which are both from the bottom of the scroll).[3] It must be admitted that we cannot reliably determine what the ancient writer might have regarded as the intent of such an expanded edition of Mosaic law, let alone what might have been deemed appropriate to include. If these fragments do belong to 4QRP, then the scroll would include extensive additional laws about festival sacrifices and the construction of the middle court of the sanctuary that are somewhat similar to the *Temple Scroll*. This raises important questions as to whether such 'additional' material was part of the scriptural source for the writer and what the purpose and status of the new writing were.

2. *Date and Provenance*

Not much can be said with certainty about either date or provenance. The earliest copies indicate that the work must have been written no later than about the middle of the first century BCE. Because it mentions festivals of fresh oil and of wood offering, it must be post-exilic (the earliest witness to a festival of wood offering is Neh. 10.35; 13.31; White Crawford 2000a: 775). This dating could be narrowed somewhat if 4QRP is dependent on the *Temple Scroll* (11QT[a] 23–24) for these festivals, as well as a common unique order to the listing of tribal offerings. 4QRP also seems to share with *Jubilees* 27 an addition concerning the departure of Jacob from his family. In both cases, White Crawford (2006: 142–44; cf. 2000a: 775–76) believes that 4QRP could be the source, in which casse it would have to date no later than about 200 BCE. However, it is not certain if these overlaps are due to literary dependence or reflect common traditions. Nothing in the content is distinctively sectarian, and the difference in scribal traditions makes it unlikely that the work was composed at Qumran.

3. *Content and Genre*

The editors (Tov and White Crawford 1994: 187) regard these five manuscripts to be copies of a single composition. It is not certain that this is the case. Although they each contain fragments from various parts of the Pentateuch, there is almost no overlap among the manuscripts to test their similarity.

M. Segal (2000) argues that they cannot be the same work or even the same genre on the basis of different ways they treat the scriptural source. (1) 4Q364, 365 are similar to SP with regard to harmonistic additions and juxtapositions; they should be regarded as a 'biblical text' and entitled 4QPentateuch. (2) 4Q158 shows a freer approach to the biblical text with some non-biblical additions; it is comparable to *Jubilees* and belongs to the genre rewritten Bible (see also Segal 1998). (3) 4Q366, 367

---

2.   J. Strugnell and H. Stegemann as cited in Tov and White Crawford 1994: 319–20, and n. 4; Brooke 1999: 227; García Martínez 1998: 237–39.

3.   This is based on an examination of photographs and inspection of the fragments at the Israel Museum in Jerusalem, 19 Sept. 2005.

have no exegetical additions but only rearrangements; they are also 'biblical text' but different in character from 4Q364, 365; 4Q367 might be an excerpted text of Leviticus. The evidence, however, is too fragmentary for such bold conclusions, and it needs to be noted that there are probably additions in 4Q366 and 4Q367, and that the reworkings in 4Q364 and 4Q365 go significantly beyond that of the Samaritan Pentateuch. Bernstein (2005b: 181, 196 n. 45; 1999: 13) also believes that 4Q158 is not a copy of 4QRP, but in contrast to Segal considers it *not* to be an example of rewritten Bible. More to the point is the argument of G. Brooke, who finds evidence for significant textual differences in the few examples of overlap, based on reconstruction of line lengths (Brooke 2001), and highlights other differences among the manuscripts as well. He argues that the five are 'separate compositions of the same genre' and should instead by designated by capital letters (4QRP A, etc.). Given the fragmentary nature of the manuscripts, none of these arguments is conclusive, but they do advise healthy caution. The relationship among these manuscripts is not settled and hopefully will become clearer with further analysis. In what follows, I treat all of this material together, but without assuming that the manuscripts are all witnesses to a single work.

One of the central debates with 4QRP is deciding whether these manuscripts should be classified as 'biblical' texts with harmonizations and expansions similar to those in Deuteronomy versus Exodus and in the Samaritan Pentateuch, or as 'extra-biblical' texts that belong to a category of rewritten Bible. As argued in the introduction, I believe it is best to avoid the anachronistic language of 'Bible' for this time period, and to regard 'rewritten Scripture' as an activity rather than a specific genre. In any case, all scholars acknowledge that 4QRP represents a borderline case that is extremely difficult to classify. White Crawford (1999: 2*–5*; 2006: 141–44), for example, considers on the one hand that the text presents itself simply as Scripture with no separation of interpretative elements. Thus, it could represent the most expanded extreme on a continuum of Pentateuchal texts. Also, there are two instances of shared traditions with *Jubilees* and the *Temple Scroll* (Isaac comforting Rebekah after Jacob's departure, in 4Q364 3 i cf. *Jub.* 24.14, 17; the festivals of wood and oil offerings, and the order of tribal offerings, in 4Q365 23 cf. 11QT^a 23–24) that may indicate acceptance of 4QRP as authoritative. On the other hand, she notes that there is no firm evidence of the acceptance and use of 4QRP as an authority (by means of quotation or commentary), and she argues that 'the scribal intervention … is drastic enough to call its divine authority in the Community that preserved it into question'. By this she means the addition of extra-scriptural material and not merely harmonizing additions from other scriptural texts, as with the Samaritan Pentateuch. Thus, she concludes '4QRP was perceived not as a biblical text, but as a commentary, an inner-biblical commentary on the text of the Torah. 4QRP took a relatively stabilized base text, in this case probably the already expansionist proto-Samaritan text, and inserted its comments and interpretations, particularly its new material, with no clear separation between text and comment'. Tov (1992) and Bernstein (2005b: 181–84; 2000: 379) also come down on this same side of the fence, emphasizing that since the major goal of the work seems to be interpretation, it should not be regarded as a scriptural text but rewritten Scripture, although it is on the boundary between the categories and, Bernstein adds, the authors may have regarded them as scriptural. The criteria of interpretation and the introduction of 'new material' are both of questionable reliability. A potentially more valuable clue is that it seems likely there were significant omissions in the presentation of the Pentateuch – thus possibly a sort of excerpted Pentateuch – although the extent of this is difficult to judge.[4]

Falling on the other side, Ulrich (2000b: 56–57), Lange (2002b: 27), and Segal (2000) believe that 4QRP is best classified as scriptural, emphasizing its self-presentation and its continuity with other expanded scriptural editions. VanderKam (2002a: 100) and Brooke (2000f: 778; 2002: 35) ride the fence, referring to 4QRP as reworked or rewritten scriptures, but arguing that there is no basis for distinguishing such texts as not scriptural. As VanderKam notes: 'on the basis of form, wording, and contents, there seem to be no strong reasons for denying *Reworked Pentateuch* the status that scrolls of Genesis to Deuteronomy had'. Given the current incomplete understanding of the manuscripts and short of being able to demonstrate that the work was an excerpted Pentateuch, this latter open approach is best.

4. *Nature of the Scriptural Source*

Since *Reworked Pentateuch* for the most part closely follows its scriptural source, the major points of interest concern the nature of the scriptural text represented, the text-critical significance of its text, interpretative traditions and methods, and implications for the boundary between Scripture and tradition. Of the major ancient biblical versions known to us (MT, SP, LXX), the 4QRP manuscripts correspond most closely to the Samaritan Pentateuch in numerous small details (Tov 1994; 1995). The correspondence is best illustrated with a few larger features that hitherto had been regarded as distinctive of the Samaritan Pentateuch.

a. *Exodus 20 with Interpolations from Deuteronomy 5 and 18*
The table below compares 4Q158 frgs. 6 and 7–8 with the SP's version of Exodus 20. In the second column, text in italics indicates material incorporated from Deuteronomy or otherwise different than MT Exodus 20. Overlaps with 4Q158 are underlined, and inexact overlaps are marked with dotted underline. Bold in the first column marks differences from the Masoretic Text. The third column provides references according to the Masoretic Text.

Table 14. *Exodus 20 in 4Q158 and the Samaritan Pentateuch*

4Q158	SP Exod 20	MT
	(Decalogue)	Exod. 20.1-17
	(Addition about altar on Mt Gerizim)	(cf. Deut. 11.29; 27.2-3, 5-7; 11.30)
	[18] When all the people *heard* the thunder and the sound of the horn, and saw the lightning and the mountain smoking, *all* the people were afraid and trembled and stood at a distance.	Exod. 20.18-19a (MT: … saw the thunder and lightning, the sound of the horn, and the mountain …)
	[19] And they said to Moses,	

---

4.   That is, it is possible that the juxtapositions of passages in some cases could be the result of selection rather than simply rearrangement.

4Q158	SP Exod 20	MT
	'Look, the Lord our God has shown us his glory and his greatness, and his voice we have heard from the midst of the fire. This day we have seen that God can speak with a human and that person may still live. So now why should we die? For this great fire will consume us. If we hear the voice of the Lord our God any longer, we will die. For who is there of all flesh who has heard the voice of the living God speaking from	Deut. 5.24-27
Frg. 6 (Strugnell 1970: 171-72) …you…	*the midst of the fire like us and lived? You go near yourself, and listen to all that the Lord our God says, then you tell us all*	
but do n]ot let [God] speak with u[s	*that the Lord our God says to you, and we will listen and do; but* do not let *God* speak with us *or we will die.'*	(Exod. 20.19b)
	²⁰ Moses said to the people, *'Do not be afraid; for it is so as to test you*	Exod. 20.20-22a
G[od] has come, [and so] th[at]f[e]ar [of him] will be[	*that* God has come, and so that fear of him will be *upon you so that you do not sin'.* ²¹ Then the people stood at a distance, while Moses drew near to the thick	
]God. And the Lord [spoke] to Moses, saying	darkness where there was God. ²² And the LORD spoke to Moses, saying.	-----
	'I have heard the words of this people, which they have spoken to you; they are right in all that they have spoken.	Deut. 5.28b-29
] they had such a mind as this, to fear[	*If only* they had such a mind as this, to fear *me and to keep all my commandments always, so that it might go well with them and with their children forever!*	
] the voice of my words. Sa[y] to them. A prophet[	*A prophet I will raise up for them from among their own people, like you. I will put my words in his mouth, and he shall speak to them everything that I command.*	Deut. 18.18-22
] who does not heed the word[s	*Anyone* who does not heed the words *of him* (MT 'me') *that he shall speak in my name, I myself will hold accountable. But any prophet who presumes to speak in my name a word that I have not commanded him*	
to sp]eak, or who spe[aks	to speak, or who speaks *in the name of another deity, that prophet shall die. You may say to yourself, 'How can we recognize a message that the LORD has not spoken?'*	
²² I]f [a prophet] speaks [	If a prophet speaks *in the name of the LORD but the thing does not happen or come about, that is a word that the LORD*	

4Q158	SP Exod 20	MT
	has not spoken. The prophet has spoken it presumptuously; do not be frightened by it.	
Frg. 7-8		
(Decalogue)		Exod. 20.1-17
And the Lord said to Moses		
Go tell them, 'Return to [	*Go tell them, 'Return to your tents'. But you, stand here with me so that I may tell you all the commandments, the statutes*	Deut. 5.30
and the ordinances,	*and the ordinances,*	
that you shall teach them to do	*that you shall teach them to do*	
in the land which [	*in the land which* I am giving you to possess.	
So the people returned to their individual tents, but Moses remained before [the Lord		
	And the Lord spoke to Moses	(cf. Exod. 20.22a)
	saying, Speak	-----
	to the children of Israel:	Exod. 20.22b-26
] 'You have seen for yourselves	'You have seen for yourselves	
that I have spoken with you	that I have spoken with you	
from heaven. You shall not	from heaven. ²³ You shall not make gods of	
ma[ke	silver alongside me, nor shall you make for yourselves gods of gold.	
	²⁴ You need make for me only an altar of	
] on it your burnt offerings and	earth and sacrifice on it your burnt	
your offerings of well-being,	offerings and your offerings of well-being	
your sheep[	*from* (not in MT) your sheep and *from* (not in MT) your oxen; in *the* (not in MT) place where I cause my name to be remembered *there* (not in MT). I will come to you and bless you.	
] you make for me [an altar of	²⁵ But if you make for me an altar of stone,	
stone,] do not build it of hewn	do not build it of hewn stones; for if you	
stones; for if you [use] a chisel [	use a chisel upon it you profane it.	
	²⁶ You shall not go up by steps to my altar, so that your nakedness may not be exposed	
] on it.	*to* it (MT: on it)'.	
(blank space)		
These are the ordinances, etc.		Exod. 21.1

The two fragments (4Q158 frgs. 6 and 7–8) belong close together, and show a similar reworking of Exodus 20 to that in the Samaritan Pentateuch. An outline of the relationship shows this clearly.

Table 15. *4Q158 Synopsis*

4Q158	Samaritan Pentateuch	
	Decalogue	Exod. 20.1-17
	Addition about altar on Mt. Gerizim	cf. Deut. 11.29; 27.2-3, 5-7; 11.30
[…]	People's fear	Exod. 20.18-19a
People's request	People's request	Deut. 5.24-27; Exod. 20.19b

4Q158	Samaritan Pentateuch	
Moses' reassurance	Moses' reassurance	Exod. 20.20-21
God's agreement	God's agreement	Exod. 20.22a; Deut. 5.28b-29
A prophet like Moses	A prophet like Moses	Deut. 18.18-22
Decalogue		Exod. 20.12, 16-17
People to return	People to return	Deut. 5.30-31
People return		-----
Instructions about altar	Instructions about altar	Exod. 20.22b-26

Two features are especially important. (1) 4Q158 and the Samaritan Pentateuch both integrate the same parallel passages from Deuteronomy 5 to create a harmonized account of the theophany on Mount Sinai. (2) They both incorporate the passage about a prophet like Moses who will teach God's commands (from Deut. 18.18-20) after the expression of God's desire that the people adhere to his commandments (from Deut. 5.28-29).

These features must belong to a harmonistic edition of Exodus that also served as the base of the Samaritan Pentateuch. 4Q158 does not share the Samaritan addition about an altar on Mount Gerizim attached to the end of the Decalogue, and agrees with the MT against the SP in a few minor details in Exod. 20.24 and 26. It also shows two exegetical changes of its own to be discussed further below: it adds a description of the people carrying out the instruction to return to their tents (cf. Deut. 5.30) and most strikingly, it places the Decalogue *after* the discussion about Moses serving as intermediary and a future prophet like Moses (see p. 118 below).

b. *Deuteronomy 2 with Interpolation from Numbers 20*
Into the account of Israel skirting Edom's territory in Deuteronomy 2, the SP integrates a passage based on Numbers 20.14, 17-18 about Moses' negotiations with the king of Edom. This same harmonizing juxtaposition appears in 4Q364 23a–b i – including several minor differences from Num. 20.17 – indicating that it is part of a pre-Samaritan edition of Deuteronomy.

c. *An Anticipatory Addition after Gen. 30.36 (4Q364 4b–e ii)*
In the Masoretic Text of Genesis, Jacob employs a curious technique of sympathetic magic to enrich his flocks while impoverishing Laban's (Gen. 30.37-43), and later boasts to his wives that he was following divine guidance through a dream (Gen. 31.10-13). In the Samaritan Pentateuch, there is an account of this dream – based on Gen. 31.10-13 – at the appropriate place in the earlier narrative (just before Gen. 30.37), with adjustments for its new context. That is, the addition supplies – in antici-pation – what is implied by a comment later in Genesis. This sort of extension is typical of the scriptural edition that served as the based for the Samaritan Pentateuch. What seems to be much the same addition, but somewhat longer (Tov and White 1994: 210), appears in 4Q364 4b–e ii 21–26. The manuscript is too fragmentary to be certain of the relation between the two additions. Most likey, the added account of Jacob's dream belonged to the scriptural source for 4Q364, but even so, it would seem that it was extended further.

4QRP is an important witness to the Jewish edition of the Pentateuch that survived only in the Samaritan Pentateuch (Ulrich [1998: 88] suggests that it may instead constitute a distinct literary edition of the Pentateuch). On the one hand, it helps demonstrate that this version of the Pentateuch was regarded as authoritative Scripture by Jews in the Second Temple period, and it may help differentiate certain readings as either belonging to the Samaritan recension or the underlying Jewish edition. For example, Exod. 20.24 and 26 in SP have several minor differences from MT:

> You need make for me only an altar of earth and sacrifice on it your burnt offerings and your offerings of well-being *from* (not in MT) your sheep and *from* (not in MT) your oxen; in *the* (MT 'every') place where I cause my name to be remembered *there* (not in MT) … You shall not go up by steps to my altar, so that your nakedness may not be exposed *to it* (MT: on it).

Although it otherwise agrees with SP on major features in Exodus 20, on these points 4Q158 7–8 agrees with MT. The textual variants in these manuscripts have been meticulously documented by E. Tov (1992: 53–82; Tov and White Crawford 1994).

5. *Interpretative Traditions*

What elements in 4QRP reflect interpretative interventions of the author, that is, beyond developments that belonged to an already extended scriptural source? This is difficult to answer since we cannot be certain of the nature of the scriptural source used by the author apart from comparison with known versions today, and we do not know what other sources (written or oral) may have been influential. The following discussion will examine select examples that are unknown in any biblical version and so are probably due to the author's interpretative activity, or may reflect the incorporation of other interpretative traditions. We will consider chiefly two main types of activity: additions to the text that are exegetically based, and juxtapositions of texts from different contexts (see further Segal 1998).

a. *Exegetical Additions*
1. In 4Q364 there is a lengthy addition of at least six lines to the story of Jacob's departure, just preceding Gen. 28.6 that is reconstructed by the editors as follows:

> him you shall see […] you shall see in peace […] your death, and to your eyes [… lest I be deprived of even] the two of you. And [Isaac] called [to Rebecca his wife and he told] her all [these] wor[ds …] after Jacob her son [and she cried …]. (4Q364 3 ii 1–6; Tov and White Crawford 1994: 207)

The editors suggest that this passage probably contains an expanded conversation of Rebekah with Jacob (lines 1-4a?, cf. Gen. 27.45–46; *Jub.* 27.2–7) and Isaac comforting his grieving wife (lines 4b-6) after the manner of *Jub.* 27.13-18, adding 'a note of human interest' to the story (White Crawford 1992: 219). It is indeed possible that this addition concerns similar content to the addition in *Jubilees* 27, addressing the emotions and anxiety of Rebekah and Isaac over the break-up of their family to flesh out the stoic report of Genesis. Particularly attractive is the similarity of the wording 'you shall see in peace' in line 2 to Isaac's reassurance to Rebekah 'until he return in peace to us, and we see him in peace'. If so, the extension might draw on *Jubilees* or other tradition, and possibly analogy with Rebekah's anxiety in Gen. 27.45-46 (cf. the extensions in 1QapGen by means of exploring emotional and psychological states). But as intriguing as this theory is, it needs to be noted that this reconstruction is highly conjectural and problematic in certain details: this produces an awkward structure, especially the abrupt switch from Rebekah's conversation with Jacob to Isaac's comfort of Rebekah without a report of Jacob's departure. It is possible to imagine alternative reconstructions, for example perhaps an angelic message to anticipate Jacob's dream and subsequent vow (Gen. 28.10-22; esp. v. 21, '… so that I come again to my father's house in peace'). In the end, it is best to regard this as a haggadic addition to the story of Jacob's departure analogous to the addition in *Jubilees* 27 at this point, but with uncertain content. It any case, the major factor in this extension would seem to be the author's imagination.

2. Genesis 32.30 succinctly mentions that the angel blessed Jacob. 4Q158 adds a passage giving the content of this blessing (4Q158 1–2 7–10).

> 'May the Lo[rd] make you fruitful, [and multiply] you [… know]ledge and insight. May he deliver you from all violence, and […] until this day and forever more […]'. Then the man went on his way, having blessed Jacob there.

The blessing seems to be expanded from Isaac's blessing of Jacob (Gen. 28.3). Thus, this addition supplies content that is implied by the narrative, and fills out the content by means of analogy to a related episode in Genesis.

3. The most extensive and interesting addition in 4QRP is the addition of Miriam's Song. After recording the Song of Moses celebrating God's victory over the Egyptians at the Red Sea (Exod. 15.1-18), Exodus briefly notes that Miriam led the women with tambourines and dancing, singing 'Sing to the Lord, for he has triumphed gloriously; horse and rider he has thrown into the sea' (Exod. 15.21). This is the opening strophe of Moses' song, and perhaps it was meant to indicate that Miriam taught the women to sing Moses' song. But it would be natural to assume that this was merely an abstract of a different song by Miriam. Such a tradition seems to be implied in Philo's descriptions of male and female Therapeutae singing the songs of Moses and Miriam antiphonally (Philo, *Vit. Cont.* 83–88; Brooks 1994b: 65). 4Q365 is the only known text, however, to attempt to supply Miriam's song in full, distinct from Moses' song (it should be noted that a somewhat expanded version appears in *Tg. Ps.-Jonathan* and *Neofiti* to Exod. 15.21). Parts of seven lines survive:

> … you despised [or: you plundered] … for the triumph of … You are great, a savior … the hope of the enemy perishes and he is … they perished in the mighty waters, the enemy … and he exalted her to their heights … you gave … wor]king a triumph … (4Q365 6a ii and c 1–7; Brooke 1994b: 63)

Brooke finds in line 6 an exaltation of a feminine figure (probably Miriam), and argues that this is a representative of songs that celebrate God's victory through the weak and lowly and effect a reversal of power (Brooke 1994b). He compares it with two other 'women's songs' – Judith 16 and the Magnificat in Luke 1.46-55 – as well as two songs in the War Scroll (1QM 11, 14). It should be noted, though, that the editors translate line 6 differently: 'Extol the one who raises up' (Tov and White Crawford 1994: 270). In any case, the concern here seems to be to supply content which is deemed to be implied by the scriptural source, and for fleshing out the gap the author makes use of language and analogy from elsewhere in scriptural writings.

4. In its treatment of Exodus 20, 4Q158 7–8 is similar to SP by incorporating the command from Deut. 5.30 for the people to return to their tents (see Table 11). But it goes further by adding a description of the people carrying out the instruction. This

type of harmonization is typical of the scriptural source on which SP was based, but this instance is unique to 4Q158.

5. Exodus 24.18 notes that Moses was with God on Mount Sinai for 40 days and nights. Following this, 4Q364 includes a two line addition before Exod. 25.1:

>] ... he made known to him everything [...] he did at the time of assembly[(4Q364 15 3–4)

The impulse for this addition would seem to be similar to that in *Jub.* 1.4: to expand on what God revealed to Moses during that time (Segal 2000: 393–94). Because of the broken context, the passage is not entirely clear, but presumably the idea is that God revealed to Moses details going back to creation. This would be based on inference combined with tradition: if Moses recorded the account of creation, God probably revealed this on Mount Sinai. A similar tradition is assumed as the setting for *Jubilees* (VanderKam 2006), except there the revelation is mediated by angels.

6. In 4Q365 23, there is a sizeable addition of at least eight lines following the passage about Sukkoth at the end of Leviticus 23. The addition is worked into the scriptural text by using the opening words from Lev. 24.1-2 (about the sanctuary lamp) as introductory to further instructions about festival sacrifices: it mentions the use of calves for Passover sacrifices as well as for other occasions, as also in Deut. 16.2 and 2 Chron. 35.7-9; it implies Passover as a public sacrifice at the Temple as was the practice in the Second Temple period; it gives prescriptions for a festival of fresh oil and probably also a festival of wood offering, two 'post-biblical' festivals legislated in the *Temple Scroll* (11QT^a 21–22, 23–24); and it gives the same unique order for offerings by tribes as in the *Temple Scroll* (11QT^a 24), starting with Levi and Judah on the first day and Reuben and Simeon on the third day (White Crawford 1992 1: 225-27). Thus, this section bears some close similarities with the *Temple Scroll*, perhaps reflecting its use as a source.

b. *Unique Juxtapositions*
In a number of places 4QRP attests unique arrangements of the scriptural source to juxtapose certain passages. Sometimes the purpose of these juxtapositions is obscure, but in at least two instances, it is clear that the author has brought together scriptural material on a single topic.

1. Inheritance law. 4Q365 36 groups together the story about an inheritance claim by Zelophehad's daughters (Num. 27.1-11) with what appears to be an appendix to the story at the end of the book (Num. 36.1-11).

2. Festival of Sukkoth. 4Q366 4 i brings together laws concerning Sukkoth from Num. 29.32–30.1 and Deut. 16.13-14. The purpose of the following examples is less clear.

3. Following the proposal of M. Segal (2000: 47–48), the curious juxtaposition of Gen. 32.25-32 and Exod. 4.27-28 on 4Q158 1-2 may be to explain the enigmatic story about 'the Lord' trying to kill Moses (Exod. 4.24-26) by means of another story about a dangerous supernatural encounter at night: Jacob's wrestling match (Gen. 32.24-32). If so, the point could be to avoid the impression that God wanted to kill Moses: it was rather a struggle with an angel sent by God and ultimately a turning point for the benefit of the man of God.

4. Segal also offers an intriguing explanation for the juxtapostion in 4Q158 4 of Exod. 3.12; 24.4-6; 6.3; and Gen. 17.7. This brings together three passages that

mention covenant, and thereby expounds the content of the 'book of the covenant' in
Exod. 24.7 in terms of the promise of offspring and land made to Abraham and
reiterated in Exodus 6. He suggests that Exod. 3.12 is adduced at the beginning as an
'exegetical citation' to show that the worship in Exodus 24 is the fulfillment of an
earlier promise by God (Segal 2000: 49–51).

5. Tov has also noted that the juxtaposition of the census of Levites and the setting
up of the tabernacle (Num. 4.47-49; 7.1) in 4Q365 28 may be to group together priestly
laws.

6. The juxtaposition of the *lex talionis* and the freeing of slaves (Lev. 24.20-22;
25.39-42) in 4Q366 2 may be harmonizing with Exod. 21.24-25, 26-27 which treats
these laws together (Tov 1994: 129).

c. *Rearrangement*

It was noted above that in its representation of Exodus 20, which otherwise closely
corresponded to SP, 4Q158 places the Decalogue *after* the people say they have heard
God speaking but now want Moses to be intermediary for them (from Deut. 5.24-27;
see Table 15). Segal proposes an attractive explanation for this puzzling displacement
of the Decalogue. He suggests that the first two commandments may have been in the
same location as in SP – that part of the manuscript is lost – and only the latter commandments were moved to a later position. The rearrangement would be exegetical
e.g., related to the midrashic tradition (*b. Mak.* 24a) that the people heard God pronounce the first two commandments, but the rest were mediated through Moses (Segal
2000: 55–58).

Alternatively – and more simply – the rearrangement could be due to connecting the
thunder and lightning which frightens the people in Exod. 20.18-20, leading to their
request to Moses to mediate, with the thunder and lightning in Exod. 19.16 leading to
fear before the declaration of the Decalogue. This could be a case of simply leveling
the narrative. Speculating further, though, it could also belong to an attempt to emphasize the status of Moses' authority as God's spokesperson: Moses is so appointed
before any of the Torah is uttered on Sinai.[5] Furthermore, the arrangement it shares
with SP makes both Moses' role and the promise of a future prophet like Moses derive
from the people's request. It is not impossible, then, that this text could have a deeper
rhetorical point to emphasize: an inspired teacher/leader is not imposed on the people
but a response to the community's need.

d. *Other Interventions*

There are omissions, but it is difficult to identify these because of the fragmentary
nature of the manuscripts, and it is difficult to distinguish an omission from a rearrangement for the purpose of juxtaposition. In the example of Lev. 15.14-15/19.1-4
(*vacat*) 9–15 (4Q367 2a–b), are the missing sections omissions, or were they somewhere else in the text?

Segal also describes a couple of examples of paraphrase, but once again, due to the
fragmentary nature, it is difficult to be certain whether a particular instance would not
better be described as an exegetical addition with some scriptural language.

---

5.   Contrast Philo's democratizing interpretation of this episode (Philo *Dec.* 32, 37), emphasizing
that in the Decalogue God revealed himself to all the people (see Bockmuehl 1990: 73; *Tg. Neof.* and
Tg. Ps.-J. Exod. 20.2).

6. *Summary*

The scriptural source for 4QRP was itself an extended edition similar to the base text for the Samaritan Pentateuch. 4QRP contains a fairly straightforward presentation of its scriptural source with some modifications. There is none of the paraphrase or substitution that is so prevalent in the *Genesis Apocryphon*, nor is there any contradiction to the plain sense of Scripture. Rather, the main modifications are simple supplements or rearrangements. Rearrangements can be either the relocation of an episode to improve the narrative flow, as with the Decalogue, or juxtaposition of passages originally distant. The latter can serve the purposes of systematizing by grouping related laws together, clarifying by means of an analogous episode, or harmonizing with the presentation in a parallel passage. Additions are for the most part supplying content that is implied, either to anticipate something mentioned later in the text, or to record the fulfillment of something mentioned in the text. The details are worked out by inference and/or analogy to another episode in Scripture with some point of contact. The addition of festivals is both an example of contemporizing the text and extending by analogy.

There is no discernible consistent theological tendency throughout 4QRP, but that does not mean that none exists. One can sense certain assumptions with regard to the scriptural text: Scripture is coherent and consistent, and should be read holistically. Therefore laws expressed in different parts of the text are complementary or supplementary. Scripture is mined for meaning intertextually. But one of the most important implications of 4QRP is that it highlights the very shadowy boundary between Scripture and tradition in the Second Temple period. It stands very close to the stage when the process of interpretation and reinterpretation is part of the development and transmission of the text.

Whether 4QRP was intended to be read as a new edition of Mosaic Torah, or as some sort of interpretative account alongside Scripture is perhaps impossible to answer with confidence. Segal's judgment (noted earlier) that the incorporation of 'extrabiblical' material into 4Q158 would disqualify it from having the status of Scripture is of questionable relevance. It might be applicable in the context of rabbinic assumptions about Scripture and exegetical authority, but would not be compatible with the context in which the Chronicler created a new edition of Samuel and Kings, nor would it be applicable for any group operating with a model of continuing revelational authority. It seems best to leave the matter open. Clues as to a possible purpose and setting for these manuscripts give slender guidance. Most of the interventions have to do with bringing together related material and to supply implied content to produce a more systematic, fleshed out and updated version of the Pentateuch. Brooke (2002: 35) suggests an educational use in a school setting, and this may be the most likely explanation, particularly if he is correct that the manuscripts are divergent examples of a similar type of work.

Chapter 4

4QCOMMENTARY ON GENESIS A–D

1. *Description of the Manuscripts*

There are four fragmentary Hebrew manuscripts now designated *Commentary on Genesis*: 4QCommGen A (=4Q252); 4QCommGen B (=4Q253); 4QCommGen C (=4Q254); 4QCommGen D (=4Q254a). The capital letters (A–D) indicate the editor's judgment that there is not sufficient evidence to regard these as copies of the same composition, but they are perhaps different compositions of the same genre (e.g., Brooke 2002a: 21; 2002b: 225). All of these contain selections from Genesis with various kinds of explicit and implicit commentary (see Bernstein 2001: 67–70).

The palaeographic dating of the manuscripts ranges from late Hasmonaean or early Herodian (4Q253) to early Herodian (4Q252, 4Q254) and developed Herodian (4Q254a; Brooke 1996b: 190–92, 209, 219–20, 233). Thus, the manuscripts were copied within a span of about a century, from approximately the middle of the first century BCE to the middle of the first century CE.

4QCommGen A, the best preserved manuscript, survives in one large and five smaller fragments that preserve parts of six columns. Brooke has demonstrated on the basis of physical observations that the first column must be the start of the scroll, with evidence for the folded edge and outer tie surviving. Also, the scroll probably consisted of just a single sheet of leather, approximately 60 cms long, containing six columns of text with 22 lines of text each (Brooke 1994a: 162–65; Brooke 1996b: 186–90, pl. XII–XIII). The first column of the scroll survives almost in its entirety, and there are parts from each of the following five columns, with only parts of a few words of the last column. The work covered from Gen. 6.3 to the blessings on Jacob's sons in Genesis 49. In col. 2.4, two spaces are left in the midst of what is a garbled text, perhaps to allow for correction. One of these fragments was originally published by J. Allegro as 4QPatriarchal Blessings (Allegro 1956).

4QCommGen B consists of three small fragments; a fourth fragment that was originally grouped with these because of its similar palaeography has been redesignated as 4QCommentary on Malachi. Fragment 1 has possible overlap with 4Q252 2.2–5 concerning Noah's exit from the ark.

Seventeen small fragments are classified as 4QCommGen C. Fragments 1, 3 and 4 contain some possible overlaps with 4Q252 with regard to the curse of Canaan, the binding of Isaac, and the blessing of Judah.

Three small fragments originally grouped with 4Q254 are now identified as part of a separate manuscript, 4QCommGen D, on the basis of palaeographic differences. Fragment 3 contains a significant overlap with 4Q252 2.2–5 concerning Noah's exit from the ark.

2. *Date and Provenance*

On the basis of the manuscript evidence, these commentaries must have been composed or compiled sometime before the middle of the first century BCE. They are probably sectarian works of the Yahad, as indicated by reference to 'Men of the Yahad' (אנשי היחד; 4Q252 5.5; 4Q254 4 4; cf. 1QS 5.1, 3, 16; 6.21; 7.20, 24; ; 8.11, 16; ; 9.6, 7, 10; 4QpIsaᵉ 9 3; 4Q177 5–6 1; CD 20.32) and possibly '[the Interpreter of] Torah' (4Q252 5.5; cf. CD 6.7; 7.18; 1QS 6.6; 4Q174 1–2 i 11; 4Q177 10–11 5), as well as calendrical and speling features(Trafton 2002: 204; Brooke 2002a: 221; 2002b: 26; 2002c: 235–36). Thus they date not earlier than about the middle of the second century BCE.

3. *Contents*

On the basis of 4Q252, it seems that 4QCommGen was a commentary on selected passages from the pronouncement of judgment in Gen. 6.3 to the blessings of Jacob on his sons in Genesis 49. The following table summarizes the content as it may be detected in the four manuscripts (see Brooke 1996b: 188; 2000d: 1).

Table 16. *Synoptic Table for 4QCommGen.*

4Q252	4Q253	4Q254	4Q254a	Subject	Scriptural Source
1.1-3				The 120 years	Gen. 6.3
			1-2 1	The Dove	Gen. 8.8-12
			1-2 2-4	Measurements of ark	Gen. 6.15
1.3-6				Flood waters	Gen. 7.10-12
1.7-8				Swelling of waters	Gen. 7.24
1.8-12				Abating of waters	Gen. 8.3-5
1.12-13		1 1-2?		Window opened	Gen. 8.6
I 14-20				Birds released	Gen. 8.6-12
1.20–II 2				Earth is dry	Gen. 8.13-14
2.2-5	1 3 ?		3 1-2	Disembarking from ark	Gen. 8.18-19
2.2-5				364 days	
			3 4-5	Message from raven?	(Gen. 8.6-12)
	2 1-4			Noah's sacrifice?	Gen. 8.20-22?
		1 2-4		Curse of Canaan	Gen. 9.24-25
2.5-8					Gen. 9.24-27 (+9.1; 2 Chron. 20.7)
2.8-10				Terah and Abram	Gen. 11.31
2.11-13				Covenant of the Pieces	Gen. 15.9, 17
3.1-2				Blessing of Ishmael?	Gen. 17.20 ?
3.2-6				Sodom and Gomorrah	Gen. 18.31-32 (+Deut. 13.16, 17; 20.11, 14)
3.6-10		3 2-8?		Binding of Isaac?	Gen 22.5-17?
				Binding of Isaac	Gen. 22.10-12
3.11-14				Blessings of Jacob	Gen. 28.3-4
4.1-3				Amalek	Gen. 36.12 (+Deut. 25.19)
4.3-7				Blessing of Reuben	Gen. 49.3-4

4Q252	4Q253	4Q254	4Q254a	Subject	Scriptural Source
5.1-7		4 1-4		Blessing of Judah	Gen. 49.8-12 (+Zech. 4.14) Gen. 49.10 (+Jer. 33.17)
		5–6 1		Blessing of Issachar	Gen. 49.15
		5–6 2-3		?	---
		5–6 3-5		Blessing of Dan	Gen. 49.16-17
6.1				Blessing of Asher	Gen. 49.20
6.2-3				Blessing of Naphtali	Gen. 49.21
		7 2-5		Blessing of Joseph	Gen. 49.24-26

There is little overlap between the different manuscripts, but there is some scope for comparison in three places:

1.   Noah's disembarking from the ark (4Q252, 4Q254a)
2.   The curse of Canaan (4Q252, 4Q254)
3.   The blesssing of patriarchs (4Q252, 4Q254)

There is enough similarity to indicate some relationship, particularly with regard to similar approaches to commenting on Genesis, but there are enough differences to make it clear that they are not identical compositions. Perhaps they are different recensions of a single work, but they could also be different compositions of the same genre (cf. Bernstein 2001: 67–70, 83–85). For example to start with the third overlap, it seems that both 4Q252 and 254 give a Messianic interpretation to the blessing of Judah, and use the sectarian designation 'Men of the Community' (4Q252 5.6 and 4Q254 4 4). But it seems that the two texts invoke different Messianic prooftexts: Jer. 33.15–17 in 4Q252 and Zech. 4.14 in 4Q254 (unless each had both).

Both similarities and differences are much clearer in the following examples.

Table 17. *Noah's Disembarking from the Ark and the Curse of Canaan.*

4Q252 2	4Q254 1	4Q254a 3	Genesis 8–9
[1] On the 17th day of the second month,		[1] On the] 17th of the month [...]	[14] In the second month, on the 27th day of the month, the earth was dry
[2] the earth was dry, on the first (day) of the week. On that day, Noah went out from the ark,		[2] Noah went out from the ark,	[18] So Noah went out with his sons and his wife and his sons' wives.
at the end of a [3] complete year of 364 days, on the first (day) of the week, In the seventh [4] *vacat* one and six *vacat* Noah from the ark			

4Q252 2	4Q254 1	4Q254a 3	Genesis 8–9
at the appointed time, a ⁵ complete year. *vacat*		at the appointed time year by year. ³ *vacat* ⁴ a ra]ven and it went forth and returned to make known to the l[atter] generations […] him because the ra[ven] had gone forth and had re[turned	
	¹ that which he said […] ² concerning the doors and the w[indows …		9 ²⁴
When Noah awoke from his wine, he knew what ⁶ his youngest son had done to him. And he said, 'Cursed be Canaan! May he be the lowest of slaves to his brothers!' He did not ⁷ curse Ham, but rather his son, because God blessed the sons of Noah.	When Noah awoke from his wine] ³ he knew wh[at his youngest son had done to him. And he said, 'Cursed be Canaan] ⁴ [May he be] the lowest of slaves [to his brothers!']		When Noah awoke from his wine he knew what his youngest son had done to him. ²⁵ And he said, 'Cursed be Canaan! May he be the lowest of slaves to his brothers!'

Between 4Q252 and 4Q254a, there is some identical wording concerning Noah's disembarking, including two significant differences from Genesis: Noah leaves the ark on the 17th rather than the 27th day, and there is an addition emphasizing that this was 'at the appointed time, a complete year'. It is probable that the phrase 'year by year' (למועד ימים ימימה) in 4Q254a3 2 is a corruption for 'a complete year' (למועד שנה תמימה, 4Q252 2.2). 4Q252 has some material before this specifying a year of 364 days and some other calendrical information that is not found in 4Q254a, but it is garbled. Both manuscripts had a corrupted text at this point. 4Q254a has some material following this about special meaning derived from the raven's flight ('to make known to the l[atter] generations …') that is not in 4Q252, which jumps abruptly to Noah's curse of Canaan. It is possible that 4Q253 1 also mentions Noah leaving the ark (line 3), followed by a reference to revelation 'to make known to No[ah …' (line 4). If so, it shows a different application of the motif of revelation, and before this has a reference to Israel that can fit in neither of the other texts. Similarly, references to the dove and measurements of the ark in 4Q254a 1-2 seem to be absent from 4Q252 col. 1. Noah's cursing of Canaan appears in both 4Q252 and 4Q254, but in the latter there is some preceding content about doors and windows – perhaps of heaven, and perhaps relating to the passage in 4Q254a – that is lacking in 4Q252.

Such differences do not necessarily indicate entirely different compositions *per se*, but they are at least not identical. There is a very close analogy in the two different recensions of the *Damascus Document* found in the Cairo Genizah: there is material in one that is missing from the other, there are passages that look garbled, and there are different proof texts used in a similar context (cf. CD A 7–8; CD B 19).

4. *Genre*

M. Bernstein notes that 4QCommGen is unique among early Jewish writings, being somewhere between 'rewritten Bible' and full-fledged 'biblical commentary', and as such represents an important stage in the development of 'biblical interpretation' (Bernstein 1994a: 4, 24). Brooke further refines the generic description by emphasizing that in it one finds implicit exegesis (the approach of rewritten Bible) and explicit exegesis intermingled, and that it includes only selected passages to be supplemented with comment. Thus, the work is best described as a selective or excerpted commentary on Genesis (Brooke 1996a: 394–395). For example, 4Q252 treats the following passages in succession: Gen. 6.3, 15; 7.10-12, 24; 8.3-14, 18-27; 9.24-25; 11.31; 15.9, 17 and so on (see Table 16 above).

Another distinctive feature of 4QCommGen is that it employs various sub-genres. In places, particularly the section on the flood, the style is like that of rewritten scripture, working supplementary comments into the narrative itself. But here, the result is not a self-standing narrative. Other places, there is a clear separation of lemma and comment, by various formal markers.

In at least one place, the interpretation is introduced by the formula 'its interpretation is' (פשרו; 4Q252 4.5), in the style of pesher texts from Qumran. Because of this, some scholars have referred to 4Q252 as a pesher, but as a whole it is not a pesher. An analogous incorporation of isolated pesher forms into a larger work of a different character is found in the *Damascus Document* (e.g., CD 4.14).

Sometimes, a comment or prooftext is simply juxtaposed following the citation of the lemma. Prooftexts may be paraphrases or direct citations. Sometimes prooftexts are introduced with various citation formulas familiar from other Qumran interpretative texts (see Bernstein 1994d): 'as it is written' (4Q252 3.1); 'as he spoke to Moses' (4Q252 4.2); 'that which he said' (4Q254 1 1). Most often, the comment is introduced by means of a demonstrative pronoun, for example 'this is' (הוא or הוא אשר; 4Q252 1.13, 19; 4.1; 5.2) a common technique in early Jewish and Christian interpretation (e.g., 1QpHab 1.13; 3.2; 10.3; 12.3; CD 6.7; 7.17-20; Acts 2.16). In one section, the scriptural lemma is broken down into parts (atomization) which are then individually identified (4Q252 5.2-3; cf. CD 6.3-7).

This diversity of style suggests that the work is compiled from various sources (Kister 1993: 289). Also in support of this impression is the abrupt beginning of the work: 'In] the year four hundred and eighty of Noah's life, their end came for Noah'. An antecedent for 'their' is lacking. If this section were excerpted from a larger commentary, such phenomena would be more readily explained.

Both the style of commentary and certain aspects of content invite comparison with the thematic commentaries known as 4QFlorilegium (4Q174) and 4QCatena (4Q177, 4Q182). In these one finds similar techniques of interpreting one passage by juxtaposition with another, atomization and identification, similar formulas to introduce supporting citations ('he said', 'it is written', 'this is'), and a limited use of the term 'pesher' (in these only to introduce quotations from the Psalms). Both also make mention of the 'Interpreter of the Law' who seems to appear in 4Q252 5.5 together with the Branch of David as in 4Q174 1–2 i 11–12. The interpretations are eschatological and refer to the 'latter days'. There are also some similarities in style and content with the Admonition section of the *Damascus Document* (CD 1–8, 19–20), especially with regard to the style of the midrash on the well in CD 6 and the admonition by means of positive and negative examples in CD 2–3. What sets 4QCommGen apart from these is that it follows the order of one scriptural source. Its selective nature, on the other hand, sets it apart from the continuous pesharim.

There remains the very important question about the purpose of such a text, and whether there is a unifying theme or principle of selection. We will consider this at the end of the chapter, after first considering its significance for understanding Genesis as scriptural text, and the interpretative traditions and methods attested in it.

5. *The Text of Genesis*

The scriptural text as cited in 4QCommGen seems most closely related to the textual type translated by the Septuagint (Brooke 1998: 25). It also preserves some readings in agreement with the Samaritan Pentateuch against the Masoretic Text, suggesting that it was based on an old Palestinian text of Genesis. In at least one place it may preserve an original reading against the three main versions. Thus, it is an important witness to the early Hebrew text of Genesis. Some of the more significant variants are as follows.

1. In Gen. 6.3, MT and SP have a puzzling word in the phrase usually translated 'my spirit shall not <u>abide</u> in humankind forever'. This is how the translations in LXX and *Jub.* 5.8 render it, but the word (ידון) looks like it could be from the verb 'to judge', and it is sometimes translated '<u>contend</u>' (e.g., *Ps.-Philo* 3.2; Jerome). 4Q252 here reads ידור, meaning 'to dwell'. This could be a variant textual reading, also reflected in LXX and *Jub.* 5.8 (Lim 1992: 292; Brooke 1998: 8–9). If so, it is easy to imagine how one form of the word is a corruption of the other due to graphic similarity of the last letter. Alternatively, 4Q252 might reflect an interpretative paraphrase of the Hebrew text rather than a variant textual reading (Bernstein 1994b).

2. 4Q252 1.10 reads 'Hurarat' (Gen. 8.4) along with SP, 1QapGen 10.12, and 1QIsaᵃ 31.19, against Ararat in MT and LXX.

3. The variant dates associated with the beginning and end of the flood have usually been explained in terms of different calendrical interpretations. The period from the 17th day of the second month of the 600th year to the 27th day of the second month in the following year, attested in MT and SP, is usually seen as resulting from discrepancy between the solar and lunar years. The dates in LXX (consistently 27/2) and 4Q252 and *Jubilees* (consistently 17/2) are then seen as harmonizations to stress that the flood lasted exactly one year.

Table 18. *Duration of the Flood* (adapted from Hendel 1995: 73).

	MT, SP	*LXX*	*4Q252*	Jubilees
Flood begins (Gen. 7.11)	600/2/17	600/2/27	600/2/17	600/2/17
Ark at rest (Gen. 8.4)	600/7/17	600/7/27	600/7/17	600/7/17
Earth is dry (Gen. 8.14)	601/2/27	601/2/27	601/2/17	601/2/17

R. Hendel instead proposes a text-critical solution (Hendel 1995). The original dates are preserved in *Jubilees* and 4Q252: the flood began and ended on the 17th day of the second month, so that the flood lasted one complete year (although the length of this year is not known). The different date for the end of the flood in MT and SP arose because of a graphical error on the part of a scribe:

בשבעה עשר יום (on the 17th day)
בשבעה ועשרים (on the 27th day)

If Hendel is correct then 4Q252 is a very important text critical witness for the chronologies. It remains more likely, however, that the differences are due to competing traditions (Zipor 1997; Caquot 2000: 355).

4. In the blessing on Judah in Gen. 49.10, MT reads that the staff will not depart from between 'his feet' (רגליו; also LXX), whereas SP reads 'his divisions' (דגליו). 4Q252 5.3 reads 'divisions', as with SP. One or the other is easily accounted for as a corruption due to graphic similarity of the first letter, a frequent mistake in manuscripts.

6. *Interpretative Traditions*

We will consider here only the best preserved passages which allow some consideration of meaning.

a. *Chronology of the Flood*
The episode of the flood is preserved almost completely in 4Q252. It covers from the warning of coming judgment in Gen. 6.3 to the disembarking from the ark in Gen. 8.19. Underlining indicates differences.

Table 19. *Chronology of the Flood.*

4Q252 (adapted from DJD 22)	Genesis (adapted from NRSV)
[In] the 480th year of Noah's life, their end came for Noah. And God said, 'My spirit shall not reside in humans forever.	6 [3] Then the LORD said, 'My spirit shall not reside (LXX) in humans forever, for they are flesh;
Their days shall be fixed at 120 years until the end of the waters of the flood.' And	their days shall be 120.' 7 [10] And after seven days
the waters of the flood came upon the earth. In the 600th year of Noah's life, in the second month, on the first of the week on its seventeenth (day), on that day	the waters of the flood came upon the earth. 7 [11] In the 600th year of Noah's life, in the second month, on the seventeenth day of the month, on that day
all the springs of the great deep burst forth, and the windows of the heavens were opened. The rain fell on the earth forty days and forty nights until the twenty sixth day of the third month, the fifth day of the week.	all the springs of the great deep burst forth, and the windows of the heavens were opened. [12] The rain fell on the earth forty days and forty nights.

4Q252 (adapted from DJD 22)	Genesis (adapted from NRSV)
And the waters prevailed over the land	7 24 And the waters prevailed over the land
150 days	150 days.
until the fourteenth of the seventh month,	
the third (day) of the week.	
At the end of 150 days	8 3 At the end of 150 days
the waters abated	the waters abated;
for two days,	
the fourth day and the fifth day, and the sixth day	
the ark rested	4 and the ark came to rest
on the mountains of Hurarat.	in the seventh month,
I[t was] the seventeenth [da]y	on the seventeenth day of the month,
of the seventh month.	on the mountains of Ararat.
The waters continu[ed] to abate	8 5 The waters continued to abate
until the [te]nth month,	until the tenth month;
	in the tenth (month),
on its first (day),	on the first day of the month,
the fourth day of the week,	
the heads of the mountains appeared.	the heads of the mountains appeared.
And at the end of forty days	8 6 At the end of forty days
after the heads of the mountain[s] appeared,	
Noah [op]ened the window of the ark	Noah opened the window of the ark
	that he had made,
the first (day) of the week;	
this is the tenth day of the elev[enth] month.	
Then he sent out the dove	8 8 Then he sent out the dove
	from him,
to see if the waters had subsided,	to see if the waters had subsided
	from the face of the ground;
but it did not find a resting place	9 but the dove did not find a resting place
	for its feet,
and it returned to him, [to] the ark.	and it returned to him, to the ark.
He waited an[other] seven days	8 10 He waited another seven days,
To send it out again	and again he sent out the dove
	from the ark.
It came to him	11 The dove came to him
	in the evening,
and a freshly plucked olive leaf (was)	and there was a freshly plucked olive leaf
in its beak.	in its beak.
[This was the twenty]-fourth [day]	
of the eleventh month,	
on the first (day) in the wee[k.	
And Noah knew that the waters had subsided]	8 11 so Noah knew that the waters had subsided
from upon the land.	from upon the land.
At the end of	8 12 Then he waited again
anoth[er] seven days	another seven days,
[he sent out] the [dove,	and sent out the dove,
and it did not] return any more.	and it did not return any more
	to him.
This was the fir[st] day [of the twelfth] month,	
[on the first day] in the week.	
At the end of thir[ty]-one [days	
after sending out the dov]e	
which did not return any mo[re],	

4Q252 (adapted from DJD 22)	Genesis (adapted from NRSV)
the wat[ers] dried up [from upon the land,	8 ¹³ In the 601st year,
a]nd Noah removed the cover of the ark.	of Noah's life (LXX)
He looked and behold	in the first (month),
[the surface of the ground was dry.	on the first (day) of the month,
on the four]th (day of the week),	
on the first (day)	the waters dried up from upon the land,
in the first month	and Noah removed the cover of the ark.
in the 601st year	He looked, and behold
of Noah's life.	the surface of the ground was dry.
On the seventeenth day	8 ¹⁴ In the second month,
of the second month,	on the twenty-seventh day of the month,
the land was dry,	the land was dry.
on the first (day) of the week.	
On that day,	8 ¹⁸
Noah went out	Noah went out
	with his sons and his wife and his sons' wives.
	8 ¹⁹ And every creature ... went out
from the ark,	from the ark.
at the end of a complete year of 364 (days),	
on the first (day) in the week.	
On the seventh *vacat* one and six *vacat*	
Noah went out from the ark,	
at the appointed time, a complete year.	
{scribal errors: the text is confused}	
When Noah awoke from his wine	9 ²⁴ When Noah awoke from his wine
and knew what his youngest son	and knew what his youngest son
had done to him,	had done to him,
he said, 'Cursed be Canaan ...'	²⁵ he said, 'Cursed be Canaan ...'

The form of the narrative is similar to that of rewritten Scripture: the text is presented in running form with short interpretative expansions, and there are no formal markers to distinguish text from comment. However, the text is not self-standing. Large sections of the scriptural text are omitted, but not to remove redundancy and render the text more fluid as with examples of rewritten Scripture. The omissions result from a severe selectivity that leaves the text unintelligible without self-conscious reference to the scriptural text. At numerous points it assumes or refers back to key parts of the story that it has left out. So although this uses the style of rewritten Scripture, it is selective commentary, and it will be important later to reflect on what the compiler has chosen to comment on.

There are three main areas of interest in this section. (1) The 120 years of Gen. 6.3 is interpreted as a period of time until God's judgment in the flood. Gen. 6.3 is ambiguous.

> Then the Lord said, 'My spirit shall not abide/contend (?) with humankind forever, for they are flesh; their days shall be one hundred twenty years.'

This most naturally reads as a reference to decreased life span, especially because of the reason given: 'for they are flesh' (e.g., Philo, *Quaest. in Gen.* 1.91; Josephus, *Ant.* 1.75; *Gen. R.* 26.6). One hundred twenty years does eventually come to be viewed as the outer limit of a normal human life; for example, it is the age of Moses at his death (Deut. 31.2; 34.7; cf. *Jub.* 23.9–11; *Ps.-Philo* 13.8). But there is an obvious problem: for many generations after the flood, people live much longer than 120 years. It became more common to interpret this verse as announcing a 120-year period until the flood brought God's judgment (e.g., LXX; targums; *Jubilees* 5.11, *Ps.-Philo* 3.2; also *Gen. R.* 30.7; *Mek. R. Ishmael, Avot R. Nathan*, Aphrahat, Jerome; see Kugel 1998: 183–85, 212–16, 220).

4Q252 makes explicit the latter interpretation.

> [In] the year four hundred eighty of Noah's life, their time/end came for Noah. And God *said, 'My spirit will not dwell among humankind forever'* (Gen. 6.3a). Their days were fixed at *one hundred twenty years* until the time/end of the waters of the flood. (4Q252 1.1–3; italics mark correspondence to Genesis)

This passage dates God's speech of Gen. 6.3 to the 480th year of Noah, a date inferred from Noah's age of 600 at the time of the flood (Gen. 7.6, 11). It should be noted that Gen. 5.32 has already mentioned that Noah became a father at the age of 500. Thus, 4Q252 presumably must assume that Gen. 5.32 is narrated out of chronological sequence.

(2) The most conspicuous feature is the addition of numerous short additions to the story. These are mostly temporal clauses, often beginning 'in the year/day …' or 'until …'; twice there is a formal marker to introduce the addition: 'it was' (והיא). Some of the additions provide chronological qualifications to clarify various ambiguities, for example the 120 years of Gen. 6.3. Most of the additions are specifically calendrical qualifications that work out the chronology of the flood according to the 364-day solar calendar and that specify the day in the week that events happened. This is also a feature of *Jubilees* (5.21-32; cf. 6.23-32), but 4Q252 is even more meticulous. The application of the 364-day calendar is made explicit at the end: Noah was in the ark 'a complete year of three hundred sixty-four days' (4Q252 2.3). It is also implicit in the identification of each date in the story with a particular day of the week. For example, the 17th day of the second month (2/17) is the first day of the week in both year 600 and year 601. This is possible only in the 364-day calendar which is perfectly divisible by seven. It also harmonizes the figures mentioned in Gen. 8.3, 4 – 150 days of water swelling, and five months until the ark comes to rest – with the 364-day calendar (Lim 1992: 292). According to the 364-day calendar described by *Jubilees*, the five months would last 152 days due to the extra memorial days at the beginning of the fourth and seventh months (see *Jub.* 6.23). 4Q252 harmonizes these data by positing two days between the end of the waters swelling (after 150 days) and the ark coming to rest (after five months):

> The waters swelled on the earth one hundred fifty days (Gen. 7.24) until the fourteenth day *in the seventh month* (Gen. 8.4a) on the third (day) of the week. At the end of *one hundred fifty days the waters receded* (Gen. 8.3b, rearranged) for two days, the fourth day and the fifth day, and on the sixth day the ark came to rest on *the mountains of Hurarat.* Th[is was the] *seventeenth* [da]y *in the seventh month.* (4Q252 1.8–10)

Brooke notes that according to this chronology, 'none of the dated events takes place on a Sabbath or on the principal days of a festival'. This may implicitly make two related theological points: that God's judgment by the flood corresponds to the order of the universe; and that Noah and his family observe the sacred calendar (Brooke 1994c: 40). The latter point is a very common motif in early Jewish texts as noted already in the discussion on the *Genesis Apocryphon*.

It should be noted that in two places, the addition of temporal qualifiers has required the writer to rearrange the order of clauses (Gen. 8.4 and 8.13-14; see Table 19 above).

The rearrangements appear to be neither text-critical or exegetical but seem to be merely for the sake of narrative flow to accommodate the additions.

(3) The treatment of this section of Genesis is very selective. Of approximately 850 words in Gen. 6.3–8.18, 4Q252 uses about 170. That is, it reproduces about 20 per cent of the text. To that it adds about 110 words. Altogether, the new text is about one third the length of the original, and about 40 per cent of that consists of short additions. The gaps between selections can be large, and include the following omitted sections:

- Gen. 6.3-10a: the sons of God, instruction about the flood and ark, and entry into the ark
- Gen. 7.13–8.3: entry into the ark, swelling of waters, the destruction of life
- Gen. 8.7: the sending out of the raven (but present in 4Q254a 3 4-5)
- Gen. 8.15-17: God's instruction to leave the ark

Following this section, it also omits Gen. 8.18b–9.23 concerning Noah's family, Noah's altar, the blessing and covenant, the law of blood, and Noah's vineyard, although both the blessing and Noah's vineyard are assumed in the remaining text. These omissions are not exegetically significant: they are simply not commented on. In order for the new text to be intelligible, it is assumed that the reader supplies the rest of the text from memory. An essential difference between this section of 4Q252 and 4QRP, then, is that the former reproduces only text to be expounded with interpretative additions. The latter reproduces the unexpounded text as well.

There are also some small minuses (one or two words) of qualifying details in comparison with other versions of Genesis, for example, 'of the month', 'that he had made', 'from him', 'from the ground', 'for its feet', 'from the ark' (see Table 19 above). It is not impossible that these minuses are due to the source text of Genesis, but more likely they are omissions of redundant details that are unnecessary for the commentary.

Four factors suggest that the flood section is largely drawn from another source (or sources). (1) The abrupt beginning of this section assumes a prior referent that is not provided, as discussed above. (2) Its formal character (excerpted rewritten Scripture) differs from other sections. (3) The two other manuscripts that overlap with this section show strong indications of relationship in terms of content, and yet have material that is clearly not in 4Q252 (measurement of the ark, 4Q254a 1; message of the raven, 4Q254a 3 4-5; Noah's sacrifice, 4Q253 2 1-4). (4) Comparison between 4Q252 2.2-5 and 4Q254a 3 4-5 suggests that both had an incomplete or corrupted text, that 4Q252 included in garbled fashion. If so, one must also be careful not to assume that all of the included text had special importance to the compiler of 4Q252.

Is it possible to discern any thematic importance of this section for the compiler? Comparison with the rest of 4Q252 shows that interest in timing and chronology run throughout many of the selections, especially with regard to expulsion of the wicked and/or possession of the land. In this section, it is likely that the 120 years until destruction and the meticulous chronology of the flood illustrate for the compiler that removal of the wicked from the land and God's deliverance of his people follow a divinely ordained timetable. It also seems that the message apparently derived from the raven's flight in 4Q254a 3 4-5 may be analogous to meaning inferred from the animals in the Covenant Between the Pieces in 4Q252 2.11-13 (see the discussion below).

b. *Curse of Canaan*

4Q252 jumps abruptly from Noah's exit from the ark (Gen. 8.18) to Noah's curse on Canaan (Gen. 9.24-27), skipping over the stories about Noah building an altar, God's blessing and covenant with Noah, the law of blood, and Noah's planting of a vineyard. In this work, such omissions do not signal a desire to silence these stories; the compiler simply moves to the next lemma he wishes to comment on. We will consider later whether the particular selection of passages has overall thematic significance. In contrast to the rewritten Scripture form of the previous section, the curse of Canaan is presented in lemma and comment form.

> 4Q252 2.5-8; cf. Gen. 9.24-27
> Lemma: *When Noah awoke from his wine, he knew what his youngest son had done to him. And he said, 'Cursed be Canaan! May he be the lowest of slaves to his brothers.'* (Gen. 9.24-25)
> Comment: He did not curse Ham, but rather his son,
> (Prooftext) because *God blessed the sons of Noah* (paraphrase of Gen. 9.1).
> Lemma: *And in the tents of Shem may He dwell* (Gen. 9.27b, rearranged).
> Comment: *A land He gave to Abraham his friend* (paraphrase of 2 Chron. 20.7).

Two lemmata are cited and commented on in this section. The compiler does not engage in a comprehensive interpretation of this passage; notably he leaves out the blessing on Japheth. Rather, he addresses precisely the two interpretative cruxes in this pericope, answering them by means of juxtaposed prooftexts.

In the first case, the scriptural text leaves a famous problem for the reader: if it was Ham that did something shameful, why does Noah curse Ham's son Canaan instead of Ham himself? The solution here is to call on Gen. 9.1 which pronounced God's blessing on Noah's sons. The inference is implicit: Ham is under God's blessing and so cannot be cursed; the curse consequently falls to his son.

This identical interpretation also appears in *Gen. R.* 36.7, attributed to R. Judah (ca. mid-second cent. CE, a student of R. Akiva), similarly citing Gen. 9.1.

> Lemma: *And he said, 'Cursed be Canaan!* (Gen. 9.25)
> Comment: (objection) Ham sins and Canaan is cursed! …
> (Authority) R. Judah said:
> (Prooftext) Because it is written, *And God blessed Noah and his sons* (Gen. 9.1).
> (Inference) there can be no curse in the place of a blessing.
> (Conclusion) Therefore, *And he said: Cursed be Canaan!*
> (my translation, edition of Theodor and Albeck 1965: 1.340–41)

The same tradition is also given in *Tanhuma* on Gen. 9.25 (Townsend 1989: 53).

4Q252 shows a more primitive form of the same argument, simply juxtaposing the lemma with the interpreting prooftext without citing an authority or making the inference explicit.

In the second case, the clause in Gen. 9.27b is ambiguous: who will dwell in the tents of Shem? Is it Japheth, mentioned in the preceding clause ('May God make space for Japheth'), so that the passage alludes to cooperation between descendents of Japheth and of Shem? Or is it God, who is the subject of the preceding clause, so that the passage alludes to God's sanctuary in the land of Israel? The latter view is explicit in *Jub.* 7.12 (also *Tg. Onq.* Gen. 9.27; *Gen. R.* 36.8 mentions both interpretations).

4Q252 rearranges the text of the lemma – verb at the end – so that the subject must be the same as that in the prooftext: God, who gave a land to Abraham (Jacobson

1993: 292 notes a similar interpretation in *b. Yoma* 9b-10a). The significance of the paraphrased prooftext from 2 Chron. 20.7 is two-fold. First, it identifies the 'tents of Shem' with the land promised to Abraham, a point also made in the *Genesis Apocryphon* and *Jubilees* (*Jub.* 8.8-21 cf. 13.19-21; 1QapGen 16.14-25; 17.7-15 cf. 21.15-19). Second, it is likely that the broader context of 2 Chronicles 20 is summoned. Under attack by the Edomites, the people of Judah feel helpless. Jehoshaphat the king appeals to the God of the heavens who has power over the nations for help:

> Did you not, O our God, drive out the inhabitants of this land before your people Israel,
> and give it forever to the descendants of your friend Abraham?
> They have lived in it, and in it have built you a sanctuary for your name, saying,
> 'If disaster comes upon us, the sword, judgment, or pestilence, or famine, we will stand
> before this house, and before you, for your name is in this house, and cry to you in our
> distress, and you will hear and save'. (2 Chron. 20.7-9, NRSV)

This may give a clue to understanding the compiler's interest in the curse on Canaan: the concern would be fulfillment of God's promise of land to Abraham, by the removal of foreigners (cf. Fröhlich 1994: 84–85). This text may assume the same tradition as in *Jubilees* and the *Genesis Apocryphon* that the land given to Abraham was Shem's rightful portion, stolen by Canaan. Brooke has suggested on this section that the exclusion of Japheth 'probably reflects an anti-Greek exclusivism (the descendants of Japheth including Javan) which is characteristic of *Jubilees* and is explicit in some of the community texts from Qumran' (e.g., 1QM 18.2; Brooke 1994c: 42).

If this hypothesis is correct, the compiler is not interested simply in solving exegetical problems in the text, that is, what Vermes terms 'pure exegesis'. Rather, there would be an external practical concern brought to the text, thus blurring the distinction between pure and applied exegesis. Like Jehoshaphat, the compiler looks forward to God's intervention to eliminate the threat of foreigners and fulfill the promise to Abraham.

We may note two other features of interest: the patriarch's name is given in the form as found in the text being cited: thus Abraham here when citing (actually paraphrasing) 2 Chron. 20.7, but subsequently Abram when citing from Genesis 15. That is, the writer is faithful to the scriptural source, even when it introduces some awkwardness into the resulting text. Secondly, the prooftext about Abraham which is used as a comment on the curse of Canaan serves also as a bridge to a new lemma about Abraham's travel to Canaan.

c. *Chronology of Abraham's Travels*
It is very difficult to determine the point of the next passage because it is too fragmentary to give a clear picture of the form. There is no distinct citation of lemma which is then commented on. Rather, there seem to be allusions to several passages which are expounded in a running narrative, without formally distinguishing between lemma and comment.

> 4Q252 2.8-13; cf. Gen. 11.31–12.5; 15.9-17
> Terah was one hundred fo[r]ty years old
> when he went *forth from Ur of the Chaldees and entered Haran* (cf. Gen. 11.31b).
> And Ab[ram was se]venty years old.
> For five years Abram *dwelled* in Haran (cf. Gen. 11.31b).
> And after he *departed* [...] *the land of Canaan* (cf. Gen. 12.5?), sixt[y years? ...]
> The *heifer* and the *ram* and the go[at ...] (cf. Gen. 15.9a)

[…] Abram […] The fire when it passed […] (cf. Gen. 15.17b)
[…] he took […] after Ab[ram] departed […] Canaan […]

At first glance, it seems to fall into two parts: expounding on the chronology of Abram's journey from Ur to Canaan (Gen. 11.31–12.5), and commenting on the elements in the Covenant Between the Pieces (Genesis 15), with a surprisingly abrupt transition between them. On closer inspection, the two stories seem to be intertwined: line 13 mentions again Abram's departure. Although much remains obscure about this passage, the close connection forged between these two passages is an important clue to at least the main concern of this section.

First we need to consider the chronological data. Genesis explicitly provides only the following chronological data related to Abram's journey:

- Terah was 70 years old when he fathered Abram (Gen. 11.26)
- Abram departed from Haran when he was 75 years old (Gen. 12.4)

4Q252 infers at least four further chronological data:

- Terah was 140 years of age, and
- Abram was 70 years of age when they traveled from Ur to Haran
- Abram stayed in Haran for 5 years
- Terah lived another 60 years after Abram's departure (Brooke 1996b, 200)

Given a 5-year stay at Haran, the rest of the figures are readily inferred from the scriptural data. But from where was inferred the 5-year stay?

The chronology of Abraham's travels was regarded by ancient chronographers to hold the key to one of the central cruxes of scriptural chronology: the dating of the exodus. Famous already in antiquity, the problem was how to reconcile two passages about the exodus (see Kugel 1998: 270–71, 317–18, 570–74; Wacholder 1964):

Genesis 15.13: 'your offspring shall be aliens in a land that is not theirs, and shall be slaves there, and they shall be oppressed for four hundred years'.

Exodus 12.40: 'The time that the Israelites had lived in Egypt was four hundred thirty years'.

Besides the two different figures here, adding up relevant dates in Genesis and Exodus reveals that the time in Egypt could not have been anywhere near as long as either figure!

- Jacob's grandson Kohat is among those who go to Egypt (Gen. 46.11)
- Kohat lived 133 years (Exod. 6.18)
- his son Amram lived 137 years (Exod. 6.20)
- his son Moses was 80 at the time of the Exodus (Exod. 7.7)

Even assuming each man fathered a son on his deathbed, this would allow a maximum of 350 years!

A common solution proposed in antiquity is that the 400 years of Gen. 15.13 dates from the birth of Isaac, and the 430 years of Exod. 12.40 dates from the covenant with Abram in Genesis 15. Thus, neither of these dates gives the time in Egypt alone – which was about half of this time. This interpretation is reflected in the versions of Exod. 12.40 in the Samaritan Pentateuch, the Septuagint, and Targum Ps.-Jonathan. It is also assumed by Paul (Gal. 3.16-17), Josephus (*Ant.* 2.318), Demetrius the

Chronographer (frg. 2, 16), and Ephraem (Commentary on Exod. 12.40). The problem is explicitly worked out in detail by the rabbis (e.g., *Mekilta of R. Ishmael*, Piska 14 on Exod. 12.40; *Seder Olam* 3).

While ingenious, this solution creates a formidable problem: the Covenant Between the Pieces of Genesis 15 then took place 30 years before the birth of Isaac. From Gen. 17.17, we are informed that Abram was 100 years old at Isaac's birth, and thus must have been 70 at the time of the covenant in Genesis 15. But according to Gen. 12.4, Abram was 75 when he departed Haran! To resolve this, the sages commonly reasoned that there must have been two journeys: one when he was 70 when the covenant of Genesis 15 took place, and one when he was 75 when the events of Genesis 12–14 took place – even though only one journey is recorded in Genesis and it necessitates assuming that the events of Genesis 15 precede the events of Genesis 12–14 (see Bernstein 1994a: 12–14).

The logic in 4Q252 appears to be the same, but perhaps without two trips. According to 4Q252, the vision of Genesis 15 must occur when Abram arrives in Haran, mentioned in Gen. 11.31, at the age of 70.

This section of 4Q252, then, does not treat two subjects, but what is for the compiler a single event (it would seem that he regards Genesis 15 as narrated out of order: the event happens when Abram arrives in Haran, before the events of Genesis 12–14). Analogously, the *Genesis Apocryphon* also introduces a detailed summary of the chronology of Abram's travels into the story of the Covenant of the Pieces (1QapGen 22.27-29). In both cases, encouragement comes from the text of Genesis itself, where in the midst of Abram's dream (Gen. 15.13-16), God outlines for Abram the chronology of the oppression in Egypt ('four hundred years') and the exodus ('in the fourth generation').

At one level, of course, this interpretative process can be seen as solving problems in the text of Genesis. But the juxtaposition of Genesis 15 with 11.31 highlights a concern about possession of land. Although no citation of it survives, the thought of Gen. 15.7-8 is in this text the central concern of Abram in Haran:

> Then He said to him, 'I am the Lord who brought you out from Ur of the Chaldeans, to give to you this land, to possess it.'
> But he said, 'O Lord God, how shall I know that I will possess it?' (Gen. 15.7-8)

It would seem that in this text, the elements of the vision (animals, fire) are understood to serve as symbolic clues to the divine plan (e.g., perhaps four rows of animals // four generations). For the compiler of 4Q252, Abraham's possession of the land is preordained and according to a precise timetable.

d. *Sodom and Gomorrah*
A short section on Sodom and Gomorrah is too fragmentary to allow a detailed analysis, but it seems to be the case that Abraham's haggling with God over the lives of the inhabitants is interpreted by means of juxtaposed prooftexts from Deut. 13.16, 17 and 20.11, 14 (Brooke 1994a: 170). The former context concerns what to do about idolatrous towns in the people's midst: they must be utterly destroyed by fire and all of their inhabitants killed (Deut. 13.12-18). The latter context concerns the law of warfare with regard to distant towns: they are to be offered the opportunity to surrender to forced labor. If they do not, the males are to be killed and the rest may be taken as plunder. It would seem, then, that the story of Sodom and Gomorrah is

interpreted as a model for the treatment of the wicked town in one's midst. As Brooke notes, it seems to assume the view that Sodom and Gomorrah are part of the land as in Ezek. 47.15-20.

e. *Amalek*
Curiously, an obscure parenthetical comment in Gen. 36.12 about Esau's grandson Amalek merits exposition.

> 4Q252 4.1-3
> Lemma: *Timna was the concubine of Eliphaz, son of Esau. She bore* him *Amalek* (Gen. 36.12a).
> Comment: This is (הוא אשר) the one whom Saul stru[ck] (allusion to 1 Sam. 14.48; 15.3, 7).
> (Authority) As He spoke to Moses,
> (Prooftext) 'In the latter days *you will wipe out the memory of Amalek from under the heavens*' (Deut. 25.19).

Once again, there is formal separation of lemma from commentary, and the citation of distant scriptural passages to exposit the lemma. First, there is an allusion to the story of Saul's attack on the Amalekites. It is the broader context that is important. Saul was to utterly destroy the Amalekites, but he did not; he allowed the king to survive and retained the valuable plunder (1 Sam. 15.8-9). For this God rejected him. The second passage cites Deut. 25.19 in which Moses urges the Israelites not to forget to destroy the Amalekites when they enter the land in recompense for their enmity (cf. Exod. 17.8-16). There is an exegetical alteration though. In place of 'when the Lord your God has given rest to you from all your enemies round about, in the land that the Lord your God is giving you as an inheritance to possess it', 4Q252 reads 'in the latter days'. That is, this passage is expounded as eschatological destruction of the enemies of Israel as precursor to the ultimate fulfillment of the possession of the land.

f. *The Blessing of Reuben*
It seems that 4QCommGen ended with interpretations of Jacob's blessings on his twelve sons. Parts of seven blessings survive: Reuben, Judah, Asher, Naphtali (4Q252); Judah, Issachar, Dan, Joseph (4Q254). They are introduced as 'The blessings of Jacob' (4Q252 4.3).

The blessing on Reuben, Jacob's eldest son, is cited in full (4Q252 4.3-5; Gen. 49.3-4) with a few small variations. Following a short space, a general interpretation on the whole is introduced with the formula familiar from the Qumran pesharim: 'its interpretation is that (פשרו אשר) he rebuked him for when he slept with Bilhah his concubine' (4Q252 4.5-6). Then it seems that the text is atomized for comment on each part, although only the first line survives.

> 4Q252 4.6-7; cf. Gen. 49.3
> Citation formula: And he [s]aid,
> Lemma: '*Y*[*ou*] *are* [*my*] *firstbo*[*rn* …] (Gen. 49.3)
> Comment: He was the firstfruits of … [

It is possible, then, that the seemingly obvious statement that the blessing is a rebuke is making a more substantial point than at first appears. Whereas in Genesis the first half appears to be a positive statement (Gen. 49.3) and only the latter half a rebuke (Gen. 49.4), this commentary might be attempting to show the whole as a rebuke.

g. *The Blessing of Judah*

The exposition of the blessing of Judah in 4QCommGen attracted early attention because of its emphasis on an eschatological Messiah (Allegro 1956; Woude 1957: 169–72; Stegemann 1967; 211–17; Schwartz 1981; Oegema 1998; Zimmerman 1998; Evans 1999).

> 4Q252 5.1-7; cf. Gen. 49.10
>
> Lemma: *A ruler shall [no]t depart from* the tribe *of Judah* (Gen. 49.10a).
>
> Comment: When Israel has dominion [*there will not*] *be cut off one who occupies David's throne* (Jer. 33.17).
>
> (Identification) For '*the staff*' (Gen. 49.10a) is (אוה) the covenant of the kingship (cf. 2 Sam. 7);
>
> the [thousa]nds of Israel are '*the divisions*' (Gen. 49.10a) *vacat* until comes the *righteous* Messiah, the *Branch of David* (Jer. 33.15). For to him and to his seed has been given the *covenant* (Jer. 33.21) of the kingship of his people for everlasting generations which he kept [… the Interpreter?] of the Law with the Men of the Yahad.
>
> For […] is the congregation of the men of […]

The lemma here is Gen. 49.10, a classic Messianic text in both early Judaism and Christianity. It is clarified by means of a partial paraphrase. The term translated 'sceptre' (metaphor for ruler) in Gen. 49.10 can also mean 'tribe'. 4Q252 incorporates both meanings: it retains the term with the meaning 'tribe' but also adds a translation equivalent 'ruler', thus 'a *ruler* shall not depart from the *tribe* of Judah'.

Using of atomization and identification, the passage is expounded by means of Jer. 33.14-26, another classic Messianic text which asserts the future fulfillment of the promise to David. That David is compared with the offspring of Judah and the covenant with Abraham at the end of the passage made it especially appropriate for expounding the blessing on Judah. Once again, the context bears on the motif of land: the Branch of David is to 'execute justice and righteousness in the land' so that 'in those days Judah will be saved and Jerusalem will live in safety' (Jer. 33.15-16).

The method and the interpretation are similar to the exposition of Num. 21.18 in CD 6.3-10. In both cases, the fulfillment seems to be associated with the sectarian community's interpretation of Torah. Although the context is too broken to tell, it may be that the blessing of Judah in 4Q252 emphasized an eschatological priestly messiah as well as a Davidic ruler, as also in the *Damascus Document*. This would find ready support in the close connection between the covenant with David and the covenant with the Levites in Jer. 33.17-22. Also, 4Q254 4 seems to use the passage about two Messiahs in Zech. 4.14 as prooftext in expounding the covenant with Judah.

7. *Thematic Unity and Tendency*

A difficult question is whether the work as a whole has a distinct structure and thematic agenda (Brooke 1994c) or whether it merely selects and comments on difficult passages in sequence (Bernstein 1994c). Brooke and Bernstein have debated the issue in detail (see also Bernstein 1994a; 2001: 67–71; Brooke 1994a; 1996a). In part, the difference is methodological and philosophical: in seeking the purpose of a work, can one sift for implicit clues to the author's interest in the selection of material, or must one require explicit indications of purpose? Brooke finds meaningful thematic unity throughout the various episodes selected for comment, centering on a concern for 'unfulfilled or unresolved blessings and curses' particularly those associated with sexual sin (Canaan, Sodom and Gomorrah, Amalek, Reuben), and the fulfillment of the promise of land (Noah, Shem, Abraham, Judah); see similarly Kister 1993: 288–89 and Fröhlich 1994.

> 4Q252 seems to suggest that its compiler considered himself and his audience as those who stand under the divine blessing; they have the right credentials to take up the promise of the land. In particular the inheritance of the promised land belongs to those who are not involved in any kind of sexual misdemeanor. (Brooke 1994c: 55–56)

Brooke finds structural and thematic similarities to the review of history in the Admonition of the *Damascus Document* (CD 2–3).

Bernstein argues against this that sexual sin is alluded to only in the rebuke on Reuben (Gen. 49.3-4; 4Q252 4.3-6), and the motif of land is explicit only in one passage (the interpretation of Gen. 9.27 by reference to the promise of land to Abraham; 4Q252 2.8). He questions why, if these were part of a message intended by the author, they would be so well hidden. Instead, he insists that the only unifying factor clearly operative is the purpose to explain exegetical difficulties in the scriptural text. He regards 4Q252 as a 'proto-biblical commentary' that provides non-ideological, simple-sense interpretation of selected scriptural difficulties.

Bernstein raises important cautions about over-interpreting a fragmentary text, but it does seem that he is overly pessimistic about finding meaning in selection. It must be admitted that the selection of passages for comment is highly unusual. There are many famously difficult passages neglected, and even Bernstein must admit that it is difficult to explain why the straightforward passage about Reuben's rebuke required comment (Gen. 35.22) and why the parenthetical passage about Amalek in Gen. 36.12 merited treatment (Bernstein 1994a: 15, 17). It is clear that the work demanded considerable familiarity with the scriptural text and the ability of the reader to supply the context. The thematic unity of the passages included here is not at all too subtle for the intended reader.

Although the fragmentary nature of the text renders precarious any hypothesis about the purpose of the composition, it does seem possible to detect a theme running through the selection of passages in 4QCommGen, concerning land and timing, at least so far as one can judge from the better preserved passages.

- Chronology of the Flood: the wicked are removed from the earth according to a precise predetermined timing. In 4Q254a there is an eschatological message found in this story.
- Curse of Canaan: the land belongs to Abraham, and God will act to remove those who illegitimately control it.
- Chronology of Abraham: there is a precise timing to Abraham's possession of the land.
- Sodom and Gomorrah: God's destruction of Sodom and Gomorrah is a model of the clearing of the land for Israel to possess it.
- Amalek: the foreign ruler who continues to exert control in Israel will ultimately be destroyed by God's eschatological action.
- Blessing of Judah: God's covenant will be fulfilled with an eschatological Messianic ruler, and this is somehow related to the Men of the Yahad, perhaps with the Yahad's Interpreter of Torah advising the king.

Brooke may be correct that there is an implicit critique of sexual sin in the choice of
negative examples, but Bernstein's caution is especially appropriate here. It should be
noted that in the example of Sodom and Gomorrah, the prooftext applied to it
concerns the sin of idolatry.

4QCommGen seems to be an eschatological and Messianic work, and we might
state its theme as follows. The wicked must be removed from the land so that God's
promise to Abraham of land and security might be fulfilled. This is an eschatological
action of God with predetermined timing and involves the establishment of Jewish
independence under a ruling Messianic king. It seems that this is to come about
through the faithful adherence to the law of the Men of the Yahad. Somewhat
similarly, Brooke suggests that 'from the point of view of the text's function, it is a
quasi-legal document, validating a claim to inheritance and possession' (1994a: 179).

If this analysis is correct – and it must readily be acknowledged that much remains
hypothetical – it perhaps opens some possibilities for speculating on a setting for the
work. It could reflect a protest against foreign control of the land of Israel, but like
Daniel and the *War Scroll* it would seem to advocate waiting for God's eschatological intervention rather than initiating armed resistance like the Maccabaean revolt.

8. *Summary*

These four manuscripts represent variant copies of a commentary on select passages in
Genesis – presented in sequence – probably produced during the first century BCE in a
similar setting as the sectarian texts found at Qumran. It seems to use as its source a
Palestinian text of Genesis similar to the Hebrew base of the Septuagint. The commentary employs diverse forms of interpretation. Part is in the form of rewritten
Scripture, implicitly interpreting the text by means of small additions to clarify chronological and calendrical matters, especially in relation to a 364-day solar calendar.
Some minor omissions and rearrangement of clauses do not appear to be interpretative, but to produce a smooth text that accommodates the additions. For the most part
the interpretation is explicit, with formal distinction between lemma and commentary
in a style that anticipates later rabbinic commentary.

Sometimes the commentary consists of proposing solutions to difficulties in the
text of Genesis, summoning support from prooftexts both within Genesis and elsewhere in Scripture, either in direct citation or paraphrase. Other times, the passage is
broken down into constituent parts that are identified by means of prooftexts. In some
instances, it provides an eschatological interpretation in the pesher form. Even in
sections of commentary form, there is also occasional use of implicit interpretation by
paraphrase and juxtaposition of analogous passages.

The formal distinction of lemma and comment implies a clear scriptural consciousness and a relatively established text, although the use of paraphrase and rewriting
indicates that it is the message not an immutable text that is authoritative. Scripture is
extended not in the form of supplementation – new stories or laws – but by bringing
to light authoritative meaning understood to be inherent in Scripture by means of
inspired interpretation. It assumes the unity of Scripture, so that the meaning of one
passage can be shown in a distant passage, and seemingly also the sufficiency of
Scripture.

The different forms suggest that the commentary draws on interpretation from various sources, but it does appear likely that in both the choice of passages and the interpretations offered there is a coherent set of concerns: emphasizing the antiquity of a sectarian sacred calendar and promoting the group's distinctive eschatology. The content is thus polemical, both in terms of practice and ideology, but there is no indication that it was intended for polemics with outsiders. It seems to be intended for internal use by the community to reinforce its identity and ideology. Some sort of study setting is most likely.

Chapter 5

SYNTHESIS

In this volume we have examined three representatives across a broad spectrum of Jewish literature from the Second Temple period that variously complement and supplement other writings revered as sacred Scripture. It remains here to draw out some general characteristics and implications for the status and use of Scripture, and to locate the phenomenon in a broader historical and cultural context.

The *Genesis Apocryphon* exemplifies the strategy of rewriting, producing a new work that still recognizably tells the story of Genesis in mostly the same order. Employing additions, omissions, and rearrangements it produces a clearer, 'problem-free', and delightful version that presents the patriarchs as examples to emulate. The main process is effectively substitution, replacing the text of Genesis with new narrative. Most prominently, the approach extends Scripture by means of supplementation, incorporating traditions from other sources – especially *Jubilees* and Enochic writings – into the story of Genesis. This shows a very high regard for these other sources, and it is not certain whether the author regarded these as authoritative interpretations or as Scripture along with Genesis. Written in Aramaic, the new narrative seems not to be intended as a new edition of Genesis, but the work is remarkable for its creative and imaginative freedom with Genesis, even to the point of directly contradicting the plain meaning. Typologically, the *Genesis Apocryphon* represents a flexible attitude to the scriptural text.

The *Reworked Pentateuch* exhibits much more constraint with regard to the text of the Pentateuch. The interpretative modifications in these manuscripts – which may not all represent the same work – are mostly simple harmonistic rearrangements and expansions to provide what is implied by the text or can be extended by analogy. There is no harmonizing with other sources, liberties or contradictions with the plain sense of Genesis. In this way it carries further the approach of its scriptural base, which is similar to the expansionistic, harmonistic base used for the Samaritan Pentateuch. In fact, it is possible that the 4QRP manuscripts – or some of them at least – were intended and/or used as an expanded scriptural edition. It is difficult to imagine how else a reader might be imagined to approach such a text. In any case, these manuscripts illustrate the extension of Scripture by centripetal force, with the scriptural base wielding an overwhelming gravity.

Further yet on our typological sequence are the divergent manuscripts designated *Commentary on Genesis*. Here, for the most part, there is clear distinction between scriptural authority and interpretation by means of formal markers. Where the commentary employs the form of rewriting, the additions are small, specific, and systematic, mostly inserting chronological and calendrical indications. These do not represent the incorporation of external traditions, but merely working out details in the text of

Genesis itself, albeit in relation to a particular assumed 364-day sacred calendar. Moreover, given the nature of the whole – a selective commentary – it is probable that a reader would recognize even these unmarked additions as added commentary in a similar way as is required of a reader of rabbinic midrash.[1] In other words, this is probably best understood as economical unmarked commentary rather than a section of rewritten Scripture included in a commentary. Thus, these commentaries assume a relatively established scriptural text and a posture of utmost deference to it. The interpretations might be regarded as inspired and authoritative in their own right, but they must be grounded in scriptural authority.

I have argued that these texts – and many others belonging to this broad phenomenon – represent various strategies of extending sacred Scriptures. Behind these are some common assumptions about Scripture: they assume a body of authoritative sacred Scriptures that are intelligible and form a consistent unity that is an inexhaustible source for law and ethical example. There are some areas of possible difference with regard to boundaries of authoritative Scriptures and its sufficiency (e.g., to what degree are traditions from external sources introduced, and what is the status of sources such as *Jubilees* and the Enochic writings?) None of the writings assume an ideology of a strictly immutable text of Scripture, although in the preceding survey I have outlined a typological trajectory heading in that direction. If so, it is possible that these different strategies could be related to different attitudes toward Scripture synchronically in different communities, or diachronically in the canonical process: from a fluid Scripture to greater sanctity attached to the text itself. It is very unlikely, for example, that these three works originated in the same community: although all were preserved at Qumran, only 4QCommGen might have been composed there.

On the other hand, we should not assume that the different strategies of extending the scriptural text are directly or simply products of different attitudes toward Scripture. A much more significant factor is that these writings are in different forms that serve different purposes. The *Genesis Apocryphon* is a very free rewriting probably for popular edification (e.g., imaginative and emotional elements). 4QRP is a much more constrained rewriting that seems most suited for an educational setting (e.g., a systematizing tendency). 4QCommGen is a formal commentary that is likely related to more advanced study (the selective style assumes and demands considerable familiarity with the narrative and its interpretive difficulties; cf. Philo's idealized portrait of the individual and group study of the Therapeutae, *Vit. Cont.* 25–26, 28–31, 75–79). It is not at all impossible that such different texts could all have had their particular uses in a single community at the same time.

In trying to understand the phenomenon of Jewish parascriptural writings that flourished in the late Second Temple period, it is necessary to consider the broader historical and cultural context in which they emerged. In the great cultural synthesis of the Hellenistic period, the histories of Hesiod and Herodotus inspired other attempts to produce national histories and to correlate with universal chronologies. Prominent among these in the fourth and third centuries BCE were the Egyptian histories of Manetho and Hecataeus of Abdera and the history of the Babylonians by Berossus. Such histories aspired to be 'scientific' in the use of sources, combined myth with

---

1. That is, the intended user of this commentary is expected to know the text of Genesis sufficiently well to fill in the gaps between the sections presented for comment; such a reader could be expected to distinguish between the added calendrical qualifiers and the running text of Genesis.

history, and included apologetic with regard to the nation's antiquity. The revolutionary advances in philosophy, sciences, and mathematics disseminated throughout Alexander's empire especially by means of school and gymnasium (Hengel 1974: 1.65–78). On classical texts, there developed significant bodies of critical scholarship, above all in Alexandria from the third century BCE. Most important for our purposes is scholarship on Homer, which was the closest thing to a 'Bible' among the Greeks (Siegert 1996: 130–41; see 133 and n. 17). As the basic text of Greek education, Homeric epic poetry stimulated philological and historical interpretation to produce clean and authoritative editions free of errors and interpolations, and to explain archaic words and background. Underlying principles include an assumption of consistency with context, freedom from redundancy, and that one should 'explain Homer from Homer' (Siegert 1996: 135–37; Porter 1992). On the other hand, use of allegorical interpretation by the Stoics was substantially apologetic, to defend Homer from criticisms of immoral and primitive presentations of the gods (e.g., Plato; cf. Josephus, *Apion* 2.238-49), and to find in Homer a message that was acceptable for the time (Siegert 1996: 130–35; Long 1992: esp. 44; Dawson 1992: 9–11; cf. Most 1989). Interpretation could take the form of text and commentary or 'questions and solutions'.

Whether enthusiastic, reluctant, or resistant, Jews were part of the mix and could not be unaffected, in Palestine as well as throughout the Diaspora (Hengel 1974). Many Jews responded to the new culture of the Hellenistic world with varying types of intentional engagement (see Barclay 1996). One result of this was the production of assorted writings seeking in various ways and to different degrees to accommodate Judaism to Hellenistic culture. Much of this was presented in historiographical form, retelling the scriptural story with implicit and explicit interpretation to correlate the stories of Israel with universal history and chronology, present the patriarchs as bringers of culture, and reconcile scriptural stories and law with the philosophy and mythology of the Hellenistic world (e.g., Demetrius on the chronology of Genesis; Eupolemus on Moses to the exile, and Pseudo-Eupolemus on Abraham; similarly the tragedic poet Ezekiel on the Exodus and the syncretistic philosopher Artapanus on Abraham and Moses). There are apologetic overtones in some of this literature, but most of these writings seem to be primarily for needs internal to the Jewish community: to nurture self-esteem among Jews and encourage retention of Jewish identity in a context where Jewish distinctiveness was a decided disadvantage to social integration and advancement.[2]

It is important to note that there are some similarities with our texts, especially the *Genesis Apocryphon*, in terms of general approach and concerns (e.g., patriarchs as paragons of virtue, antiquity of the Jews and their law, and that these have commanded universal admiration and respect) but also in terms of specific motifs (especially the tradition that Abraham taught the Egyptians astrology and other sciences transmitted to him by Enoch who had learned them from the angels, and that Pharaoh was prevented from having intercourse with Sarai, attested in Pseudo-Eupolemus).

---

2.   For a useful summary of the debate around these writings, see Rajak 2001, who argues that these mostly serve the internal needs of the community, following Tcherikover, Hengel, and Wacholder. Gruen (1998, esp. 110–88) likewise argues that their purpose is to encourage Jewish self-esteem. For the opposite view that these are apologetic writings meant to engage non-Jews, as Bickerman had argued, see now Feldman 2006c. Specifically on the chronologies, see Wacholder 1974: 97–128.

Unquestionably the most significant product of this engagement was the translation of the Torah into Greek around the middle of the third century BCE. Such a large-scale translation of sacred texts was unprecedented in the Hellenistic world, and that it was carried out is a profound testimony to the unique function of the Jewish Scriptures as the basis for a practical way of life.[3] As a further reflection of assumptions that Scripture must be comprehensible and applicable, the Septuagint can be regarded as an interpretative extension of the Hebrew Scriptures, in a way significantly beyond the truism that all translation is interpretation (see Wevers 1996; Jobes and Silva 2000: 93–101; Greenspoon 2003). For example, Wevers (1996: 95–107) notes that the Greek translation of Genesis shows a 'tendency to level out or harmonize the text', in such ways as anticipating comments later in the text and in parallel accounts, eliminating inconsistencies in the Hebrew text, and rearranging the text 'into a more sensible order'. Other modifications include small additions to make explicit what is implicit in the Hebrew, replacement of obscure and ambiguous language, updating practices and place names to reflect contemporary conditions, altered language about God for theological reasons, and giving a different nuance in portraying the patriarchs. As the work of multiple translators, the Septuagint as a whole varies in character considerably between books, ranging from literal translation so slavish as to produce very awkward Greek to rather free paraphrase. Seeligmann meticulously showed that the translation of Isaiah reflects the contemporary historical and cultural context in Alexandria: updating geographical details and place names, making allusion to contemporary persons and events, and making a 'conscious attempt to transpose from the Biblical to the Hellenistic sphere of thought [the] nuclear idea of every Jewish theological concept: God, Torah and Israel' (Seeligmann 1948: 96). He furthermore argued that some of this is polemical, directed against another Jewish group (105–107). In relation to the Hebrew source, the book of Job is an abridged addition, whereas the book of Esther is an expanded edition with the inclusion of haggadic additions.

One may recognize among these features numerous similarities in interpretative methods and motifs with the *Reworked Pentateuch* and the more restrained sections of the *Genesis Apocryphon*; the differences are more in terms of degree than kind. Nevertheless, the translators were conscious that they were producing not 'just a translation' but the Scriptures in Greek, and that is certainly how they were received by those who embraced them. Of special interest is the effusive endorsement in the *Epistle of Aristeas* 310–11 (probably ca. mid-second cent. BCE, Alexandria), according to which the resulting translation is a product of divine inspiration and perfectly accurate, such that no alteration of any kind – addition, change, deletion – must be allowed, on pain of curse, 'as was their custom'. On the surface this would seem to claim a theory of an immutable text of Scripture among Jews, but unless we are to imagine that the author expects no one to notice the variations of the Greek from its Hebrew source we should more likely understand the claim to be that the Septuagint is true to the scriptural revelation. That is, *its extension inherently belongs to Scripture*. On the other hand, the enthusiastic defense of the Septuagint in the *Epistle of Aristeas* probably

---

3. More typically there is resistance to the translation of sacred texts because of the religious significance of the language itself in ritual and liturgy. Comparable projects in the ancient world are the translation of Sumerian sacred texts into Akkadian around the beginning of the second millennium BCE, and of Buddhist scriptures from Sanskrit into Chinese starting in the second century CE, besides Christian translations (see Smith 1993: 154–56 and 245 n. 13).

reflects apologetic: some were evidently uncomfortable with the freedom of the Septuagint in relation to the Hebrew, as is also suggested by the emergence of revisions
(see Tov 2001: 143–48). But this matter is perhaps best understood diachronically as
reflecting an increasing concern for textual uniformity: the translators in the third
century BCE show sensitivity to the current social–political situation, and reflect
assumptions that *Scripture is a living revelation* that is comprehensive and relevant.
Around the middle of the second century BCE the translation of the Pentateuch required
some defense as to its accuracy and authority, but it is unlikely that either side of the
polemic assumes a word-by-word immutable text. A century later (ca. mid-first cent.
BCE) we find evidence for the beginning of revision toward the Hebrew (*kaige*
revision), and following the emergence of a dominant Hebrew text there is in the
second and third centuries CE a marked increase in the activity of revision (Aquila,
Symmachus, Theodotion, Origen).

In Alexandria in the first half of the first century CE, Philo represents the high
point of this intellectual tradition of engagement with Hellenism, standing firmly in
both worlds to offer a learned synthesis of Greek philosophy and Torah (see Borgen
1997a and 2003; Amir 1988; Siegert 1996: 162–88). He addresses intellectual Jews
as well as Greeks with concern for both apologetics and instruction. With regard to
his Greek audience, he wishes to improve Jewish–Gentile relations and to nurture the
interest and support of sympathizers. In a context where Judaism was viewed with
suspicion as a new religion and Jewish practices excluded them from society, Philo
takes great pains to show recognition of the antiquity and moral excellence of Judaism.
He furthermore presents the Greek Bible as divine wisdom for the instruction of the
Greek world (Philo, *Vit. Mos.* 2.25-40, esp. 36 and 44; Borgen 2003: 114–15, 118).
With regard to his Jewish audience, he seeks to encourage both actual practice of
Torah and the pursuit of deeper spiritual meanings acquired by allegory (see Dawson
1992: 73–126), drawing on the earlier precedents of Aristeas and Aristobulus. Out of
concern to stave off the abandonment of Jewish practice and tradition in the process
of assimilation, he polemicizes against other interpreters who demean Torah, whether
literalists or extreme allegorists (e.g., Philo, *Conf. Ling.* 2–14; *Migr. Abr.* 89–93, *Abr.*
99, 178), and instructs on allegorical meaning in the law and the lives of the patriarchs,
which serve as models for emulation.

Philo's expository writings are of two main types: exegetical commentaries in the
form of running commentary or questions and solutions, and rewriting scripture in
continuous narrative (Borgen 2003: 115–16).[4] He shows fluency with the Hellenistic
methods of interpretation, for example in the correspondence between macrocosm
and microcosm, use of etymologies, presenting individuals as embodiments of virtues
and vices, and use of question and solution form (Borgen 2003: 122–29; Lamberton
1986: 48–51; cf. Long 1997). But Philo also shows thorough familiarity with Jewish
interpretative traditions in Palestine (Borgen 1992: 338; 1997b). For our purposes
here, it will be sufficient to list as examples a number of distinctive traditions in
common with the *Genesis Apocryphon* in the Abraham section:

- Abram heard of corn in Egypt (1QapGen 19.10 cf. Philo, *Abr.* 92)
- Sarah was the most beautiful woman (1QapGen 20.6-7 cf. Philo, *Abr.* 93)

---

4. Dawson (1992: 73–74) notes that even Philo's allegorical interpretation can be seen as a type
of rewriting.

- Abram was powerless to help Sarai, but prayed to God (1QapGen 20.10-16 cf. Philo, *Abr.* 95–96)
- Pharaoh was prevented from sexual advances on Sarai, so that her chastity was protected (1QapGen 20.16-17 cf. Philo, *Abr.* 98)
- Lot instigated the quarrel with Abram's shepherds by his greed; Abram responded generously (1QapGen 21.5-6 cf. Philo, *Abr.* 208–16)

In terms of form, Philo's commentaries show some general formal similarities with the lemma-based commentary in the pesharim and 4QCommGen (Dimant 1992: 5.250), and his use of rewritten Scripture – while more explicitly interpretative – belongs to the same broad phenomenon as *Jubilees*, the *Genesis Apocryphon*, *Pseudo-Philo*, and Josephus's *Antiquities* (Borgen 2003: 132–33). In contrast to the Alexandrian philologists but consistent with other Jewish commentators of the time, he does not engage in textual criticism but assumes the integrity of the Septuagint as revealed Scripture (Philo, *Vit. Mos.* 2.34-39). Although he uses allegory, he rejects any mythological explanation of the Torah and stresses that it is law to be practiced.

Toward the end of the first century CE, the Palestinian Jew Josephus did with historiography what Philo had done with philosophy. His *Jewish Antiquities* presents the history of the Jews from creation to the eve of the war with Rome (66 CE), consciously modeled on Greek historiography, especially the *Roman Antiquities* of Dionysius of Halicarnasus and the methods of Thucydides, and indicating familiarity with other attempts to write national histories (Feldman 1998a: 3–23). Characteristics influenced by Hellenistic historiography include 'scientific' use of sources, the incorporation of invented speeches, digressions on a theme, use of tragedy, moralizing and psychologizing tendencies, emphasis on piety and divine providence, and use of biography to exemplify virtues (Feldman 1998a: 12–13). Similar to Philo, his purpose is explicitly apologetic: he seeks to inform Gentile readers about Jews and their history to cultivate respect for Jewish people, and so emphasizes the antiquity of the Jewish race, the nobility of the people, and excellence of their laws and institutions. But he also seeks to impart moral and religious instruction on a proper view of God and divine providence at work in history to motivate a life of piety as modeled in certain figures (Attridge 1984: 217–18; see *Ant.* 1.14-15).

For the parts covering scriptural history (primarily books 1–10), the *Jewish Antiquities* is a rewriting of the Septuagint. Josephus intends his narrative to serve as a self-standing, complete, and accurate account of the Jewish Scriptures for those not familiar with them. His claim to relate the Mosaic scriptures without any change – neither adding nor omitting anything (Jos., *Ant.* 1.17; 4.196-98) – may strike the modern reader as disingenuous since he does indeed add, omit, and change a good deal. He readily admits that he rearranges the material into chronological order (indicating that he regards the Mosaic Scriptures as not chronological but presented in the order that Moses received revelation; Josephus, *Ant.* 4.196-98), and that he has enhanced his account with language and exposition to render a more readily understood and engaging story (Josephus, *Ant.* 14.2-3).[5] Feldman is probably correct to suggest that Josephus follows the lead of the Septuagint itself, and that he 'conceived

---

5. He makes this comment in the course of relating the history of the latter Hasmonaean dynasty, but it describes as well how he has treated the scriptural narratives.

of his task as not merely translating but also interpreting the Scriptures, and therefore he did not conceive of himself as adding or subtracting anything if he continued the Septuagint's tradition of liberal clarification' (Feldman 1998a: 46; see 37–46; see Feldman 2006a). Josephus, though, exercises a much more aggressive interpretative control on his narrative, 'strategically restructuring the biblical material' and omitting problematic material to reinforce his presentation of history as evidencing the reward of the pious and ruin of the impious (Niehoff 1996: 37; see Feldman 2006b). Besides sounding this theological message throughout his narrative and enhancing the presentation of scriptural figures as exemplary, other features of the *Jewish Antiquities* in relation to Scripture include the addition of etymologies and geographical details, and smoothed out genealogies and chronologies (but without systematically reconciling difficulties), and occasional appeal to external authorities (Franxman 1979: 9–21, 24–27). Josephus 'condenses and systematizes non-narrative material' (legal, prophetic) while expanding narrative material, enhancing vocabulary and style, making the story 'more comprehensible to the Hellenistic world generally by hellenizing "barbaric" names and by using common literary and philosophical themes', making the narratives 'more dramatic, by focusing explicitly on the psychological dimensions of the leading characters, by heightening the emotional impact of important scenes, by introducing rhetorical set-pieces, and by highlighting the erotic possibilities of several episodes" (Attridge 1984: 212–13).

Josephus incorporates into his rewriting a wealth of haggadic traditions in common with other interpretative works such as *Jubilees*, the *Genesis Apocryphon*, Philo, *Pseudo-Philo*, the targums and later rabbinic midrash (see Rappaport 1930; Feldman 1971: LI–LXX; Feldman 1998a: 51–56, 65–73; 1998b; Franxman 1979; see Feldman 1998a and 1998c for a comprehensive treatment of Josephus's interpretation of scriptural characters). Specifically in comparison with the *Genesis Apocryphon*, there are numerous similarities including interest in psychological, emotional, and erotic overtones, and certain haggadic traditions:

- Abram settled in Hebron (1QapGen 19.9-10 cf. Josephus, *Ant*. 1.170; *Jub*. 13.10)
- Abram was inspired to move to Egypt during the famine by reports of abundance there (1QapGen 19.10 cf. Josephus, *Ant*. 1.161)
- In Egypt, Abram consulted with the intellectuals and instructed them (1QapGen 19.24-25 cf. Josephus, *Ant*. 1.161, 165; *Ps.-Eupolemus*)
- Pharaoh gave gifts to Abram after the return of Sarai (1QapGen 20.29-30 cf. Jos. *Ant*. 1.165)
- The king of Sodom and his allies had paid tribute to the Mesopotamian kings for 12 years before rebelling (1QapGen 21.25-27; Josephus, *Ant*. 172-73)
- Abram was moved with emotion at the news of Lot's capture (1QapGen 22.5; Josephus, *Ant*. 176)
- Salem is Jerusalem (1QapGen 22.13; Josephus, *Ant*. 180)
- Abram gave a tithe to Melchizedek only from the spoil of the Mesopotamian kings, not the rescued property (1QapGen 22.17; Josephus, *Ant*. 181)
- The king of Sodom requests only his people rescued by Abram (1QapGen 22.18-20; Josephus, *Ant*. 182; *Jub*. 13.28)

So far in this survey, we have considered examples of Jewish writers consciously engaging the broader Hellenistic culture, variously concerned to help non-Jews understand Judaism and to help Jews to situate themselves in the larger Hellenistic world. To this end, we notice deliberate use of Hellenistic models and methods, and specifically we find literature in forms generally corresponding to the two types of literature studied in this volume – rewritten Scripture and scriptural commentary – influenced by standards of Hellenistic historiography and the interpretation of classics, especially the epic poetry of Homer. All of these writers show continuity with other streams of Jewish interpretation, and both Philo and Josephus indicate that they regard their project as an act of piety flowing from the nature of divine revelation, and that they regard it as having didactic value (e.g., Philo, *Op. Mund.* 1–12; Josephus, *Ant.* 1.10-26).

In the inner-Jewish world, the counterpart to the Greek school and gymnasium was traditional education focused on the Torah beginning with young children, progressing to other Scriptures and oral traditions (*T. Levi* 13.2; Sir. 51.23; *4 Macc.* 18.10-19; *Ps.-Philo* 22.5-6; Philo, *Leg. Gai.* 115, 210; Josephus, *Apion* 1.60; 2.240; Josephus, *War* 1.648; see *HJP*[2] 2.332–34, 417–22). It is this education – which Josephus credits for his mastery of Torah by the age of fourteen (Josephus, *Life* 9) – that probably most accounts for the continuity of Jewish interpretative traditions attested among the Hellenistic Jewish writers with Palestinian writers as well as the targums and later rabbinic midrash. When Ben Sira summons young men to his instruction (51.23-30), equating the pursuit of wisdom with the study of Torah, a significant part of the instruction he offers is a rehearsal of exemplars of piety, starting with Enoch, Noah, and Abraham, shown to be observant of Torah. The presentation of scriptural characters as Jewish heroes and models of pious life is a feature of many texts (e.g., *Jubilees, Testaments of the Twelve Patriarchs*, Philo, Josephus), and it was probably especially prominent in the education of children, as explicitly portrayed in 4 Macc. 18.10-19. It is also important to recognize that the Torah here operates not merely as part of a curriculum of classics, but as authoritative source of law and identity (e.g., Sir. 24.22-23; Josephus, *Apion* 1.60; 2.204).

We may recognize in the cosmopolitan Ben Sira at the beginning of the second century BCE, a genteel protest against the liberalizing effects of Hellenistic culture, by identifying wisdom with Torah (Hengel 1974, 1: 131–53). Among others, however, the resistance was much more strident, especially following the clash with Hellenistic reformers that led to the suppression of traditional Jewish observance under Antiochus IV Epiphanes and the subsequent Maccabaean Revolt. For these, the answer to Hellenism must be to separate and return to Torah (1 Macc. 1.27; *Jub.* 23.26). This intentional disengagement from the broader Hellenistic world and retreat into the world of Torah places an even greater burden on interpretation and application, which eventually diverges in two directions: authority grounded in exegesis as ultimately championed by the rabbinic movement, and appeal to revelation for ultimate authority, as especially in apocalyptic movements (e.g., Daniel, the Enochic literature, *Jubilees*, the Dead Sea Scrolls, and early Christianity). In the Hellenistic context, the latter is a particularly sharp polemical position: it represents rejection of other bases of authority such as universal wisdom or Greek reason (see Heger 2005, 81).

A particularly relevant example is *Jubilees* because of its many correspondences to the *Genesis Apocryphon*. The *Book of Jubilees* is a product of a separatist Palestinian

Jewish community in the aftermath of the Antiochan crisis (around 160–150 BCE; VanderKam 1997: 20). It represents a community with relatively high boundaries, and its rewriting of Genesis 1–Exodus 12 is intended to reinforce the boundaries of the covenant, in distinction from non-Jews as well as from other Jews (Endres 1987: 210–13). There is some reflection of (indirect) contact with Hellenistic geography, science, and medicine (Ruiten 2000: 374).

The main distinctive concerns of *Jubilees*, reinforced repeatedly through additions and substitutions in its rewriting of Genesis 1–Exodus 12 are as follows.[6]

1. To reinforce a particular view of the predetermined divine order, expressed in a chronological progression of history based on 49-year Jubilee periods and a symmetrical 364-day solar calendar

2. To present the Torah and covenant as eternal rather than originating with Moses, by dating it to the time of creation (e.g., *Jub.* 1.29; 2.19-22, 33) and showing the earliest patriarchs observing Torah and the covenant signs of circumcision and Sabbath

3. To advocate separatism from Gentiles, by such means as additions of speeches (God's intent at creation, *Jub.* 2.19-20; exhortation by patriarchs, *Jub.* 21.21-23), extending the range of laws in Torah and heightening penalties (e.g., prohibition on intermarriage in general; death penalty on a father who gives his daughter in marriage to a Gentile [*Jub.* 30.7, on analogy with Lev. 20.2]; death for any breach of Sabbath [*Jub.* 2.27; 50.8, 12, an extension of Exod. 35.2]; death penalty for eating blood [*Jub.* 7.29, cf. Lev. 17.10]; and by new laws [e.g., prohibition on nakedness, *Jub.* 3.31, cf. Gen. 3.7, 21])

4. To emphasize the distinction of a pure Levitical priestly line that guarantees the authoritative transmission of divine law

5. To authorize its teaching through association with Mosaic Torah and presentation as direct revelation, by means of placing the whole in the narrative framework of direct revelation to Moses on Sinai (e.g., *Jub.* 1; 2.24; 6.22)

6. To motivate observance and study of Torah by means of an eschatology in which the turning point of the sin–punishment–repentance–salvation cycle is diligent Torah study and observance by all Israel, leading to a return of long life and peace and independence in the land (*Jub.* 1.22-25; 23.26-29; 50.2-5; cf. the additions in *Jub.* 8.11–9.15 and 10.27-34 to the effect that possession of the land by Israel was pre-ordained, and that occupation by others is unnatural)

It seems likely, as VanderKam (1997: 20–22) and others have noted, that *Jubilees* reflects a struggle with assimilationist Jews similar to those mentioned in 1 Macc. 1.11: 'In those days certain renegades came out from Israel and misled many, saying, "Let us go and make a covenant with the Gentiles around us, for since we separated from them many disasters have come upon us"' NRSV. That is, the argument is with Jews who advocate full assimilation with Hellenistic culture on the grounds that it is a return to an ideal golden age of human unity before the particularism of Mosaic law isolated the Jews from others, which is to blame for their troubles and subordination to others. The author of *Jubilees* counters this by emphasizing that the law and covenant

---

6. For the first four I follow VanderKam 1997: 16–19; on the fifth, see Najman 2003: 41–69 and VanderKam 2006.

5. *Synthesis*   149

that make them a people set apart are from creation, that the sacred authority of their instruction is secure, and that the divine plan is for a return to separation and independence from Gentiles.

The main audience was probably the author's own community, with a purpose to reinforce their distinctive outlook and practice in the face of opposition from other Jews ('They will persecute those too who study the law diligently', *Jub.* 1.12 [*VBJ*]). Whether the conciliatory and encouraging tone toward Jewish sinners in some passages (*Jub.* 1. 5-6, 15-18, 25; 23.26) implies that the work was also at least partly intended as an apologetic appeal to other Jews to repent, or merely rhetoric aimed at insiders, is unclear.

With *Jubilees*, then, there is a clear *Tendenz* that guides much of the rewriting, but it would be a mistake to think that this accounts for the book. It is above all a work of exegesis, the product of close reading and interpretation by 'those too who study the law diligently' (*Jub.* 1.12), to make clear what is understood to be the meaning of the text (see Endres 1987, esp. 219–25; VanderKam 1993; Ruiten 2000, esp. 368–75). Simultaneously *Jubilees* assumes the authority of preceding Scriptures and asserts its own authority alongside them as revelation. As Najman (2003, esp. 117–26) makes clear, *Jubilees* establishes its authority in a dialectical relationship with the Scriptures it rewrites; by grounding its own authority in imitation and exegesis, it both appropriates and reaffirms the authority of those Scriptures (see Najman 2003). In a way, *Jubilees* relates to Genesis 1–Exodus 12 similarly to how Deuteronomy relates to Exodus. Exegetical authority and revelational authority in appeal to heavenly tablets are here interrelated (see Heger 2005: 84–85). As Ruiten notes (2000: 370), even the additions almost always have a basis in the scriptural text.

It is useful also to consider briefly the Qumran pesharim, which represent an even more exclusive community than that of *Jubilees*. The pesharim ground their authority in Scripture by employing the form of explicit commentary, but the interpretations are at the same time inspired revelation. They do constitute a distinct genre, with the following common characteristics: a lemmatic form (quotation of Scripture text to be commented on), commentary marked usually with the term '*pesher*' (e.g., 'its interpretation is …'), identification of person or event in the lemma with a contemporary person or event, and often an eschatological significance to the interpretation (see Dimant 1992: 250; Lim 2002: 40, 52–53). Despite their uniqueness in particular details having to do with the distinctive outlook of the Qumran community, the pesharim belong to broader phenomena of the time. As lemmatic commentaries they show similarities with Philo's exegetical techniques (Dimant 1992: 250) as well as the Hellenistic commentary tradition more generally. As prophetic interpretation they have analogies to dream interpretation in the Hellenistic Near East (Dimant 1984: 506–507; see Gnuse 1996: 34–128) and especially the Demotic Chronicle of the early Ptolemaic period, as noted by Daumas (1961) and Collins (1975: 32).

The Demotic Chronicle interprets a sacred text line by line, distinguishing commentary from lemma by means of a formula ('this means'). The interpretation largely consists of identifying elements in the text with contemporary events in an eschatological scheme anticipating the removal of foreign domination (Greeks) and renewal of the nation under a native ruler. Moreover, rulers are evaluated throughout on the basis of whether they abandon or adhere to the divine law (see McCown 1925: 387–92). In sum, the text is remarkably similar to the Qumran pesharim in form and content.

This survey of the broader literary and cultural context for the phenomenon of parascriptural writings is too brief to do justice to any of the writings mentioned and it is by no means intended to be comprehensive. I have focused on the Hellenistic context, which might seem to take us rather far afield since the parascriptural writings that are the focus of this book belong near the end of the spectrum that stresses conscious disengagement from Hellenistic culture. But I wish to emphasize that most of the features that we find in the parascriptural literature among the Dead Sea Scrolls are not uniquely Jewish let alone unique to a particular movement within Judaism. In a general way they reflect concerns and issues of the larger milieu in the Hellenistic world of the time. I am not suggesting any direct lines of influence or dependency, as might be possible to establish for the more cosmopolitan of Jewish writers like Aristeas, Philo, and Josephus. Rather, the commonalities are to be explained by a common *Zeitgeist* due to two factors. First, they belong to the same cultural and intellectual world, and whether or not there is a conscious concern to be competitive in the marketplace of ideas, many of the questions and concerns are set by the common culture. Thus, we find in the parascriptural writings reflection of widely attested methods and concerns of historiographical approach to national myth and commentary on classics. These include:

- Emphasis on antiquity
- Concern to relate to the understanding of the larger world (e.g., chronology, geography, science, and philosophy)
- Concern to present a compelling story (e.g., with details of psychological and emotional interest)
- Concern to present a moral message (e.g., characters as clear models of virtue or vice, often emphasized through inserted speeches and dreams)[7]
- Concern for clarity and meaning (e.g., streamlining a narrative; plain-sense interpretation)

Secondly, they are responding to similar circumstances, most significantly the 'demise of the native monarchies' across the Near East in the wake of Alexander's conquest, resulting in a widespread 'sense of alienation and loss of meaning in the present, and a conviction that bygone ages had greater wisdom' (Collins 1975: 28, 33). Thus, the phenomenon of various parascriptural writings belongs to wider trends of turning to the past for authoritative guidance and the use of pseudepigraphy that take root in 'a new world view in which the present is valued less than the remote past or the idealized future' (Collins 1975: 34).

This is not to ignore what is unique to the Jewish situation. It is true that there are parallels between the treatment of Homer and Jewish Scripture, for example with regard to the respect for the text and the hermeneutical principle of interpreting 'Homer by Homer' (Siegert 1996: 136), but there are significant differences. Even

7.   We may notice that the frank presentation in the Hebrew Scriptures of the imperfection of the patriarchs is an important distinctive of its theological message. During the Hellenistic period, though, when Jewish communities are conscious of competition to maintain self-identity and there is some degree of mutual awareness of the traditions of others, we find a proliferation of retellings that seek to renovate the scriptural characters and emphasize them as models for pious life. In the later rabbis we find both tendencies, but on the whole they are more willing to acknowledge the imperfections of the patriarchs.

among those who are very much immersed in Hellenistic culture, there is no evidence of Jews engaging in textual criticism of the Jewish Scriptures. They do not treat their Scriptures as an old classic in need of editing from corruptions (see Dawson 1992: 74–75) but as the living word of God. Moreover, the intertextual hermeneutics applied to Scripture are far greater in scope than what is applied to Greek classics. All of the sacred writings are seen to be a unity of divine origin so that the counterpart to 'Homer by Homer' is not interpreting Moses by Moses, but interpreting God by God. That is, there are some unique features that flow from the status of Jewish Scripture not only as national myth and classical writings but also divine law for a practical way of life incumbent on all Israel, and as dynamic revelation.

The parascriptural literature reflects common assumptions about Scripture. Implicit in all of this activity – and explicit in Philo and Josephus – is 'the belief that sacred texts have a bearing on the present' (Kugel and Greer 1986: 38). This has at least two aspects: that the study of Scripture as divine revelation has religious value in and of itself, and also that it has ethical value as instruction in the right way to live. The activities of harmonization, anticipation, and interpreting Scripture in light of Scripture attest an assumption of the unity of Scripture. The attempt to flesh out what is deemed to be implicit in Scripture, whether in the allegorical interpretations of Philo or the prophetic interpretation of Qumran, reflect a conviction of the dynamic sufficiency and inexhaustible depth of Scripture. We should add that for the time period under investigation, there is no evidence of a theory of an immutable text, but rather a focus on Scripture as sacred story which the community appropriates dynamically by means of various strategies of extension (see Sanders 1976).

Also distinctive to the Jewish situation in general are specific shared haggadic traditions and interpretations of law, the patriarchs presented as models specifically of Torah observance and not merely virtues, and the religious significance given to study for its own sake.

As we have noted, parascriptural writings can be related to intra-Jewish competition by means of authorizing one's own position by writing it directly into Torah or more generally by association with Moses (Najman 2003). This can have an outward orientation of apologetic aimed at a rival group in the hopes of affecting a change (perhaps *Jubilees*) or – more often, it would seem – an inward orientation for the purpose of defining and reinforcing boundaries of one's own community. A particularly relevant reflection of competing claims to Scripture and the legitimate authority to interpret it is explicitly reflected in the *Epistle of Enoch* from the second century BCE.

> Woe to you who alter the true words and pervert the everlasting covenant. (*1 En.* 99.2)

> And now I know this mystery, that sinners will alter and copy the words of truth, and pervert many and lie and invent great fabrications, and write books in their own names. Would that they would write all my words in truth, and neither remove nor alter these words, but write in truth all that I testify to them. And again I know a second mystery, that to the righteous and pious and wise my books will be given for the joy of righteousness and much wisdom. Indeed, to them the books will be given, and they will believe in them, and in them all the righteous will rejoice and be glad, to learn from them all the paths of truth. (*1 En.* 104.10–13; Nickelsburg and VanderKam 2004: 151, 162–63)

These are extraordinary passages, especially since the author claims authority for his own writing as revealed wisdom for all ages but rejects other writings making such claims on the grounds that they are human in origin (Nickelsburg, 2001: 534).

Nickelsburg contemplates that the polemic might be against such writings as *Jubilees* and *Temple Scroll*. Whether or not this is so, it does press the question how such rewritten scriptural texts – as also the *Genesis Apocryphon*, the Enochic writings themselves, and even restrained rewritings such as *Reworked Pentateuch* – could be defended against the charge leveled in these passages? Did the authors really believe their writings to be the product of divine revelation (and in a way that the writings of their rivals were not)? We have no way of getting to the answer of that because we cannot ascertain the experience of the authors. But we can take stock that such writings were involved in competing claims for authority, that there was concern to distinguish valid and invalid claims to scriptural authority, and that the phenomenon as a whole reflects a dynamic rather than static view of Scripture.

This intersects with observations about the absence of textual criticism among Jews of the Second Temple period – at least as far as is known. Even Aristeas, Philo, and Josephus, who would be well familiar with philological scholarship on the Greek classics, and all of whom take pains to assert perfect accuracy in the transmission of Scripture (specifically the Septuagint) beyond the standard of other writings, there is no hint of a need to intervene in the transmission by means of textual criticism.[8] It is highly unlikely that the authors just naively believed the Septuagint to be without variation from the Hebrew, or that they were deliberately intending to mislead. Rather, it is best to accept that their conception of Scripture and its transmission does not involve word-by-word exactitude; they have in mind above all a faithful rendering of the message (see Mason 1996: 227).

We may return finally to reflect further on the implications of the phenomenon of these parascriptural writings in the Second Temple period for understanding the development of Jewish Scriptures. In majestic simplicity, the scriptural writings are often mysteriously restrained. Seemingly indifferent to their readers' natural curiosities, they tease, but tell their own stories. Ancient Jews were drawn to wrestle with these very openings in the text. Philo and later the rabbis tackled them directly, explicitly asking questions and proposing solutions. But much earlier, Jews more often wrestled with the puzzles of Scripture by retelling the stories. We find this already in the Scriptures themselves: virtually all the phenomena described in this book are to be found in some form in Chronicles. To pick just one example, how is it that Manasseh, one of the most evil of the kings of Judah, has a remarkably long and prosperous reign and goes to his grave in peace (2 Kgs 21.1-18), whereas Josiah, one of the most godly of the kings of Judah suffers a violent death (2 Kgs 23.1-30)? The stories are retold in Chronicles in a manner to resolve the apparent discrepancy. Here we are told that Manasseh repented at the end of his life and God forgave him (2 Chron. 33.18-20), but Josiah at the end of his life opposed God by recklessly going into battle against the divine will and thus suffered the fate of his own folly (2 Chron. 35.20-27). These pieces of evidence show us that Scripture was in the beginning somewhat fluid and dynamic. Scripture was a community project and a process. It was owned by successive generations who made it speak to their situation. Increasingly, however, Scripture became static, a fixed thing, a text. Thus we see two aspects that are flip-sides of the

---

8.   Aristeas notes that the translators reached agreement by comparing versions (*Ep. Arist.* 302), but it is not correction of corruptions that is in view here. In Philo's version of the legend, each translator writes exactly the same thing as a proof that it is a miraculous event (Philo, *Vit. Mos.* 2.37-40). Josephus's version is in *Ant.* 12.101-13.

same coin. On the one hand, reworking is part of the process in the formation of Scripture. Like a stone that is rubbed until smooth, it seems that the handling of a text by successive generations hones it to the timeless quality necessary for it to be Scripture. On the other hand, the open character that calls forth further interpretation and application is an essential aspect of what constitutes Scripture. It is from this openness to give rise to multiple interpretations that comes its remarkable power to sustain different communities throughout the harsh realities of history.

> Therefore every scribe who has been trained for the kingdom of heaven is like the master of a household who brings out of his treasure what is new and what is old. (Mt. 13.52, NRSV)

BIBLIOGRAPHY

Albani, Matthias, Jörg Frey, and Armin Lange (eds)
    1997   *Studies in the Book of Jubilees* (TSAJ, 65; Tübingen: Mohr–Siebeck).
Alexander, Philip S.
    1972   'The Targumim and Early Exegesis of "Sons of God" in Genesis 6', *Journal of Jewish Studies* 23: 60–71.
    1982   'Notes on the "Imago Mundi" of the Book of Jubilees', *Journal of Jewish Studies* 33: 197–213.
    1988   'Retelling the Old Testament', in D. A. Carson and H. G. M. Williamson (eds), *It is Written: Scripture Citing Scripture. Essays in Honour of Barnabas Lindars, SSF.* (Cambridge: Cambridge University Press): 99–121.
    1992   'Targum, Targumim', in *The Anchor Bible Dictionary*, VI (New York: Doubleday): 320–31.
    2000   'The Bible in Qumran and Early Judaism', in Mayes (ed.) 2000: 35–62.
    2002   'The Enochic Literature and the Bible: Intertextuality and Its Implications', in Herbert and Tov (eds) 2002: 57–69.
Allegro, John M.
    1956   'Further Messianic References in Qumran Literature', *Journal of Biblical Literature* 75: 174–87.
    1968   'Biblical Paraphrase: Genesis, Exodus', in DJD 5: 1–6.
Altheim, Franz, and Ruth Stiehl
    1958   'Das Genesis-Apokryphon vom Toten Meer', in *Philologia Sacra* (Untersuchungen zur klassischen Philologie und Geschichte des Altertums; Tübingen: M. Niemeyer): 49–55.
Amir, Yehoshua
    1988   'Authority and Interpretation of Scripture in the Writings of Philo', in Mulder (ed.) 1988: 421–53.
Anderson, George W.
    1970   'Canonical and Non-Canonical', in P. R. Ackroyd and C. F. Evans (eds), *The Cambridge History of the Bible.* I. *From the Beginnings to Jerome* (Cambridge: Cambridge University Press): 113–59.
Anderson, Gary A.
    1992   'The Interpretation of the Purification Offering (חטאת) in the *Temple Scroll* (11QTemple) and Rabbinic Literature', *Journal of Biblical Literature* 111: 17–35.
Attridge, Harold W.
    1984   'Josephus and his Works', in Stone (ed.) 1984: 185–232.
Auwers, J.-M., and H. J. de Jonge (eds)
    2003   *The Biblical Canons* (BETL 163; Leuven: Leuven University Press).
Avigad, Nahman
    1958   'The Paleography of the Dead Sea Scrolls and Related Documents', in C. Rabin and Y. Yadin (eds), *Aspects of the Dead Sea Scrolls* (Scripto Hierosolymitana 4; Jerusalem: Magnes): 56–87.

Avigad, Nahman, and Yigael Yadin
    1956   *A Genesis Apocryphon: A Scroll from the Wilderness of Judaea* (Jerusalem: Magnes Press).
Barclay, John M. G.
    1996   *Jews in the Mediterranean Diaspora from Alexander to Trajan (323 BCE–117 CE)* (Edinburgh: T&T Clark).
Barr, James
    1983   *Holy Scripture: Canon, Authority, Criticism* (Philadelphia: Westminster Press).
Barthélemy, Dominique
    1984   'L'état de la Bible juive depuis le début de notre ère jusqu'a la deuxième révolte contre Rome (131–135)', in J.-D. Kaestli and O. Wermelinger (eds), *Le canon de l'ancien testament: sa formation et son histoire* (Le Monde de la Bible; Geneva: Labor et Fides): 9–45.
Barton, John
    1986   *Oracles of God: Perceptions of Ancient Prophecy in Israel After the Exile* (London: Darton, Longman and Todd).
    1996   'Significance of a Fixed Canon of the Hebrew Bible', in Sæbø 1996: 67–83.
    2000a   'Canons of the Old Testament', in Mayes (ed.) 2000: 200–22.
    2000b   'Intertextuality and the "Final Form" of the Text', in *Congress Volume: Oslo 1998* (VTSup, 80; A. Lemaire and M. Sæbø; Leiden: E. J. Brill): 33–37.
Bearman, Gregory, and Sheilo Spiro
    1995   'Appendix', *Abr-Nahrain* 33: 53–54.
    1999   'Imaging Clarified', in D. W. Parry and E. Ulrich (eds), *The Provo International Conference on the Dead Sea Scrolls: Technological Innovations, New Texts, and Reformulated Issues* (STDJ 30; Leiden: E. J. Brill): 5–12.
Beckwith, Roger
    1986   *The Old Testament Canon of the New Testament Church* (Grand Rapids, MI: Eerdmans).
Berman, Samuel A.
    1996   *Midrash Tanhuma-Yelammedenu. An English Translation of Genesis and Exodus from the Printed Version of Tanhuma-Yelammedenu with an Introduction, Notes, and Indexes* (Hoboken, NJ: KTAV).
Bernstein, Moshe J.
    1994a   '4Q252: From Rewritten Bible to Biblical Commentary', *Journal of Jewish Studies* 45: 1–27.
    1994b   '*4Q252* i 2 לעולם באדם רוחי ידור לא: Biblical Text or Biblical Interpretation?' *Revue de Qumran* 16: 421–27.
    1994c   '4Q252: Method and Context, Genre and Sources', *Jewish Quarterly Review* 85: 61–79.
    1994d   'Introductory Formulas for Citation and Re-Citation of Biblical Verses in the Qumran Pesharim: Observations on a Pesher Technique', *Dead Sea Discoveries* 1: 30–70.
    1996   'Re-Arrangement, Anticipation and Harmonization as Exegetical Features in the Genesis Apocryphon', *Dead Sea Discoveries* 3: 37–57.
    1998   'Pentateuchal Interpretation at Qumran', in P. W. Flint and J. C. VanderKam (eds), *The Dead Sea Scrolls After Fifty Years: A Comprehensive Assessment*, Vol. 1 (Leiden: E. J. Brill): 128–59.
    1999a   'Noah and the Flood at Qumran', in D. W. Parry and E. C. Ulrich (eds.), *The Provo International Conference on the Dead Sea Scrolls: Technological Innovations, New Texts, and Reformulated Issues* (STDJ 30; Leiden: Brill): 199–231.
    1999b   'Pseudepigraphy in the Qumran Scrolls: Categories and Functions', in Chazon and Stone (eds) 1999: 1–26.

2000   'Interpretation of Scriptures', in *EDSS* 1: 376–83.

2001   'Contours of Genesis Interpretation at Qumran: Contents, Context, and Nomen-
           clature', in J. L. Kugel (ed.), *Studies in Ancient Midrash* (Cambridge, MA:
           Harvard University Center for Jewish Studies): 57–85.

2005a   'From the Watchers to the Flood: Story and Exegesis in the Early Columns of
           the *Genesis Apocryphon*', in Chazon *et al.* 2005: 39–63.

2005b   ' "Rewritten Bible": A Generic Category Which Has Outlived Its Usefulness?',
           Textus 22: 169–96.

Betz, Otto
1960   *Offenbarung und Schriftforschung in der Qumransekte* (Tübingen: Mohr–
           Siebeck).

Beyer, Klaus
1984   *Die Aramäischen Texte Vom Toten Meer* (Göttingen: Vandenhoeck & Ruprecht).

Black, Matthew
1961   *The Scrolls and Christian Origins: Studies in the Jewish Background of the
           New Testament* (London: Thomas Nelson and Sons).

1968   'Aramaic Studies and the Language of Jesus', in M. Black and G. Fohrer (eds),
           In Memoriam Paul Kahle (BZAW, 103; Berlin: Töpelmann): 17–28.

Boccaccini, Gabriele
1998   *Beyond the Essene Hypothesis. The Parting of the Ways Between Qumran and
           Enochic Judaism* (Grand Rapids: Eerdmans).

Bockmuehl, Markus N.A.
1990   *Revelation and Mystery in Ancient Judaism and Pauline Christianity* (WUNT,
           2, 36; Tübingen: Mohr–Siebeck; republished 1997, Grand Rapids: Eerdmans).

Borgen, Peder
1992   'Philo of Alexandria', in *The Anchor Bible Dictionary*, V (New York: Double-
           day): 333–42.

1997   *Philo of Alexandria: An Exegete for His Time* (NovTSup. 86; Leiden: E. J. Brill).

2003   'Philo of Alexandria as Exegete', in Alan J. Hauser and Duane F. Watson (eds),
           A History of Biblical Interpretation. I. *The Ancient Period* (Grand Rapids:
           Eerdmans): 114–43.

Bowker, John
1969   *The Targums and Rabbinic Literature. An Introduction to Jewish Interpretations
           of Scripture* (Cambridge: Cambridge University Press).

Bowley, James E., and John C. Reeves
2003   'Rethinking the Concept of "Bible": Some Theses and Proposals', *Henoch* 25:
           3–18.

Brewer, David I.
1992   *Techniques and Assumptions in Jewish Exegesis Before 70 CE* (Texte und
           Studien Zum Antike Judentum, 30; Tübingen: Mohr–Siebeck).

Brooke, George J.
1985   *Exegesis at Qumran: 4Q Florilegium in Its Jewish Context* (Dead Sea Scrolls
           Project of the Institute for Antiquity and Christianity at Claremont 2; Sheffield:
           JSOT Press).

1987   'The Biblical Texts in the Qumran Commentaries: Scribal Errors or Exe-getical
           Variants?', in C. A. Evans and W. F. Stinespring (eds), *Early Jewish and Chris-
           tian Exegesis. Studies in Memory of William Hugh Brownlee* (Homage Series;
           Atlanta: Scholars Press): 85–100.

1994a   'The Genre of 4Q252: From Poetry to Pesher', *Dead Sea Discoveries* 1(2):
           160–79.

1994b   'Power to the Powerless – a Long-Lost Song of Miriam', *Biblical Archaeology Review* 20(3): 62–65.

1994c   'The Thematic Content of 4Q252', *Jewish Quarterly Review* 85: 33–59.

1996a   '*4Q252* as Early Jewish Commentary', *Revue de Qumran* 17: 385–401.

1996b   'Commentaries on Genesis and Malachi', in DJD 22: 185–236.

1997a   'Exegetical Strategies in Jubilees 1–2: New Light from 4QJubilees[a]', in Albani *et al.* (eds), 1997: 39–57.

1997b   ' "The Canon Within the Canon" at Qumran and in the New Testament', in Porter and Evans (eds) 1997: 242–66.

1998   'Some Remarks on 4Q252 and the Text of Genesis', *Textus* 19: 1–25.

1999   Review of *Qumran Cave 4. VIII. Parabiblical Texts, Part 1*, ed. by H. Attridge *et al* (DJD 13), *Journal of Near Eastern Studies* 58(3): 226–28.

2000a   'Biblical Interpretation in the Qumran Scrolls and the New Testament', in L. H. Schiffman, E. Tov, and J. C. VanderKam (eds), *The Dead Sea Scrolls: Fifty Years After Their Discovery 1947–1997. Proceedings of the Jerusalem Congress, July 20–25, 1997* (Jerusalem: Israel Exploration Society in cooperation with the Shrine of the Book, Israel Museum): 60–73.

2000b   '*E Pluribus Unum*: Textual Variety and Definitive Interpretation in the Qumran Scrolls', in Lim *et al.* 2000: 107–19.

2000c   'Florilegium', in *EDSS* 1: 297–98.

2000d   'Genesis, Commentary On', in *EDSS* 1: 300–302.

2000e   'Reading the Plain Meaning of Scripture in the Dead Sea Scrolls', in G. J. Brooke (ed.), *Jewish Ways of Reading the Bible* (JSS Sup 11; Oxford: Oxford University Press on behalf of the University of Manchester): 67–90.

2000f   'Rewritten Bible', in *EDSS* 2: 777–81.

2001   '4Q158: Reworked Pentateuch[a] or Reworked Pentateuch A?' *Dead Sea Discoveries* 8(3): 219–41.

2002a   'Commentary on Genesis B (4Q253 = 4QCommGen B)', in J. H. Charlesworth (ed.) 2002: 220–23.

2002b   'Commentary on Genesis C (4Q254 = 4QCommGen C)', in J. H. Charlesworth (ed.) 2002: 224–33.

2002c   'Commentary on Genesis D (4Q254a = 4QCommGen D)', in J. H. Charlesworth (ed.) 2002: 235–39.

2002d   'The Rewritten Law, Prophets and Psalms: Issues for Understanding the Text of the Bible', in Herbert and Tov 2002: 31–40.

2005a   'Between Authority and Canon: The Significance of Reworking the Bible for Understanding the Canonical Process', in E. G. Chazon, D. Dimant, and R. A. Clements (eds), *Reworking the Bible: Apocryphal and Related Texts at Qumran* (Studies on the Texts of the Desert of Judah, 58; Leiden: E. J. Brill): 85–104.

2005b   'The Qumran Scrolls and the Demise of the Distinction Between Higher and Lower Criticism', in J. G. Campbell, W. J. Lyons, and L. Pietersen, K. (eds), *New Directions in Qumran Studies. Proceedings of the Bristol Colloquium on the Dead Sea Scrolls, 8–10 September 2003* (LSTS, 52; London/New York: T&T Clark [A Continuum imprint]): 26–42.

Bruce, F. F.

1960   *Biblical Exegesis in the Qumran Texts* (London: Tyndale [1959]).

Campbell, Jonathan G.

2004   *The Exegetical Texts* (Companion to the Qumran Scrolls, 4; London: Continuum).

2005   ' "Rewritten Bible" and "Parabiblical Texts": A Terminological and Ideological Critique', in J. G. Campbell, W. J. Lyons, and L. K. Pietersen, (eds), *New*

Directions in Qumran Studies. Proceedings of the Bristol Colloquium on the Dead Sea Scrolls, 8–10 September 2003 (LSTS, 52; London/New York: T & T Clark [A Continuum imprint]): 43–68.

Caquot, André
    2000   'Suppléments Qoumrâniens à la Genèse', *Revue d'Histoire et de Philosophie Religieuses* 80:339–58.

Carr, David M.
    1996   'Canonization in the Context of Community: An Outline of the Formation of the Tanakh and the Christian Bible', in R. D. Weis and D. M. Carr (eds), *A Gift of God in Due Season: Essays on Scripture and Community in Honor of James A. Sanders* (JSOTSup, 225; Sheffield: Sheffield Academic Press): 22–64.

Charles, R.H.
    1912   *The Book of Enoch or 1 Enoch. Translated from the Editor's Ethiopic Text* (Anecdota Oxoniensia; Oxford: Clarendon Press).

Charlesworth, James H.
    1993   'In the Crucible: The Pseudepigrapha as Biblical Interpretation', in Charlesworth and Evans (eds) 1993: 20–43.

Charlesworth, J. H. (ed.)
    2006   *The Bible and the Dead Sea Scrolls, Vol. 1, Scripture and the Scrolls* (Princeton Symposium on Judaism and Christian Origins 2; Waco, TX: Baylor University Press).

Charlesworth James H. and Craig A. Evans (eds)
    1993   *The Pseudepigrapha and Early Biblical Interpretation* (JSPSup, 14; Studies in Scripture in Early Judaism and Christianity, 2; Sheffield: JSOT Press).

Charlesworth, James H. (ed.) and H.W. Rietz (asst. ed.), with D. Elledge and L. Novakovic
    2002   *The Dead Sea Scrolls. Hebrew, Aramaic, and Greek Texts with English Translations., Vol. 6B, Pesharim, Other Commentaries, and Related Documents* (Princeton Theological Seminary Dead Sea Scrolls Project; Tübingen: Mohr Siebeck; Louisville: Westminster John Knox).

Chazon, Esther G., Devorah Dimant and Ruth A. Clements (eds)
    2005   *Reworking the Bible: Apocryphal and Related Texts at Qumran: Proceedings of a Joint Symposium by the Orion Center for the Study of the Dead Sea Scrolls and Associated Literature and the Hebrew University Institute for Advanced Studies Research Group on Qumran, 15–17 January, 2002* (STDJ, 58; Leiden: Brill).

Chazon, Esther G. and Michael E. Stone (eds)
    1999   *Pseudepigraphic Perspectives: The Apocrypha and Pseudepigrapha in Light of the Dead Sea Scrolls. Proceedings of the International Symposium of the Orion Center, 12–14 January 1997* (with A. Pinnick; STDJ, 31; Leiden: E. J. Brill).

Chiesa, Bruno
    1998   'Biblical and Parabiblical Texts from Qumran', *Henoch* 20(2): 131–51.

Coburn, T.
    1989   'Scripture in India', in Levering (ed.) 1989: 102–28.

Collins, John J.
    1975   'Jewish Apocalyptic Against Its Hellenistic Near Eastern Environment', *Bulletin of the American Schools of Oriental Research* 220 (In Memoriam George Ernest Wright, ed. E. F. Campbell, Jr and Robert G. Boling): 27–36.

Cook, Edward M.
    1993   'Remarks on the Testament of Kohath from Qumran Cave 4', *Journal of Jewish Studies* 44: 205–19.

Coppens, Joseph
    1959   'Allusions historiques dans la Genèse Apocryphe trouvée à Qumrân', in
              J. P. M. v. d. Ploeg (ed.), *La secte de Qumrân et les origines du Christianisme*
              (Recherches Bibliques, 4; Bruges: Brouwer): 109–12.
Cowling, G.
    1972   'Notes, Mainly Orthographical, on the Galilean Targum and 1QGenAp', *Austra-
              lian Journal of Biblical Archaeology* 2: 35–49.
Cross, Frank M.
    1995   *The Ancient Library of Qumran* (Sheffield: Sheffield Academic Press, 3rd edn
              [1958]).
    2006   'The Biblical Scrolls from Qumran and the Canonical Text', in Charlesworth
              (ed.), 2006: 67–75.
Daumas, F.
    1961   'Littérature prophétique et exegétique égyptienne et commentaires esséniens',
              in A. Barucq (ed.), *A la Rencontre de Dieu: Memorial Albert Gelin* (Biblio-
              theque de la Faculté Catholique de Theologie de Lyon 8; Le Puy: Editions
              Xavier Mappus, 1961): 203–21.
Davies, Philip R.
    1998   *Scribes and Schools: The Canonization of the Hebrew Scriptures* (Library of
              Ancient Israel; Louisville, KY: Westminster John Knox Press).
    2002   'The Jewish Scriptural Canon in Cultural Perspective', in L. M. McDonald and
              J. A. Sanders (eds), *The Canon Debate* (Peabody, MA: Hendrickson): 36–52.
    2003   'Biblical Interpretation in the Dead Sea Scrolls', in A. J. Hauser and D. F.
              Watson (eds), *A History of Biblical Interpretation. I. The Ancient Period*
              (Grand Rapids: Eerdmans): 144–66.
Dawson, David
    1992   *Allegorical Readers and Cultural Revision in Ancient Alexandria* (Berkeley:
              University of California Press).
Dimant, Devorah
    1984   'Qumran Sectarian Literature', in Stone (ed.) 1984: 483–550.
    1988   'Use and Interpretation of Mikra in the Apocrypha and Pseudepigrapha', in
              Mulder 1988: 379–419.
    1992   'Pesharim, Qumran', in *The Anchor Bible Dictionary*, V (New York: Double-
              day): 244–51.
    1998   'Noah in Early Jewish Literature', in M. E. Stone and T. A. Bergren (eds),
              Biblical Figures Outside the Bible (Harrisburg, PA: Trinity Press): 123–50.
Doubles, Malcolm C.
    1968   'Indications of Antiquity in the Orthography and Morphology of the Fragment
              Targum', in M. Black and G. Fohrer (eds), *In Memoriam Paul Kahle* (BZAW,
              103; Berlin: Töpelmann): 79–89.
Doudna, Greg
    1998   'Dating the Scrolls on the Basis of Radiocarbon Analysis', in P. W. Flint and J.
              C. VanderKam (eds), *The Dead Sea Scrolls After Fifty Years: A Comprehen-
              sive Assessment*, Vol. 1 (A.E. Alvarez, with assistance of; Leiden: E. J. Brill):
              430–71.
Endres, John C.
    1987   *Biblical Interpretation in the Book of Jubilees* (CBQMS, 18; Washington, DC:
              Catholic Biblical Association).
Eshel, Esther
    1997   'Hermeneutical Approaches to Genesis in the Dead Sea Scrolls', in Judith
              Frishman and Lucas van Rompay (eds), *The Book of Genesis in Jewish and*

Oriental Christian Interpretation. A Collection of Essays (Louvain: Peeters): 1–12.

Evans, Craig A.

1988 'The Genesis Apocryphon and the Rewritten Bible', *Revue de Qumran* 13: 153–65.

1999 '"The Two Sons of Oil": Early Evidence of Messianic Interpretation of Zechariah 4:14 in 4Q252 4 2', in D. W. Parry and E. Ulrich (eds), *The Provo International Conference on the Dead Sea Scrolls: Technological Innovations, New Texts, and Reformulated Issues* (STDJ, 30; Leiden: Brill): 566–75.

2001 'The Dead Sea Scrolls and the Canon of Scripture in the Time of Jesus', in P. W. Flint (ed.), *The Bible at Qumran: Text, Shape, and Interpretation* (SDSSRL; Grand Rapids: Eerdmans): 67–79.

Evans, Craig A. (ed.)

2000 *The Interpretation of Scripture in Early Judaism and Christianity: Studies in Language and Tradition* (JSPSup, 33; Sheffield: Sheffield Academic Press).

Feldman, Louis H.

1971 'Prolegomenon', in M. R. James, *The Biblical Antiquities of Philo: Now First Translated from the Old Latin Version* (New York: KTAV): IX–CLXVIII.

1998a *Josephus' Interpretation of the Bible* (Berkeley: University of California Press).

1998b 'Josephus' Portrait of Noah and Its Parallels in Philo, Pseudo-Philo's *Biblical Antiquities*, and Rabbinic Midrashim', *Proceedings of the American Academy of Jewish Research* 55: 31–57.

1998c *Studies in Josephus' Rewritten Bible* (JSJSup, 58; Leiden: E. J. Brill).

2006a 'Josephus' Liberties in Interpreting the Bible in the *Jewish War* and in the *Antiquities*', in *Judaism and Hellenism Reconsidered* (JSJSup, 107; Leiden: E. J. Brill): 361–411.

2006b 'Rearrangement of Pentateuchal Material in Josephus' *Antiquities*, Books 1–4', in *Judaism and Hellenism Reconsidered* (JSJSup, 107; Leiden: E. J. Brill): 343–60.

2006c 'The Reshaping of Biblical Narrative in the Hellenistic Period', in *Judaism and Hellenism Reconsidered* (JSJSup, 107; Leiden: E. J. Brill): 103–27.

Feldman, Louis H., and Meyer Reinhold

1996 *Jewish Life and Thought among Greeks and Romans: Primary Readings* (Minneapolis: Fortress Press).

Fishbane, Michael

1985 *Biblical Interpretation in Ancient Israel* (Oxford: Oxford University Press, Clarendon Press).

1988 'Use, Authority and Interpretation of Mikra at Qumran', in Mulder 1988: 339–77.

2000 'Types of Biblical Intertextuality', in *Congress Volume: Oslo 1998* (VTSup, 80; A. Lemaire and M. Sæbø; Leiden: E. J. Brill): 39–44.

Fisk, Bruce N.

2000a 'One Good Story Deserves Another: The Hermeneutics of Invoking Secondary Biblical Episodes in the Narratives of *Pseudo-Philo* and the *Testaments of the Twelve Patriarchs*', in Evans (ed.) 2000: 217–38.

2000b 'Rewritten Bible', in C. A. Evans and S. E. Porter (eds), *Dictionary of New Testament Background* (Downers Grove, IL: InterVarsity Press): 947–53.

2001 *Do You Not Remember? Scripture, Story and Exegesis in the Rewritten Bible of Pseudo-Philo* (JSPSup, 37; Sheffield: Sheffield Academic Press).

Fitzmyer, Joseph A.
1971   *The Genesis Apocryphon of Qumran Cave 1: A Commentary* (BibOr; Rome: Biblical Institute Press, 2nd rev.edn).
1974   'The Contribution of Qumran Aramaic to the Study of the New Testament', *New Testament Studies* 20: 382–407.
2000   'Aramaic', in *EDSS* 1: 48–51.
2004   *The Genesis Apocryphon of Qumran Cave 1 (1Q20): A Commentary* (Biblica et Orientalia 18/B; Rome: Biblical Institute Press, 3rd edn).

Flusser, David
1957   'Healing Through the Laying-on of Hands in a Dead Sea Scroll', *IEJ* 7: 107–108.

Folkert, Kendall W.
1989   'The "Canons" of Scripture', in Levering (ed.) 1989: 170–79.

Franxman, Thomas W.
1979   *Genesis and the Jewish Antiquities of Flavius Josephus* (BibOr, 35; Rome: Biblical Institute Press).

Freedman, R. D. H.
1983   *Midrash Rabbah* (New York: The Soncino Press).

Frey, Jorg
1997   'Zum Weltbild im Jubiläenbuch', in Albani *et al.* (eds), 1997: 261–92.

Friedlander, Gerald
1981   *Pirkê de Rabbi Eliezer. Translated and Annotated with Introduction and Indices* (The Judaic Studies Library; New York: Sepher-Hermon Press, 4th edn).

Fröhlich, I.
1994   'Themes, Structure and Genre of Pesher Genesis. A Response to George J. Brooke', *Jewish Quarterly Review* 85: 81–90.

Gabrion, Henri
1979   'L'Interprétation de l'Ecriture dans la Littérature de Qumrân', *Aufstieg und Niedergang der Römischen Welt* 19.1 (Berlin: de Gruyter): 779–848.

García Martínez, Florentino
1992   '4QMess Ar and the Book of Noah', in *Qumran and Apocalyptic: Studies on the Aramaic Texts from Qumran* (STDJ 9; Leiden: E. J. Brill): 1–44.
1994   *The Dead Sea Scrolls Translated. The Qumran Texts in English* (trans. Wilfred G.E. Watson; Leiden: E. J. Brill).
1995   'Biblical Borderlines', in *The People of the Dead Sea Scrolls* (trans. Wilfred G.E. Watson; Leiden: E. J. Brill): 123–38.
1998   'New Perspectives on the Study of the Dead Sea Scrolls', in Florentino García Martínez and Edward Noort (eds), *Perspectives in the Study of the Old Testament and Early Judaism. A Symposium in Honour of Adam S. Van der Woude on the Occasion of His 70th Birthday* (VTSup; Leiden: E. J. Brill): 230–48.
2004   'Apocryphal, Pseudepigraphal and Para-Biblical Texts from Qumran', *Revue de Qumran* 21(3): 365–77.

Gevirtz, Marianne L.
1992   'Abram's Dream in the Genesis Apocryphen: Its Motifs and Their Function', *Maarav* 8: 229–43.

Ginsberg, H.L.
1967   Review of J. A. Fitzmyer, *The Genesis Apocryphon of Qumran Cave I: A Commentary*, *Theological Studies* 28(1): 574–77.

Ginzberg, Louis
1937–67 *The Legends of the Jews* (H. Szold, trans.; Philadelphia: Jewish Publication Society of America).

Gnuse, Robert Karl
1996   *Dreams and Dream Reports in the Writings of Josephus: A Traditio-Historical Analysis* (AGAJU 36; Leiden: E. J. Brill).

Graham, William A.
1987   *Beyond the Written Word. Oral Aspects of Scripture in the History of Religion* (Cambridge: Cambridge University Press).

Greenfield, Jonas C.
1978   'Aramaic and Its Dialects', in H. H. Paper (ed.), *Jewish Languages: Theme and Variations* (Cambridge, MA: Association for Jewish Studies): 29–43.

Greenfield, Jonas C., and Elisha Qimron
1992   'The Genesis Apocryphon Col. XII', in T. Muraoka (ed.), *Studies in Qumran Aramaic* (*Abr-Nahrain* Supp. 3; Louvain: Peeters): 70–77.

Greenfield, Jonas C., Michael E. Stone, and Esther Eshel
2004   *The Aramaic Levi Document: Edition, Translation, Commentary* (SVTP 19; Leiden: E. J. Brill).

Greenspoon, Leonard
2003   'Hebrew Into Greek: Interpretation in, by, and of the Septuagint', in Alan J. Hauser and Duane F. Watson (eds), *A History of Biblical Interpretation*, Vol. 1, *The Ancient Period* (Grand Rapids: Eerdmans): 80–113.

Gruen, Erich S.
1998   *Heritage and Hellenism: The Reinvention of Jewish Tradition* (Hellenistic Culture and Society 3; University of California Press).

Halpern-Amaru, Betsy
1994   *Rewriting the Bible: Land and Covenant in Postbiblical Jewish Literature* (Valley Forge, PA: Trinity Press International).

Harrington, Daniel J.
1986   'The Bible Rewritten (Narratives)', in R. A. Kraft and G. W. E. Nickelsburg (eds), *Early Judaism and Its Modern Interpreters* (The Bible and Its Modern Interpreters; Philadelphia: Fortress Press): 239–47, 253–55.

Hays, Richard B.
1989   *Echoes of Scripture in the Letters of Paul* (New Haven: Yale University Press).

Heger, Paul
2005   'Qumran Exegesis: "Rewritten Torah" or Interpretation?, *Revue de Qumran* 22: 61–87.

Helmer, Christine, and Christoff Landmesser (eds)
2004   *One Scripture or Many? Canon from Biblical, Theological, and Philosophical Perspectives* (Oxford: Oxford University Press).

Hendel, Ronald S.
1995   '4Q252 and the Flood Chronology of Genesis 7–8: A Text Critical Solution', *Dead Sea Discoveries* 2(1): 72–79.

1998   *The Text of Genesis 1–11: Textual Studies and Critical Edition* (New York: Oxford University Press).

Hengel, Martin
1974   *Judaism and Hellenism: Studies in their Encounter in Palestine During the Early Hellenistic Period* (trans. J. Bowden; Philadelphia: Fortress Press).

Henze, Matthias (ed.)
2005   *Biblical Interpretation at Qumran* (Studies in the Dead Sea Scrolls and Related Literature; Grand Rapids: Eerdmans).

Herbert Edward D., and Emanuel Tov (eds)
2002   *The Bible as Book: The Hebrew Bible and the Judaean Desert Discoveries* (London: British Library).

Hogan, Larry P.
  1992 *Healing in the Second Temple Period* (NTOA, 21; Göttingen: Vandenhoeck & Ruprecht).
Holdrege, Barbara A.
  1989 'The Bride of Israel: The Ontological Status of Scripture in the Rabbinic and Kabbalistic Traditions', in Levering (ed.) 1989: 180–261.
Hölscher, Gustav
  1949 *Drei Erdkarten. Ein Beitrag zur Erdkenntnis des hebräischen Altertums* (Heidelberg: Carl Winter/Universitätsverlag).
Horgan, Maurya P.
  1979 *Pesharim: Qumran Interpretations of Biblical Books* (Washington: CBA).
Jacobson, Howard
  1993 '4Q252 fr. 1: Further Comments', *Journal of Jewish Studies* 44: 291–93.
  1996 *A Commentary on Pseudo-Philo's Liber Antiquitatum Biblicarum. With Latin Text and English Translation* (2 vols; AGAJU, 31; Leiden: E. J. Brill).
Jobes, Karen H. and Moisés Silva
  2000 *Invitation to the Septuagint* (Grand Rapids: Baker).
Jobling, David K.
  1972a ' "And Have Dominion...": The Interpretation of Genesis 1, 28 in Philo Judaeus', *Journal for the Study of Judaism* 8(1): 50–82.
  1972b ' "And Have Dominion...": The Interpretation of Old Testament Texts Concerning Man's Rule Over the Creation (Genesis 1:26, 28, 9:2–2, Psalm 8:7–9) from 200 B.C. to the Time of the Council of Nicea' (ThD dissertation; New York: Union Theological Seminary).
Kaestli, Jean-Daniel, and Otto Wermelinger (eds)
  1984 *Le canon de l'ancien testament: sa formation et son histoire* (Le Monde de la Bible; Geneva: Labor et Fides).
Kaufman, Stephen A.
  1992 'Languages (Aramaic)', in *The Anchor Bible Dictionary*, IV (New York: Doubleday): 173–78.
Kister, Menahem
  1992 'Some Aspects of Qumran Halacha', in Trebolle Barrera and Vegas Montaner (eds) 1992, vol. 2: 571–88.
  1993 'Notes on Some New Texts from Qumran', *Journal of Jewish Studies* 44: 280–90.
  1998 'A Common Heritage: Biblical Interpretation at Qumran and Its Implications', in Stone and Chazon (eds) 1998: 101–11.
Kooij, Arie van der, and K. van der Toorn (eds)
  1998 *Canonization and Decanonization. Papers Presented to the International Conference of the Leiden Institute for the Study of Religions (LISOR), Held at Leiden 9–10 January 1997* (Studies in the History of Religions, 82; Leiden: E. J. Brill).
Kugel, James L.
  1997 *The Bible as It Was* (Cambridge, MA: Harvard University Press).
  1998 *Traditions of the Bible: A Guide to the Bible as It Was at the Start of the Common Era* (Cambridge, MA: Harvard University Press).
Kugel, James L., and Rowan A. Greer
  1986 *Early Biblical Interpretation* (LEC, 3; Philadelphia: Westminster Press).
Kugler, Robert A.
  1996 *From Patriarch to Priest: The Levi-Priestly Tradition from Aramaic Levi to Testament of Levi* (SBLEJL, 9; Atlanta: Scholars Press).

2001   *The Testaments of the Twelve Patriarchs* (Guides to Apocrypha and Pseudepigrapha; Sheffield: Sheffield Academic Press).

2003   'Rethinking the Notion of "Scripture" in the Dead Sea Scrolls: Leviticus as a Test Case', in R. Rendtorff and R. A. Kugler (eds), *The Book of Leviticus: Composition and Reception* (VTSup, 93; Leiden: E. J. Brill). 342–57.

Kuiper, G.J.
1968   'A Study of the Relationship Between *A Genesis Apocryphon* and the Pentateuchal Targumim in Genesis 14:1–12', in Matthew Black and Georg Fohrer (eds), *Memoriam Paul Kahle* (*BZAW* 103; Berlin: A. Töpelmann): 149–61.

Kutscher, Eduard Y.
1965   'The Language of the Genesis Apocryphon: A Preliminary Study', in Chaim Rabin and Yigael Yadin (eds), *Aspects of the Dead Sea Scrolls* (ScrHier, 4; Jerusalem: Magnes Press, 2nd edn): 1–35.

Lamberton, Robert
1986   *Homer the Theologian: Neoplatonist Allegorical Reading and the Growth of the Epic Tradition* (Berkeley: University of California Press).

Lamberton, Robert and John J. Kearney (eds)
1992   *Homer's Ancient Readers: The Hermeneutics of Greek Epic's Earliest Exegetes* (Princeton: Princeton University Press).

Lange, Armin
2002a   'Annotated List of the Texts from the Judaean Desert Classified by Content and Genre', with U. Mittmann-Richert, in DJD 39: 115–64.

2002b   'The Status of the Biblical Texts in the Qumran Corpus and the Canonical Process', in Herbert and Tov 2002: 21–30.

2003   'The Parabiblical Literature of the Qumran Library and the Canonical History of the Hebrew Bible', in Shalom M. Paul, Robert A. Kraft, Lawrence H. Schiffman, and Weston W. Fields (eds), *Emanuel: Studies in Hebrew Bible, Septuagint, and Dead Sea Scrolls in Honor of Emanuel Tov* (Leiden: E. J. Brill): 305–21.

2004   'From Literature to Scripture: The Unity and Plurality of the Hebrew Scriptures in Light of the Qumran Library', in Helmer and Landmesser (eds) 2004: 51–107.

Forthcoming   *Einleitung in die Textfunde vom Toten Meer* (Tübingen: Mohr–Siebeck).
Leiman, Sid Z.
1976   *The Canonization of Hebrew Scripture: The Talmudic and Midrashic Evidence* (TCAAS, 47; Hamden, CT: Archon).

Levering, Miriam
1989   'Scripture and Its Reception: A Buddhist Case', in Levering (ed.) 1989: 58–101.
Levering, Miriam (ed.)
1989   *Rethinking Scripture: Essays from a Comparative Perspective* (Albany, NY: SUNY press).

Lewis, Jack P.
1978   *A Study of the Interpretation of Noah and the Flood in Jewish and Christian Literature* (Leiden: E. J. Brill, repr. edn [1968]).

Lim, Timothy H.
1992   'The Chronology of the Flood Story in a Qumran Text (4Q252)', *Journal of Jewish Studies* 43: 288–98.

2002   *Pesharim* (CQS 3; London: Continuum, Sheffield Academic Press).
Lim, Timothy H., L. W. Hurtado, A. G. Auld, and A. Jack (eds)
2000   *The Dead Sea Scrolls in Their Historical Context* (Edinburgh: T&T Clark)
Long, A. A.
1992   'Stoic Readings of Homer', in Lamberton and Kearney (eds) 1992: 41–66.

1997 'Allegory in Philo and Etymology in Stoicism: A Plea for Drawing Distinctions', in Runia and Sterling (eds) 1997: 198–210.

Lundberg, Marilyn, and Bruce Zuckerman
1996 'New Aramaic Fragments from Qumran Cave One', *Newsletter for the Comprehensive Aramaic Lexicon* 12: 1–5.

Maier, Johann
1996a 'Early Jewish Biblical Interpretation in the Qumran Literature', in Sæbø 1996: 108–29.

1996b *Die Qumran Essener: Die Texte vom Toten Meer. III. Einführung, Zeitrechnung, Register und Bibliographie* (München: Reinhardt).

Mandel, P.
2001 'Midrashic Exegesis and Its Precedents in the Dead Sea Scrolls', *Dead Sea Discoveries* 8(2): 149–68.

Martone, Corrado
2004 'Biblical or not Biblical? Some Doubts and Questions', *Revue de Qumran* 21(3): 386–94.

Mason, Steve
1996 'Josephus on Canon and Scriptures', in Sæbø (ed.) 1996: 217–35.

Mayes, A. D. H. (ed.)
2000 *Text in Context: Essays by Members of the Society for Old Testament Study* (Oxford: Oxford University Press).

McCown, C. C.
1925 'Hebrew and Egyptian Apocalyptic Literature', *Harvard Theological Review* 18.4: 357–411.

McDonald, Lee M., and James A. Sanders (eds)
2002 *The Canon Debate* (Peabody, MA: Hendrickson).

Milgrom, Jacob
1994 'Qumran's Biblical Hermeneutics: The Case of the Wood Offering', *Revue de Qumran* 16 (1994): 449–56.

Milik, J. T.
1955 'Apocalypse de Lamech', in DJD 1: 86–87.

1959 *Ten Years of Discovery in the Wilderness of Judaea* (trans. J. Strugnell; London: SCM).

1976 *The Books of Enoch: Aramaic Fragments of Qumrân Cave 4* (in collaboration with M. Black; Oxford: Clarendon Press).

Morgenstern, Matthew
1996 'A New Clue to the Original Length of the Genesis Apocryphon', *Journal of Jewish Studies* 47: 345–47.

Morgenstern, Matthew, Elisha Qimron, and D. Sivan
1995 'The Hitherto Unpublished Columns of the Genesis Apocryphon', G. Bearman and S. Spiro (appendix by), *Abr-Nahrain* 33: 30–54.

Most, Glenn W.
1989 'Cornutus and Stoic Allegoresis: A Preliminary Report', in Wolfgang Haase (ed.), *ANRW* II.36.3 (Berlin: Walter de Gruyter): 2014–65.

Mulder, Martin J. (ed.)
1988 *Mikra: Text, Translation, Reading and Interpretation of the Hebrew Bible in Ancient Judaism and Early Christianity* (CRINT, 2.1; Assen: Van Gorcum; Minneapolis: Fortress Press).

Najman, Hindi
2000 'Torah of Moses: Pseudonymous Attribution in Second Temple Writings', in Evans (ed.) 2000: 202–16.

2003   *Seconding Sinai: The Development of Mosaic Discourse in Second Temple Judaism* (JSJSup, 77; Leiden: E. J. Brill).

Nickelsburg, George W. E.
1981   'The Gebesis Apocryphon', in *Jewish Literature Between the Bible and the Mishnah* (Philadelphia: Fortress Press): 263–65
1984   'The Bible Rewritten and Expanded', in Stone (ed.) 1984: 89–156.
1998   'Patriarchs Who Worry About Their Wives. A Haggadic Tendency in the Genesis Apocryphon', in Stone and Chazon (eds) 1998: 137–58.
1999   'The Nature and Function of Revelation in 1 Enoch, Jubilees, and Some Qumranic Documents', in Chazon and Stone (eds) 1999: 91–119.
2001   *1 Enoch 1: A Commentary on the Book of 1 Enoch, Chapters 1–36, 81–108* (Hermeneia; Minneapolis: Fortress Press).
2003a   'Patriarchs Who Worry About Their Wives: A Haggadic Tendency in the Genesis Apocryphon', in J. Neusner and A. J. Avery-Peck (eds), *George W. E. Nickelsburg in Perspective: An On-Going Dialogue of Learning*, Vol. 1 (JSJSup, 80; Leiden: E. J. Brill): 177–99.
2003b   'Response to Eileen Schuller', in J. Neusner and A. J. Avery-Peck (eds), *George W. E. Nickelsburg in Perspective: An On-Going Dialogue of Learning*, Vol. 1 (JSJSup, 80; Leiden: E. J. Brill): 213–15.

Nickelsburg, George W. E. and James C. VanderKam
2004   *1 Enoch: A New Translation* (Minneapolis: Fortress Press).

Niehoff, Maren R.
1996   'Two Examples of Josephus' Narrative Technique in his "Rewritten Bible"', *Journal for the Study of Judaism* 27: 31–45.

Oegema, Gerbern S.
1998   'Tradition-Historical Studies on 4Q252', in J. H. Charlesworth, H. Lichtenberger and G. S. Oegema (eds), *Qumran-Messianism: Studies on the Messianic Expectations in the Dead Sea Scrolls* (Tübingen: Mohr Siebeck).

Parry, Donald W., and Emanuel Tov (eds)
2004–2005 *The Dead Sea Scrolls Reader* (Leiden: E. J. Brill).
2004   *Exegetical Texts*, in *The Dead Sea Scrolls Reader. Part 2* (Assisted by N. Gordon and C. Anderson; Leiden: E. J. Brill).
2005   *Parabiblical Texts*, in *The Dead Sea Scrolls Reader. Part 3* (Assisted by C. Anderson; Leiden: E. J. Brill).

Perrot, Charles, and Pierre-Maurice Bogaert
1976   *Introduction littéraire, commentaire et index*, in *Pseudo-Philon: les antiquités bibliques* (SC 230; With D. J. Harrington; Paris: Les éditions du Cerf).

Porter, James I.
1992   'Hermeneutic Lines and Circles: Aristarchus and Crates on the Exegesis of Homer', in Lamberton and Keaney (eds) 1992: 67–114.

Porter, Stan E. and Craig A. Evans (eds)
1997   *The Scrolls and the Scriptures: Qumran Fifty Years After* (JSPSup, 26; Sheffield: Sheffield Academic Press).

Porton, Gary G.
1992   'Midrash', in *The Anchor Bible Dictionary*, IV (New York: Doubleday): 818–22.

Puech, Émile
2001   '534–536. 4QNaissance de Noé$^{a-c}$ ar: Introduction', in *Qumrân Grotte 4. XXII. Textes Araméens: première partie, 4Q529–549* (À la mémorie de Jean Starcky; Discoveries in the Judaean Desert, 31; Oxford: Clarendon Press): 117–27.

Qimron, Elisha
1992   'Towards a New Edition of the Genesis Apocryphon', *JSP* 10: 11–18.

1999 'Toward a New Edition of 1Q "Genesis Apocryphon"', in D. W. Parry and E. Ulrich (eds), *The Provo International Conference on the Dead Sea Scrolls: Technological Innovations, New Texts, and Reformulated Issues* (STDJ, 30; Leiden: E. J. Brill): 106–109.

Rajak, Tessa
2001 'The Sense of History in Jewish Intertestamental Writing', in *The Jewish Dialogue with Greece and Rome: Studies in Cultural and Social Interaction* (AGAJU, 48; Leiden: E. J. Brill): 3–37.

Rappaport, S.
1930 Agada und Exegese bei Flavius Josephus (Veröffentlichungen der Oberrabbiner Dr. H. P. Chajes "Preisstiftung an der Israelitisch-theogischen Lehranstalt in Wien", 3; Vienna: Alexander Kohut Memorial Foundation).

Reed, Annette Y.
2005 *Fallen Angels and the History of Judaism and Christianity: The Reception of Enochic Literature* (Cambridge: Cambridge University Press).

Reed, Stephen A.
1994 *The Dead Sea Scrolls Catalogue. Documents, Photographs and Museum Inventory Numbers* (SBLRBS, 32; rev. and ed. by M. J. Lundberg, with M. B. Phelps; Atlanta: Scholars Press).

Rendsburg, Gary A.
2005 'The Vegetarian Ideal in the Bible', in L. J. Greenspoon, R. A. Simkins and G. Shapiro (eds), *Food and Judaism* (Omaha, NE: Creighton University Press): 319–34.

Ruiten, J. T. A. G. M. van
2000 *Primaeval History Interpreted: The Rewriting of Genesis 1–11 in the Book of Jubilees* (JSJSup, 66; Leiden: E. J. Brill).

Runia, David T. and Gregory E. Sterling (eds)
1997 *Wisdom and Logos: Studies in Jewish Thought in Honor of David Winston* (The Studia Philonica Annual, 9; BJS, 312; Atlanta: Scholars Press).

Sæbø, Magne (ed.), in cooperation with Chris Brekelmans and Menahem Haran
1996 *Hebrew Bible/Old Testament: The History of its Interpretation. I. From the Beginnings to the Middle Ages (Until 1300)*, Part 1: *Antiquity* (Göttingen: Vandenhoeck & Ruprecht).

Sanders, James A.
1976 'Adaptable for Life: The Nature and Function of Canon', in *Magnalia Dei: The Mighty Acts of God. Essays on the Bible and Archaeology in Memory of G. Ernest Wright* (Garden City, NT: Doubleday): 531–60; reprinted in James A. Sanders, *From Sacred Story to Sacred Text* (Philadelphia: Fortress Press, 1987): 9–39.
1984 *Canon and Community: A Guide to Canonical Criticism* (Guides to Biblical Scholarship; Philadelphia: Fortress Press).
1991 'Stability and Fluidity in Text and Canon', in G. J. Norton and S. Pisano (eds), *Tradition of the Text: Studies Offered to Dominique Barthélemy in Celebration of His 70th Birthday* (OBO, 109; Göttingen: Vandenhoeck & Ruprecht): 201–17.
1992 'Canon', in *The Anchor Bible Dictionary*, I (New York: Doubleday): 837–52.
2002 'The Issue of Closure in the Canonical Process', in L. M. McDonald and J. A. Sanders (eds), *The Canon Debate* (Peabody, MA: Hendrickson): 252–63.
2006 'The Impact of the Judean Desert Scrolls on Issues of Text and Canon of the Hebrew Bible', in Charlesworth (ed.) 2006: 25–36.

Schiffman, L. H.
1994 *Reclaiming the Dead Sea Scrolls: The History of Judaism, the Background of*

Christianity, the Lost Library of Qumran (Philadelphia: Jewish, Publication
Society).

Schuller, Eileen
2003   'Response to "Patriarchs Who Worry About Their Wives: A Haggadic Ten-
        dency in the Genesis Apocryphon"', in J. Neusner and A. J. Avery-Peck (eds),
        George W. E. Nickelsburg in Perspective: An On-Going Dialogue of Learning,
        Vol. 1 (JSJSup, 80; Leiden: E. J. Brill): 200–12.

Schwartz, Daniel
1981   'The Messianic Departure from Judah (4QPatriarchal Blessings)', *Theologische
        Zeitschrift* 37: 257–66.

Scott, James M.
1997   'Geographic Aspects of Noachic Materials in the Scrolls', in Porter and Evans
        (eds) 1997: 368–81.
2002   *Geography in Early Judaism and Christianity: The Book of Jubilees* (Society
        for New Testament Studies Monograph Series, 113; Cambridge: Cambridge
        University Press).

Seeligmann, Isaac L.
1948   *The Septuagint Version of Isaiah: A Discussion of its Problems* (MVEOL, 9;
        Leiden: E. J. Brill).

Segal, Michael
1998   'Biblical Exegesis in 4Q158: Techniques and Genre', *Textus* 19: 45–62.
2000   '4QReworked Pentateuch or 4QPentateuch?' in L. H. Schiffman, *et al.* (eds),
        *The Dead Sea Scrolls Fify Years After Their Discovery. Proceedings of the Jeru-
        salem Congress, July 20–25, 1997* (Jerusalem: Israel Exploration Society, in
        cooperation with The Shrine of the Book, Israel Museum): 391–99.
2005   'Between Bible and Rewritten Bible', in Henze (ed.) 2005: 10–28.

Sheppard, Gerald T.
1987   'Canon', in *Encyclopedia of Religion*, Vol. 3 (New York: Macmillan): 62–69.

Siegert, Folker
1996   'Early Jewish Interpretation in a Hellenistic Style', in Saebø 1996: 130–98.

Smith, Jonathan Z.
1982   'Sacred Persistence: Toward a Redescription of Canon', in *Imagining Religion:
        From Babylon to Jonestown* (Chicago: University of Chicago Press): 36–52.

Smith, Wilfred C.
1989   'Scripture as Form and Concept: Their Emergence for the Western World', in
        Levering (ed.) 1989: 29–55.
1993   *What is Scripture? A Comparative Approach* (Minneapolis: Fortress Press).

Stegemann, Hartmut
1967   'Weitere Stücke von 4QpPsalm 37, von 4Q Patriarchal Blessings und Hinweis
        auf eine unedierte Handschrift aus Höhle 4Q mit Exzerpten aus dem Deuter-
        onomium', *Revue de Qumran* 6: 193-227.
1990   'Methods for the Reconstruction of Scrolls from Scattered Fragments', in
        L. Schiffman (ed.), *Archaeology and History in the Dead Sea Scrolls. The New
        York University Conference in Memory of Yigael Yadin* (JSOT/ASOR Mono-
        graph Series, 2; Sheffield: Sheffield Academic Press): 189–220.

Steiner, R.C.
1995   'The Heading of the Book of the Words of Noah on a Fragment of the Genesis
        Apocryphon: New Light on a "Lost" Work', *Dead Sea Discoveries* 2: 66–71.

Stone, Michael E.
1999   'The Axis of History at Qumran', in Chazon and Stone (eds) 1999: 133–49.
2006   'The Book(s) Attributed to Noah', *Dead Sea Discoveries* 13.1: 4–23.

Stone, Michael E. (ed.)
  1984   *Jewish Writings of the Second Temple Period. Apocrypha, Pseudepigrapha,*
          Qumran Sectarian Writings, Philo, Josephus (CRINT, 2.2; Assen: Van Gorcum).
Stone Michael E. and Esther G. Chazon (eds)
  1998   *Biblical Perspectives: Early Use and Interpretation of the Bible in Light of the*
          Dead Sea Scrolls. Proceedings of the First International Symposium of the
          Orion Center, 12–14 May 1996 (Leiden: E. J. Brill).
Stone, Michael E., and Jonas C. Greenfield
  1996   'Aramaic Levi Document', in DJD 22: 1–72.
Strack, Hermann L., and Günter Stemberger
  1996   *Introduction to the Talmud and Midrash* (second printing, with emendations
          and updates; ed. and trans. M. Bockmuehl; Edinburgh: T&T Clark).
Strugnell, John
  1970   'Notes en marge du volume V des 'Discoveries in the Judaean Desert of
          Jordan'', *Revue de Qumran* 7(2): 163–276.
Sukenik, Eleazar L.
  1950   *Megillot Genuzot II* (Jerusalem: Bialik).
Sundberg, Albert C., Jr
  1968   'The "Old Testament": A Christian Canon', *Catholic Biblical Quarterly* 30:
          143–55.
Swanson, Dwight D.
  2004   'How Scriptural is Re-Written Bible?' *Revue de Qumran* 21(3): 407–27.
Talmon, Shemaryahu
  2000   'Textual Criticism: The Ancient Versions', in Mayes (ed.) 2000: 141–70.
  2002   'The Crystallization of the "Canon of Hebrew Scriptures" in the Light of
          Biblical Scrolls from Qumran', in Herbert and Tov 2002: 5–20.
Theodor, Julius, and Chaim Albeck
  1965   *Midrash Bereshit Rabba. Critical Edition with Notes and Commentary* (2nd
          printing with additional corrections by Ch. Albeck; Jerusalem: Wahrmann
          Books).
Tov, Emanuel
  1992   'The Textual Status of 4Q*364–367* (4QPP)', in Trebolle Barrera and Vegas
          Montaner (eds) 1992, vol. 1: 43–82.
  1994   'Biblical Texts as Reworked in Some Qumran Manuscripts with Special
          Attention to 4QRP and 4QParaGen-Exod', in E. Ulrich and J. VanderKam
          (eds), *The Community of the Renewed Covenant. The Notre Dame Symposium*
          on the Dead Sea Scrolls (CJA, 10; Notre Dame, IN: University of Notre Dame
          Press): 111–34.
  1995   '4QReworked Pentateuch: A Synopsis of Its Contents', *Revue de Qumran* 16:
          647–53.
  1998a   'Rewritten Bible Compositions and Biblical Manuscripts, with Special Attention
          to the Samaritan Pentateuch', *Dead Sea Discoveries* 5: 334–54.
  1998b   'Scribal Practices and Physical Aspects of the Dead Sea Scrolls', in J. L. Sharpe
          III and Kimberly van Kampen (eds), *The Bible as Book: The Manuscript Tradi-*
          tion (London: British Library; Newcastle, DW: Oak Knoll Press, in association
          with the Scriptorium, Center for Christian Antiquities): 9–33.
  2000   'Further Evidence for the Existence of a Qumran Scribal School', in L. H.
          Schiffman, E. Tov, and J. C. VanderKam (eds), *The Dead Sea Scrolls Fifty*
          Years After Their Discovery. Proceedings of the Jerusalem Congress, July 20–
          25, 1997 (Jerusalem: Israel Exploration Society in cooperation with The Shrine
          of the Book, Israel Museum): 199–216.

2001   *Textual Criticism of the Hebrew Bible* (2nd revised edition; Minneapolis: For-
        tress Press).

2002   'The Status of the Masoretic Text in Modern Text Editions of the Hebrew
        Bible', in L. M. McDonald and J. A. Sanders (eds), *The Canon Debate* (Pea-
        body, MA. Hendrickson): 234–51.

Tov, Emanuel, and Sidnie White Crawford

1994   'Reworked Pentateuch', in DJD 13: 187–351.

Townsend, John T.

1989   *Midrash Tanḥuma. Translated Into English with Introduction, Indices, and
        Brief Notes (S. Buber Recension). I. Genesis* (Hoboken, NJ: KTAV).

Trafton, Joseph L.

2002   'Commentary on Genesis A (4Q252 = 4QCommGen A = 4QPBless)', in J. H.
        Charlesworth (ed.) 2002: 203–19

Trebolle Barrera, Julio

1998   *The Jewish Bible and the Christian Bible: An Introduction to the History of the
        Bible* (trans. W. G. E. Watson; Leiden: E. J. Brill).

2000   'Qumran Evidence for a Biblical Standard Text and for Non-Standard and
        Parabiblical Texts', in Lim, *et al.* (eds) 2000: 89–106.

Trebolle Barrera, Julio and L. Vegas Montaner (eds)

1992   *The Madrid Proceedings of the International Congress on the Dead Sea
        Scrolls, Madrid, 18–21 March 1991* (2 vols; STDJ, 11; Leiden: E. J. Brill).

Trever, John C.

1948   'The Discovery of the Scrolls', *Biblical Archaeologist* 11: 46–57.

1949   'Identification of the Aramaic Fourth Scroll from "Ain Feshkha" ', *Bulletin of
        the American Schools of Oriental Research* 115: 8–10.

Ulrich, Eugene C.

1992   'The Canonical Process, Textual Criticism, and Latter Stages in the Composition
        of the Bible', in M. Fishbane and E. Tov (eds), *"Sha'arei Talmon": Studies in
        the Bible, Qumran, and the Ancient Near East Presented to Shemaryahu Talmon*
        (with the assistance of Weston W. Fields; Winona Lake, IN: Eisenbrauns):
        267–91.

1998   'The Dead Sea Scrolls and the Biblical Text', in P. W. Flint and J. C. Vander-
        Kam (eds), *The Dead Sea Scrolls After Fifty Years: A Comprehensive Assess-
        ment*, Vol. 1 (Leiden: E. J. Brill): 79–100.

1999a   'The Community of Israel and the Composition of the Scriptures', in *The Dead
        Sea Scrolls and the Origins of the Bible* (SDSSRL; Grand Rapids: Eerdmans):
        3–16.

1999b   'Multiple Literary Editions: Reflections Toward a Theory of the History of the
        Biblical Text', in *The Dead Sea Scrolls and the Origins of the Bible* (SDSSRL;
        Grand Rapids: Eerdmans): 99–120.

1999c   'Pluriformity in the Biblical Text, Text Groups, and Questions of Canon', in
        The Dead Sea Scrolls and the Origins of the Bible (SDSSRL; Grand Rapids:
        Eerdmans): 79–98.

2000a   'The Qumran Biblical Scrolls – the Scriptures of Late Second Temple Judaism',
        in Lim, *et al.* 2000: 67–87.

2000b   'The Qumran Scrolls and the Biblical Text', in L. H. Schiffman, E. Tov and J.
        C. VanderKam (eds), *The Dead Sea Scrolls: Fifty Years After Their Discovery
        1947–1997. Proceedings of the Jerusalem Congress, July 20–25, 1997* (Jeru-
        salem: Israel Exploration Society in cooperation with the Shrine of the Book,
        Israel Museum): 51–59.

2001   'The Bible in the Making: The Scriptures Found at Qumran', in P. W. Flint (ed.),
          The Bible at Qumran: Text, Shape, and Interpretation (Studies in the Dead Sea
          Scrolls and Related Literature; Grand Rapids: Eerdmans): 51–66.
2002a   'The Notion and Definition of Canon', in L. M. McDonald and J. A. Sanders
          (eds), *The Canon Debate* (Peabody, MA: Hendrickson): 21–35.
2002b   'The Text of the Hebrew Scriptures at the Time of Hillel and Jesus', in
          Congress Volume Basel 2001 (VTSup, 92; A. Lemaire; Leiden: E. J. Brill): 85–
          108.
2003a   'From Literature to Scripture: Reflections on the Growth of a Text's Authorita-
          tiveness', *Dead Sea Discoveries* 10(1): 3–25.
2003b   'Qumran and the Canon of the Old Testament', in J.-M. Auwers and H. J. de
          Jonge (eds), *The Biblical Canons* (Bibliotheca Ephemeridum Theologicarum
          Lovaniensium 163; Leuven: Leuven University Press): 57–80.
2006   'The Dead Sea Scrolls and the Hebrew Scriptural Texts', in Charlesworth (ed.)
          2006: 77–99.
Van Seters, John
2000   'Creative Imitation in the Hebrew Bible', *Studies in Religion* 29(4): 395–409.
VanderKam, James C.
1977   *Textual and Historical Studies in the Book of Jubilees* (Harvard Semitic Mono-
          graphs, 14; Missoula, MT: Scholars Press).
1978   'The Textual Affinities of the Biblical Citations in the Genesis Apocryphon',
          Journal of Biblical Literature 97: 45–55.
1980   'The Righteousness of Noah', in J. J. Collins and G. W. E. Nickelsburg (eds),
          Ideal Figures in Ancient Judaism: Profiles and Paradigms (SBLSCS, 12; Chico,
          CA: Scholars Press): 13–32.
1989   *The Book of Jubilees* (CSCO, 511, Scriptores Aethiopici 88; Lovanii: Aedibus
          E. Peeters).
1993   'Biblical Interpretation in 1 Enoch and Jubilees', in Charlesworth and Evans
          (eds) 1993: 96–125.
1995   *Enoch: A Man for All Generations* (Studies on Personalities of the Old Testa-
          ment; University of South Carolina Press).
1997   'The Origins and Purposes of the Book of Jubilees', in Albani *et al.* (eds),
          1997: 3–24.
1999   'The Angel Story in the Book of Jubilees', in Chazon and Stone (eds) 1999:
          151–70.
2000   'Revealed Literature in the Second Temple Period', in *From Revelation to
          Canon: Studies in the Hebrew Bible and Second Temple Literature* (JSJSup,
          62; Leiden: E. J. Brill): 1–30.
2001   *The Book of Jubilees* (Guides to the Apocrypha and Pseudepigrapha; Sheffield:
          Sheffield Academic Press).
2002a   'Questions of Canon Viewed Through the Dead Sea Scrolls', in L. M. McDonald
          and J. A. Sanders (eds), *The Canon Debate* (Peabody, MA: Hendrickson):
          91–109.
2002b   'The Wording of Biblical Citations in Some Rewritten Scriptural Works', in
          Herbert and Tov 2002: 41–56.
2006   'The Scriptural Setting of the Book of Jubilees', *Dead Sea Discoveries* 13:
          61–72.
Vermes, Geza
1973   *Scripture and Tradition in Judaism: Haggadic Studies* (Studia Post-Biblica, 4;
          Leiden: E. J. Brill, 2nd rev. edn [1961]).

| 1975a | 'Bible and Midrash: Early Old Testament Exegesis', in *Post-Biblical Jewish Studies* (Studies in Judaism in Late Antiquity, 8; Leiden: E. J. Brill): 59–91. |

1975a   'Bible and Midrash: Early Old Testament Exegesis', in *Post-Biblical Jewish Studies* (Studies in Judaism in Late Antiquity, 8; Leiden: E. J. Brill): 59–91.
1975b   *Post-Biblical Jewish Studies* (Leiden: E. J. Brill).
1976   'Interpretation, History of: At Qumran and in the Targums', in K. Crim (ed.), *Interpreter's Dictionary of the Bible Supplementary Volume* (Nashville, TN: Abingdon Press): 438–43.
1986   'Biblical Midrash', in E. Schürer, *The History of the Jewish People in the Age of Jesus Christ. A New English Edition*, Vol. 3.1 (rev. and ed. by G. Vermes, *et al.*; Edinburgh: T & T Clark): 308–41.
1989   'Bible Interpretation at Qumran', *Eretz-Israel (Yigael Yadin Memorial Volume)* 20: 184–91.
1997   *The Complete Dead Sea Scrolls in English* (London: Penguin).

Wacholder, Ben Zion
1964   'How Long Did Abram Stay in Egypt? A Study in Hellenistic, Qumran, and Rabbinic Chronography', *HUCA* 35: 43–56.
1974   *Eupolemus: A Study of Judaeo-Greek Literature* (Monographs of the Hebrew Union College 3; Cincinnati, New York, Los Angeles, Jerusalem: Hebrew Union College-Jewish Institute of Religion).

Werman, Cana
1999   'Qumran and the Book of Noah', in Chazon and Stone (eds) 1999: 171–81.

Westermann, Claus
1984   *Genesis 1–11. A Commentary* (J. J. Scullion SJ; Minneapolis: Augsburg).

Wevers, John W.
1996   'The Interpretative Character and Significance of the Septuagint Version', in Sæbø 1996: 84–107.

White Crawford, Sidnie A.
1992   '4Q*364 &367*: A Preliminary Report', in Trebolle Barrera and Vegas Montaner (eds) 1992, vol. 1: 217–28.
1999   'The 'Rewritten' Bible at Qumran: A Look at Three Texts', *Eretz-Israel* 26 (Festschrift for F. M. Cross): 1*–8*.
2000a   'Reworked Pentateuch', in *EDSS* 2): 775–77.
2000b   'The Rewritten Bible at Qumran', in J. H. Charlesworth (ed.), *The Hebrew Bible and Qumran* (N. Richland Hills, TX: BIBAL Press): 173–95.
2006   'The Rewritten Bible at Qumran', in Charlesworth (ed.) 2006: 131–47.

Wise, Michael O.
1992   'Qumran Aramaic and Aramaic Dialectology', in T. Muraoka (ed.), *Studies in Qumran Aramaic* (Abr-Nahrain Sup, 3; Louvain: Peeters): 124–67.

Woude, A. S. and der
1957   *Die messianischen Vorstellungen der Gemeinde von Qumrân* (Studia Semitica Neelandica, 3; Assen: Van Gorcum).

Yadin, Yigael
1983   *The Temple Scroll* (3 vols; Jerusalem: Israel Exploration Society).

Zimmermann, J.
1998   *Messianische Texte aus Qumran: Königliche, priesterliche und prophetische Messiasvorstellungen in den Schriftfunden von Qumran* (WUNT, 2. Reihe 104; Tübingen: Mohr Siebeck).

Zipor, M.A.
1997   'The Flood Chronology: Too Many an Accident', *Dead Sea Discoveries* 4: 207–10.

Zuckerman, Bruce, and Marilyn Lundberg
    2002   'Ancient Texts and Modern Technology: The West Semitic Research Project of the University of Southern California', *AJS Perspectives*, Fall/Winter, 13–15.
Zuckerman, Bruce, and Michael O. Wise
    1991   'The Trever Fragment: Recovery of an Unstudied Piece of the Genesis Apocryphon', AAR/SBL Annual Meeting; Kansas City, Missouri.

HEBREW BIBLE

178